Anonymous

Golden Thoughts on Mother, Home, and Heaven

From Poetic and Prose Literature of All Ages and All Lands

Anonymous

Golden Thoughts on Mother, Home, and Heaven
From Poetic and Prose Literature of All Ages and All Lands

ISBN/EAN: 9783744689656

Printed in Europe, USA, Canada, Australia, Japan

Cover: Foto ©Thomas Meinert / pixelio.de

More available books at **www.hansebooks.com**

GOLDEN THOUGHTS

ON

MOTHER, HOME

AND

HEAVEN.

FROM

POETIC AND PROSE LITERATURE

OF

ALL AGES AND ALL LANDS.

WITH AN INTRODUCTION
By REV. THEO. L. CUYLER, D.D.

"If from our side the first has fled,
And Home be but a name,
Let's strive the narrow path to tread,
That we the last may gain!"
Page 29.

ILLUSTRATED.

NEW-YORK:
E. B. TREAT, 757 BROADWAY.
R. C. TREAT, CHICAGO.   W. H. THOMPSON & CO., BOSTON.
N. D. THOMPSON & CO., ST. LOUIS.   SOUTHERN PUBLISHING CO., NEW ORLEANS.
N. G. HAMILTON, CLEVELAND, O.

Presented

TO

INTRODUCTION

BY

Rev. THEODORE L. CUYLER.

The compiler of this volume has rendered a most valuable service by collecting into one sheaf these golden gleanings. In order to give his work the greatest richness and variety he has laid under contribution more than three hundred widely-known authors on both sides of the Atlantic. In the main, his selections seem to have been made with excellent taste; the ruling motive being to choose these things which would be the most practical and the most profitable. Many of them are already familiar to us all—but that very fact proves their value. There are other readers coming on the stage of life who need to know these "household words" and one object of this volume is to carry these coined thoughts of standard value into a wide and permanent circulation.

My friend who orginated and compiled this work has chosen three grand themes. They blend together beautifully, and interlock each other as light, heat and electricity are interlocked in a sun-beam. The *Mother* is the fountain-head of the *Home*. The home is the fountain head of society and of the Church of Christ. And no influences in the universe contribute so much toward guiding immortal souls *Heavenward* as the Home and the Mother.

If I were asked to name any one principle that seems to have an almost universal application, it would be this one—show me the mother and I will show you the man! Next to the sovereign grace of God, the influence of a mother's teachings and example is the most effective in moulding character and shaping destiny. Intellectual power even descends most commonly on the maternal side. Nearly all the most remarkable men have had mothers of more than ordinary mental calibre. Great men often have weak children; great women seldom have.

But it is in the direction of moral training and the development of character that the mother is most powerfully felt. What a faithful suggestion lies hid in that brief line from Holy Writ—" his mother made him a little coat!" The woman who wove that little tunic was Hannah. The lad who wore it was Samuel, who grew from a beautiful boyhood into the holy prophet and the upright ruler. No doubt that it was a modest and a comely garment which the Jewish matron made; for she was a woman of too much piety and good sense to treat her consecrated child as if he were a plaything or a doll.

But that "little coat" has a figurative application to every mother's high calling. For she not only provides her child from infancy's first moments with clothing for the body, but moral "habits" of character and conduct. The mother, more than any one else, helps to clothe the immortal soul in garments of light and loveliness, or else in garments of sin and sorrow and shame. She makes "little coats" which no moth can consume, which never wear out, and which are worn by her offspring long after she has mouldered into dust. She weaves her child's *habits* of thought and conduct; and does it too, as clothes are made, stitch by stitch. She does this not only by direct deliberate teachings, but by little words and acts, and by silent unconscious influence. Hannah's daily life helped to weave Samuel's noble character. The mother made the man.

What a debt of gratitude the world owes to godly-minded Monica! She trained up Augustine to be the champion-defender of the gospel in a day of dark apostasies. But for good, faithful Susannah Wesley, the world might never have been enriched with John and Charles, the twain founders of Methodism. Richard Cecil says that in his early manhood he tried hard to be an infidel. But he never could get over the unanswerable argument of his own mother's godly life and influence. They were too much for him: they conquered him for Christ. On the other hand, how many lives have been disfigured by the wretched "botch-work" or the deformities of such mind-garments as weak or wicked mothers have woven for their children. The brilliant Byron might have been a very different man if he had had a different mother, and a wiser early training. Children seldom rise higher than the fountain-head of the mother's character. Occasional exceptions do not shake the solid certainty of this rule. Show me the mother and I will show you the man—is a veracious maxim after all. There are tens of thousands of others who can testify,—with the author of this Introduction,—that a faithful mother's prayers and teachings were worth more to them than the fortunes of a score of Girards or Vanderbilts. Even the diadem which Victoria wears as Queen of Great Britian and Empress of India shines not with such enviable lustre as that higher crown of the pure wife and exemplary mother.

While the relation is so vitally important in shaping lives and determining human destinies, everything which helps to instruct and inspire mothers for their high calling is of great moment. This is one purpose for which this volume was complied. Not for the amusement of a listless hour, but for quickening, reproof, instruction and encouragement. Amid her routine of home cares, a busy mother may sometimes take up this book, and open to a page which shall be to her a word in season—an "apple of gold in a basket of silver." A single sentence may furnish her food for thought. A brief hint may give her most valuable assistance in the discharge of her sacred duties. If she is under the shadow of a dark sorrow, with an empty cradle in her house or the playthings of a lost darling carefully treasured in her drawer, she may open these pages, and find some precious words of consolation. There is hardly a house in which, at some time or other, there has not "been one dead." No touch makes all of us kin like the touch of bereavement. No writings have such perennial interest as those which treat of our home joys and sorrows, and which are inspired by the cradle, the fireside, the ring of wedlock, the family record, or the casket which holds our beloved dead.

This volume was prepared for home-use and home-reading. It treats not only of her who is the queen of the household, but of the rules by which home may be governed. If the mother is the fountain-head of the household, it is equally true that the household is the fountain-head of society. Both the commonwealth and the church grow out of the family. They both take their character from the family. The real seed-corn whence our republic sprang was the Christian households, which stepped forth from the cabin of the "Mayflower," or which set up the family-altar of the Hollander and the Huguenot on Manhattan Island or in the sunny South. All our best characters, best legislation, best institutions, and best church-life were cradled in those early homes. They were the tap-root of the republic, and of the American churches.

For one, I care but little for the government which presides at Washington in comparison with the government which rules the eight or ten millions of American homes. No administration can seriously harm us if our home-life is pure, frugal, and godly. No statesmanship or legislation can save us, if once our homes become the abodes of ignorance or the nestling-places of profligacy. The home rules the nation. If the home is demoralized it will ruin it.

There are several essentials to a good home. Wealth is not one of those essentials, for in many an abode of honest poverty contentment dwells. Out of such lowly cottages and cabins have sprung our greatest, noblest men and women. The little clapboarded farm houses of New England have been the nurseries of our greatest divines, most useful philanthropists and devoted missionaries. The riches of those humble dwellings were industrious hands and praying hearts. God's Word was the light of the homestead. The Bible, the spinning-wheel, and the family altar stood side by side. The growing refinements of later years have introduced into many rural habitations the piano, the pictures, and the pile of books. But let our people see to it that the increase of culture, money and refinement is not attended with any decrease of homespun frugality, domestic purity, and the fear of God.

A truly good home is not only one in which God reigns, but it must be an *attractive* spot. Even all the conscientious Christian parents do not seem to find this out. The result is that the theater, the billiard-saloon, the club, the convivial party manage to "out-bid" the home, and to draw away the sons and the daughters. It is too often the fault of his parents, that a sprightly boy prefers some other evening resort to the stupid or disagreeable place in which he eats and sleeps. If his home were made more attractive he would not seek the haunts of danger and depravity. And one of the surest methods of keeping a husband out of a dramshop, or a son out of the haunts of sin, is the "expulsive power of a new affection" for their *home.* Everything that attracts our children to their homes is very apt to be, in the end, an attraction towards Heaven.

As a citizen of Brooklyn, I am proud of the fact that in our chief public park there stands a monument to the author of "Home, sweet Home." Those immortal lines have made delicious music by many an humble fireside. They have inspired encouragement under many a lowly roof. But John Howard Payne struck a deeper truth than he may have intended when he wrote, "*there is no place like home.*" This applies to something more enduring than the heart's attachment to the spot which sheltered our childhood. For all our after lives, and our eternal destinies—for shaping the character, forming the habits, determining the choice for good or evil, and for the salvation or ruin of the soul "there is no place like home." Nothing is so dangerous and damning as a bad home. Nothing is so effective in fitting us for usefulness here and for heaven hereafter as a pure, happy Christ-lighted home;—for like heaven "the LAMB is the light thereof."

It is because this volume contains so many valuable truths for fireside reading; in short, because it is such an excellent *home book*, that I have been drawn to it and have written these words of honest commendation. When one has not time enough to read an extended treatise, he may take up this book and find some savory morsel of wisdom—some sweet touch of poetry—some timely hint for the hour, or some rich cluster of truths that shall be like a bunch of grapes from the King's own garden. Into the cleanly pages of my friend's volume "nothing entereth which defileth." And there is many a precious truth here which—with God's blessing—may make one "wise unto salvation."

LIST OF AUTHORS.

	PAGE
Abbott, Rev. Dr. John S. C.	363
Ackers, Elizabeth	878
Addison, Joseph	215
Aldrich, James	290
Alexander, J. Addison	818
Alexander, Rev. Dr. James W.	344
Bacon, Lord	261
Barbauld, Anna Letitia	321
Barker, David	214
Barr, Mrs. Amelia E.	219
Barton, Bernard	353
Baxter, Richard	357
Beecher, Henry Ward	73, 203, 298
Birkins, Rev. H. H.	87
Blair	222
Blanchard, Laman	24
Bonar, Horatius	409
Booth, Rev. B. F.	116
Bowring, John	334
Brainard, Mary G.	308
Brooks, Rev. Phillips	205
Browning, Mrs. Elizabeth B.	328
Bryant, William C.	323
Burchard, Rev. Dr. Samuel D.	106
Burr, Mrs.	179
Bushnell, Rev. Dr. Horace	65
Byron, Lord	260, 321
Campbell, Thomas	43
Carlyle, Thomas	246
Cary, Phœbe	204

	PAGE
Cassanovia, E. L.	80
Cato	201
Chaffee, Ada A.	268
Chesterfield, Lord	190, 331
Cicero	205
Clarendon, Lord	205
Clay, Henry	269
Colfax, Schuyler	128
Collyer, Rev. Dr. Robert	111
Cook, Rev. Joseph	229
Cook, Eliza	74
Colton, George H.	243
Cowper, William	83, 210, 213
Cromwell, Oliver	331
Crosby, Fanny J.	27, 103, 343
Crosby, Rev. Dr. Howard	349
Cummings, Rev. Dr. John	361
Cuyler, Rev. Dr. Theo. L.	5, 270, 306, 360, 381
Dane, H. C.	121
Deems, Rev. Dr. Charles F.	402
Dickens, Charles	136, 245
Downing, Rev. Dr.	112
Dryden, John	193
Dwight, Rev. Dr. Timothy	243
Faber, Rev. Dr. F. W.	246, 379, 397
Farman, Ella	85
Fields, James T.	182
Franklin, Benjamin	235
Fuller	241

LIST OF AUTHORS.

	PAGE
Gladstone, W. E.	263
Goethe	328
Goldsmith, Oliver	114, 190, 197
Gough, John B.	261
Guthrie, Rev. Dr. Thomas	345, 346
Guyon, Madame.	324
Hale, Mrs. Sarah J.	77
Hall, Rev. Dr. John	297
Hamilton, Rev. Dr.	132
Hamilton, R. W.	405
Harris, Rev. J. L.	354
Haven, Bishop Gilbert	94
Helps, Sir Arthur	197
Hemans, Mrs. Felicia D.	309
Henderson, Rev. M. C.	96
Henry, Rev. Dr. Matthew	195, 375
Herschel, Sir John	235
Hodge, Rev. Dr. A. A.	35, 242
Holland, J. G.	233
Holm, Saxe	34
Holmes, Oliver Wendell	100, 128, 322
Hood, Thomas	58, 170, 412
Hopkins, Jane Ellis	149
Horne, Bishop	340
Houghton, Mary H.	281
Humboldt	242
Hunt, Leigh	181
Hunter, William	399
Huntington, C.	366
Huntington, Bishop F. D.	228
Janes, Bishop E. S.	230
Jay, Rev. William	323
Jocelyn, Mrs. Elizabeth H.	393
Johnson, Dr.	185
Keble, John	126, 243, 407
Ken, Bishop Thomas	352
King, Henry	320
Lamb, Charles	367
Langé, Rev. Dr. Ernst	407
Lason, A. A.	216

	PAGE
Lathrop, Mary F.	155
Lincoln, Abraham	24
Longfellow, Henry W.	138, 261, 291
Lonsdale, Bishop of	340
Lover, S.	28
Lowell, James Russell	301
Lytton, Bulwer	369
Macaulay, Lord	80
MacDonald, George	213
Mackay, Charles	347
Mann, Horace	162, 191
March, Rev. Dr. Daniel	232, 346, 411
Marsh, Miss	362
Marzials, Frank T.	160
Mason, John	322
Matthews, Rev. Dr. J. M.	36
McLeod, Mrs. Georgie A. H.	302
Millman, Dean	367
Mills, Mrs. Elizabeth	386
Milton, John	313, 328
Mitchell, John K.	290
Montgomery, James	53, 104, 335, 392
Moody, D. L.	119, 206
Moore, Thomas	391, 398
More, Hannah	344
Morris, George P.	79, 93
Moultrie, John	297
Muckle, Mary J.	29
Mulock, Miss	331
Murray, Rev. W. H. H.	159, 166
Newton, John	356
Northrop, Prof. B. G.	262
Orrery, Earl of	100
Parnell, Thomas	280
Paxton, Rev. Dr. W. M.	203
Payne, John Howard	333
Pearce, William	351
Penn, William	358
Penrose, Richard	249
Perry, Mrs. S. T.	292

LIST OF AUTHORS.

	PAGE
Pierpont, John	304
Pliny	222
Planche, J. R.	315
Pollock, Robert	280
Pope, Alexander	71, 200, 210
Porter, Rev. Dr. Noah	202
Prentice, George D.	97, 408
Preston, Mrs.	311
Priest, Nancy A. W.	406
Proctor, Bryan W.	332
Punshon, Rev. Dr. W. Morley	231, 253, 267, 831, 385
Read, T. Buchanan	338
Reed, Rev. Dr. Alexander	320
Rice, Mrs. C. L.	301
Robertson, Rev. Dr. F. W.	242
Rogers, Samuel	129, 215
Rounds, William M. F.	199
Sangster, Margaret E.	146
Saxe, John G.	327
Scott, Sir Walter	195
Seneca	267, 328
Shakespeare, William	191, 225, 244, 314
Sidney, Sir Philip	237
Sigourney, Mrs. L. H.	65, 225, 236
Simpson, Bishop	269
Smith, Sidney	244
Southey, Robert	336, 352
Sprague, Charles	337
Spurgeon, Rev. C. H.	212, 278

	PAGE
Stillings, Henrich	405
Stowe, Mrs. H. B.	348
Swain, Charles	105
Talmage, Rev. T. De Witt	76, 194, 215, 263, 267, 273, 323
Taylor, Bishop	134
Taylor, Rev. Dr. William M.	240
Tennyson, Alfred	110, 280
Thomson, James	122, 129, 184, 331
Tillotson	57
Todd, Rev. Dr. John	202
Trafton, Rev. Mark	90, 92
Tupper, Martin F.	128, 295
Turgot	244
Tweedie, Rev. Dr. W. K.	274
Wadsworth, Rev. Dr. Charles	296
Walker, Delia E.	358
Walker, Dr. James	331
Watts, Rev. Dr. Isaac	357
Webster, Daniel	203, 388
White, Henry Kirke	79
Whittier, John G.	249, 289
Wilcox, Carlos	336
Willis, Nathaniel P.	75, 258
Williams, Rev. Dwight	387
Woodworth, Samuel	113
Yoemans, William H.	109
Young, Edward	322

CONTENTS.

Poetical Selections are indicated by bold-face numbers.

Mother.

		PAGE
A Mother's Large Affection	Laman Blanchard	24
My Mother	Abraham Lincoln	24
Mother	Fanny Crosby	27
My Mother Dear	S. Lover	28
Mother	Joanna Baillie	28
Mother, Home and Heaven	Mary J. Muckle	29
Mother	E. L. Cassanovia	30
The Mother at Home	Mother's Treasury	31
A Mother's Love	Saxe Holm	34
A Mother's Heart	Macmillan's Magazine	35
The Love Principle	A. A. Hodge, D.D.	35
A Mother's Influence	J. M. Matthews, D.D.	36
A Mother's Prayer	Anonymous	42
The Mother	Thomas Campbell	43
Tired Mothers	Mrs. May Riley Smith	44
Mothers of Distinguished Men	Anonymous	46
Mothers and Sons	Christian Intelligencer	50
The Mother's Prayer	Anonymous	52
A Mother's Love	James Montgomery	53
The Mother's Opportunity	Anonymous	54
Mothers, Put Your Children to Bed	Mother's Magazine	56

CONTENTS.

		PAGE
The Good-Night Kiss	Anonymous	57
A Good Word	Tillotson	57
Mother and Child	Thomas Hood	58
Our Mother	Rural New Yorker	59
Parental Authority	Mother's Treasury	61
Courtesies to Parents	S. S. Times	63
The Mother's Charge	Mrs. L. H. Sigourney	65
Authority of Parents	Horace Bushnell, D. D.	65
The Dying Mother	J. A. Dacus	66
Responsibility of Parents	T. F. W.	68
Visit your Parents	Anonymous	69
A Word with Parents about their Children	Anonymous	70
Charms versus Merit	Alexander Pope	71
The Mother's Sorrow	Methodist	72
Sorrows	H. W. Beecher	73
The Old Arm-Chair	Eliza Cook	74
Mary, the Mother of Jesus	N. P. Willis	75
Mother's Vacant Chair	T. De Witt Talmage	76
The Mother's Wondrous Power	Mrs. Sarah J. Hale	77
Respect for Mothers	Anonymous	78
To My Mother	Henry Kirke White	79
My Mother	George P. Morris	79
Tribute to a Mother	Lord Macaulay	80
The Mother's Mission	Anonymous	80
Old Age	M. W. B.	81
My Mother's Hands	Anonymous	82
My Mother's Picture	William Cowper	83
The Mother as Teacher	A. W. K.	84
How Mamma Plays	Ella Farman	85
Mother's Empire	Rev. H. H. Birkins	87
For His Mother's Sake	Anonymous	89
Wife and Mother	Rev. Mark Trafton	90
Be Kind unto the Old	Anonymous	90
The Old Folks	Congregationalist	91

CONTENTS.

		PAGE
MOTHER, THE QUEEN OF HER HOME.......	Rev. Mark Trafton........	92
MY MOTHER'S BIBLE....................	George P. Morris..........	93
MY MOTHER'S BIBLE....................	Bishop Gilbert Haven.......	94
MY MOTHER'S GRAVE...................	Rev. M. C. Henderson......	96
MOTHERS, SPARE YOURSELVES...........	Anonymous...............	97
MY MOTHER'S GRAVE...................	George D. Prentice.........	97

Home.

HOME.......................	Oliver Wendell Holmes......	100
DOMESTIC HAPPINESS..................	Earl of Orrery............	100
HOME....	Fanny Crosby.............	103
HOME.............................	James Montgomery.........	104
HOME DEFINED.....................	Charles Swain............	105
THE HOME OF CHILDHOOD..............	Samuel D. Burchard, D.D...	106
HOME SONGS	Anonymous..............	109
THE OLD HOME	Alfred Tennyson..........	110
HOME SHADOWS.....................	Robert Collyer, D.D.......	111
HOME ADORNMENTS...................	Rev. Dr. Downing.........	112
✓ SCENES OF MY CHILDHOOD............	Samuel Woodworth.........	113
LONGINGS FOR HOME..................	Oliver Goldsmith..........	114
HOME GOVERNMENT—WHAT IS IT?........	Mother's Treasury.........	115
HOME GOVERNMENT—ITS IMPORTANCE.....	Rev. B. F. Booth..........	116
HOME TRAINING OF CHILDREN...........	D. L. Moody.............	119
HOME AFFECTION	H. C. Dane..............	121
HOME TEACHING	James Thomson...........	122
HOME INSTRUCTION...................	Hon. Schuyler Colfax......	123
HOME INFLUENCES...................	Saturday Evening Post.... ..	124
THE SMILES OF HOME.................	John Keble....	126
HOME COURTESY.....................	Anonymous..............	127
THE HAPPY HOME	Martin F. Tupper.........	128
HOME OF OUR CHILDHOOD.............	Oliver Wendell Holmes.....	128
AN IDEAL HOME....................	Samuel Rogers.......... ...	129

CONTENTS.

		PAGE
HOME	James Thomson	129
HOME RELIGION	Mother's Treasury	130
KIND WORDS AT HOME	Anonymous	132
A HAPPY HOME DEFINED	Rev. Dr. Hamilton	132
FAMILY PRAYERS	Christian at Work	133
FREQUENT PRAYER	Bishop Taylor	134
NO TIME TO PRAY	Anonymous	135
THE CHILDREN	Dickenson	136
THE CHILDREN	H. W. Longfellow	138
THE RIGHTS OF CHILDREN	Littell's Living Age	139
SUFFERINGS OF CHILDHOOD	Appleton's Journal	140
GOVERNMENT OF CHILDREN	Boston Post	142
KIND WORDS	Saturday Evening Post	143
NOT ONE CHILD TO SPARE	Mrs. Ethel L. Beers	144
BABIES AND THEIR RIGHTS	M. E. Sangster	146
THE CHILDREN'S BED-TIME	Jane Ellis Hopkins	149
THE EVENING PRAYER	Anonymous	151
HOME AND ITS QUEEN	Scribner's Monthly	152
GIRLS' INFLUENCE	Anonymous	153
TO OUR GIRLS	Mary F. Lathrop	155
A PLEA FOR THE BOY	New York Evening Post	156
BOYHOOD	Rev. W. H. H. Murray	159
MY BOY	Frank T. Marzials	160
CHILDREN OF THE RICH AND POOR, CONTRASTED	James Russell Lowell	161
BE KIND, BOYS	Horace Mann	162
GOOD MANNERS	Anonymous	163
KIND MANNERS AT HOME	Anonymous	164
HOME, NEXT TO HEAVEN	Anonymous	165
HOME AMUSEMENTS	Rev. W. H. H. Murray	166
A CHEERFUL HOME	Friends' Intelligencer	168
THE FARMER'S HOME	William H. Yeomans	169
HOME MEMORY	Thomas Hood	170
SINGING IN THE FAMILY	Anonymous	172
ART IN THE FAMILY	Baltimore American	173

CONTENTS.

		PAGE
CONVERSATION	Churchman	175
SPEAK CHEERFUL WORDS	Anonymous	176
NONE LIVETH TO HIMSELF	Anonymous	177
SPEAK A GOOD WORD	Anonymous	178
SMILE	Mrs. Burr	179
JOY BRINGERS	Anonymous	180
GRUMBLERS	Anonymous	180
LOVE TO OUR FELLOW MEN (Abou Ben Adhem)	Leigh Hunt	181
WORDS TO BOYS	James T. Fields	182
THE LIGHT OF A CHEERFUL FACE	Anonymous	183
DOMESTIC BLISS	James Thomson	184
THE BRIGHT SIDE	The Interior	185
WORTH OF LOOKING ON THE BRIGHT SIDE	Dr. Johnson	185
THE EVENING HEARTHSTONE	Anonymous	186
CHEERFULNESS	Anonymous	187
COURTESY AT HOME	Christian Weekly	188
CHRISTIAN COURTESY	Anonymous	190
SELF-RESPECT IN COMPANY	Lord Chesterfield	190
MODELS	Oliver Goldsmith	190
THE MORALITY OF MANNERS	Horace Mann	191
THE WITCHERY OF MANNER	Anonymous	192
BEST MEN, MOULDED OUT OF FAULTS	Shakespeare	192
CULTIVATE PATIENCE	Anonymous	193
BEWARE THE FURY OF A PATIENT MAN	John Dryden	193
A WOMAN'S CARES	T. De Witt Talmage	194
WOMAN'S EQUALITY	Matthew Henry, D.D.	195
WOMAN	Sir Walter Scott	195
TELL YOUR WIFE	Pacific Rural Press	196
HOSPITALITY	Oliver Goldsmith	197
TRUE HOSPITALITY	Sir Arthur Helps	197
THE RULE OF HOSPITALITY	William M. F. Round	199
NEVER BE ASHAMED TO OWN THE WRONG	Alexander Pope	200
DON'T BE TOO SENSITIVE	Anonymous	201
THE FIRST VIRTUE IS TO RESTRAIN THE TONGUE	Cato	201

CONTENTS.

		PAGE
Advice to a Young Man	John Todd, D.D.	202
Advice to Young Men	Noah Porter, D.D.	202
Education	H. W. Beecher	203
Principles versus Horsemen or Chariots	W. M. Paxton, D.D.	203
The Security of the Nation	Daniel Webster	203
Counsels to the Young	Anonymous	204
The Problem of Life	Phillips Brooks	205
Example	Lord Clarendon	205
Great Men Inspired	Cicero	205
To Young Men	D. L. Moody	206
Ability and Opportunity	Herald and Presbyter	208
Happiness	Alexander Pope	210
Domestic Happiness	William Cowper	210
Family Life, a Test of Piety	Golden Rule	211
Aim and Object in Life	Rev. C. H. Spurgeon	212
Selfishness	William Cowper	213
Life and Religion are One	George MacDonald	213
Make Your Mark	David Barker	214
The Uses of Adversity	Joseph Addison	215
The Good are Better Made by Ill	Samuel Rogers	215
Troubles Strengthen the Soul	T. De Witt Talmage	215
Folly of Fretting	A. A. Lason	216
Never Mind	Anonymous	218
Little Troubles	Mrs. Amelia E. Barr	219
Anxiety is the Poison of Life	Blair	222
Many Dishes Bring Many Diseases	Pliny	222
Transient Troubles	Anonymous	223
Working and Waiting	Anonymous	224
Content	Mrs. L. H. Sigourney	225
Discordance	Shakespeare	225
Let Bygones be Bygones	Chambers' Journal	226
The Christian at Home	Anonymous	227
Religion in the Family	Bishop F. D. Huntington	228
Certainties in Religion	Rev. Joseph Cook	229

CONTENTS.

		PAGE
Winning Souls	Bishop E. S. Janes	230
The Agencies for Good	W. Morley Punshon, LL.D.	231
Your Mission	Daniel March, D.D.	232
The Nobility of Service	J. G. Holland	233
Whatever You Do, Do it Well	Anonymous	234
Industry	Benjamin Franklin	235
Art—Its Application	Sir John Herschel	235
Know Thyself	Mrs. L. H. Sigourney	236
Noble Thoughts	Sir Philip Sidney	237
Importance of Character	Methodist Recorder	238
Influence of Character	Wm. M. Taylor, D.D.	240
A Guilty Conscience is Like a Whirlpool	Fuller	241
Strength of Character	F. W. Robertson, D.D.	242
Character, We Take with Us	Humboldt	242
Tendency of Character	A. A. Hodge, D.D.	242
Worth of Character	George H. Colton	243
Spotless Reputation	Shakespeare	243
Earnestness of Purpose	Timothy Dwight, D.D.	243
Ambition	John Keble	243
Want of Decision	Sidney Smith	244
Columbus' Faith	Turgot	244
Don't be Discouraged	Anonymous	245
Influence	Charles Dickens	245
Earthly Influence	Thomas Carlyle	246
Power of Influence	F. W. Faber, D.D.	246
Power of Influence	Christian Weekly	247
Perpetuity of Influence	J. G. Whittier	249
Doing Good	Richard Penrose	249
Sympathy, Not Lost	Anonymous	251
Trials	Anonymous	252
Trials, A Test of Character	W. Morley Punshon, LL.D.	253
Elements of Success in Life	A. D. F.	254
Press On!	N. P. Willis	258
Ambition	Anonymous	259

CONTENTS.

		PAGE
TEARS OF SYMPATHY	Byron	260
A WORTHY AMBITION	John B. Gough	261
COMMON TRUTHS	Lord Bacon	261
THE SUMMIT GAINED BY SLOW DEGREES	H. W. Longfellow	261
MAKE HOME LIFE BEAUTIFUL	Prof. B. G. Northrop	262
WOMAN AT HOME	T. De Witt Talmage	263
THE CHARM OF WOMAN	W. E. Gladstone, M.P.	263
THE HOMESTEAD	Phœbe Cary	264
HOME	T. De Witt Talmage	267
THE POWER OF KINDNESS	Wm. Morley Punshon, LL.D.	267
RULE OF CONDUCT	Seneca	267
FIRESIDE MUSINGS	Ada A. Chaffee	268
EARLY INFLUENCES	Bishop Simpson	269
PREFERENCE FOR THE RIGHT	Henry Clay	269
A PLEA FOR HOME	Theodore L. Cuyler, D.D.	270
MAKE SOME ONE HAPPY	T. De Witt Talmage	273
MAN'S BEST POWERS POINT HIM GODWARD	Rev. C. H. Spurgeon	273
THE TRIALS OF HOME	W. K. Tweedie, D.D.	274
SANCTIFIED AFFLICTIONS	Watchman and Reflector	278
'TIS BETTER TO HAVE LOVED AND LOST	Alfred Tennyson	280
IMMORTALITY	Robert Pollock	280
DEATH, THE PATH TO GOD	Thomas Parnell	280
CONSOLATION	Mary H. Houghton	281
OUR LAMBS	Anonymous	284
MY BABY	Evangelist	287
CHILDHOOD	John G. Whittier	289
OUR DEAR ONES	James Aldrich	290
'TIS A BLESSING TO LIVE	John K. Mitchell	290
THE LITTLE CHILDREN	Henry W. Longfellow	291
ARE ALL THE CHILDREN IN?	Mrs. S. T. Perry	292
ARE THE CHILDREN AT HOME?	Mrs. M. E. Sangster	293
A LINK BETWEEN ANGELS AND MEN	Martin F. Tupper	295
DEATH OF CHILDREN	Charles Wadsworth, D.D.	296
MY BOY	John Moultrie	297

CONTENTS.

		PAGE
QUIET USEFULNESS	John Hall, D.D.	297
HOME BEREAVEMENTS	Henry Ward Beecher	298
THE ANGEL-CHILD	Mrs. C. L. Rice	301
AN ANGEL MET MY GAZE	James Russell Lowell	301
EMPTY CRADLES	Mrs. G. A. H. McLeod	302
MY CHILD	John Pierpont	304
SUNSHINE FOR THE SORROWING	Theo. L. Cuyler, D.D.	306
WE KNOW NOT WHAT IS BEFORE US	Mary G. Brainard	308
PASSING AWAY	Mrs. F. D. Hemans	309
BY-AND-BYE	Mrs. Preston	311
BROKEN TIES	Christian Weekly	312
LIVE WELL	John Milton	313
LIFE—A PLAY	Shakespeare	314
COMPUTATION OF LIFE	J. R. Planche	315
LIFE'S EPITAPH	Congregationalist	316
THE LIFE CLOCK	Anonymous	317
LIFE'S BOUNDARY LINE, OR THE DOOMED MAN	J. A. Alexander, D.D.	318
BREVITY OF LIFE	Henry King	320
RESPONSIBILITIES OF LIFE	Alexander Reed, D.D.	320
LIFE	Lord Byron	321
MYSTERY OF LIFE	Anna Letitia Barbauld	321
BOUNDARIES OF LIFE	Oliver Wendell Holmes	322
THE VANITY OF LIFE	Edward Young	322
LIFE. A BOOK	John Mason	322
OUR LIFE A SERMON	T. De Witt Talmage	323
HOW TO LIVE	William C. Bryant	323
GOD'S DEMANDS	Rev. William Jay	323
THE VOYAGE OF LIFE	Madame Guyon	323
CHRISTIAN LIVING	N. Y. Observer	327
FALSE PRIDE IN LIFE	John G. Saxe	327
LIFE REACTING UPON LIFE	Mrs. E. B. Browning	328
OUR LIVES ARE ALBUMS	John Milton	328
MUTUAL DEPENDENCE	Seneca	328
DO TO-DAY THY NEAREST DUTY	Goethe	327

CONTENTS.

		PAGE
YOUNG MEN LEAVING HOME	*Christian Voices*	329
WORLDLY PLEASURES AND THEIR INFLUENCE	*Dr. James Walker*	331
THE RESULT OF ACTIONS, THE CRITERION OF JUDGMENT	*Lord Chesterfield*	331
SCORN PLEASURE WHICH GIVES PAIN	*James Thomson*	331
LABOR IS THE TRUE ALCHEMIST	*W. Morley Punshon, LL.D.*	331
STRIKE WHILE THE IRON IS HOT	*Oliver Cromwell*	331
RETURNING HOME	*Miss Mulock*	332
TRAVELLING HOME	*Bryan W. Proctor*	332
HOME, SWEET HOME	*John Howard Payne*	333
MEMORY OF HOME	*T. Buchanan Read*	333
JOYS OF HOME	*John Bowring*	334
HARVEST HOME	*James Montgomery*	335
OUR LAST FAREWELLS	*Carlos Wilcox*	336
FAREWELL TO HOME	*Robert Southey*	336
THE FAMILY MEETING	*Charles Sprague*	337

Heaven.

THE WAY TO HEAVEN	*Bishop of Lonsdale*	340
THOUGHTS OF HEAVEN	*Bishop Horne*	340
HEAVEN	*Fanny J. Crosby*	343
THE APOSTLE JOHN'S IDEA OF HEAVEN	*J. W. Alexander, D.D.*	344
PAUL'S ESTIMATE OF HEAVEN	*Hannah More*	344
HEAVEN, A HOME	*Thomas Guthrie, D.D.*	345
IN HEAVEN, HANDS CLASP FOREVER	*Greek Proverb*	345
HEAVEN	*Daniel March, D.D.*	346
HEAVEN, A CITY	*Thomas Guthrie, D.D.*	346
HEAVEN, A RESTING-PLACE	*Charles Mackay*	347
MY FATHER'S HOUSE	*Mrs. H. B. Stowe*	348
THE HEAVENLY PLACE	*Howard Crosby, D.D.*	349
THOUGHTS OF HEAVEN	*William Pearce*	351

CONTENTS.

		PAGE
RECOGNITION IN HEAVEN	*Robert Southey*............	352
HEAVENLY RECOGNITION	*Bishop Thomas Ken*........	352
ATTRACTIONS OF HEAVEN.................	*Bernard Barton*............	353
THE TRUEST END OF LIFE................	*William Penn*.............	353
ENTERING HEAVEN......................	*Rev. J. L. Harris*..........	354
THE WONDERS OF HEAVEN..............	*John Newton*..............	356
DELIGHTS OF HEAVEN	*Dr. Isaac Watts*............	357
IGNORANCE OF THE FUTURE LIFE........	*Richard Baxter*............	357
BEAUTIFUL HEAVEN....................	*Delia E. Walker*...........	358
SONGS IN HEAVEN.......................	*M. T. B*..................	359
HYMNS OF HEAVEN.....................	*Theo. L. Cuyler, D.D*......	360
ECHOES FROM HEAVEN...................	*John Cumming, D.D*.......	361
HEAVENLY REALITIES....................	*Miss Marsh*	362
THE CHRISTIAN IN HEAVEN........	*John S. C. Abbott, D.D*.....	363
THE LAND OF BEULAH	*C. Huntington*.............	366
THE SILENT SHORE.....................	*Charles Lamb*..............	367
THE DEATH OF THE RIGHTEOUS...........	*Dean Millman*.............	367
HEAVEN—NOT FAR AWAY................	*Anonymous*	368
THERE IS NO DEATH.....................	*Bulwer Lytton*.............	369
OUR FRIENDS IN HEAVEN.................	*Anonymous.*	371
MINISTERING ANGELS...................	*Kingswood Chronicle*.......	374
THREE UNCHANGEABLES	*Matthew Henry, D.D*.......	375
THE STARLESS CROWN..................	*J. L. H*...................	376
BRINGING OUR SHEAVES WITH US.........	*Elizabeth Ackers*...........	378
THE SHORE OF ETERNITY................	*F. W. Faber, D. D*.........	379
HYMNS OF LONGING FOR REST............	*Theo. L. Cuyler, D.D*......	381
AT EVENTIDE IT SHALL BE LIGHT.........	*Anonymous*.......	384
REUNION IN HEAVEN	*W. Morley Punshon, LL.D*...	385
WHAT MUST IT BE TO BE THERE !.........	*Mrs. Elizabeth Mills*........	386
JOY IN THE MORNING	*Rev. Dwight Williams*......	387
MY RESPONSIBILITY TO GOD..............	*Daniel Webster*............	388
THE SUNSET HOUR OF LIFE	*Anonymous*	389
THE JOY OF INCOMPLETENESS	*Sunday Magazine*..........	390
THERE'S NOTHING TRUE BUT HEAVEN......	*Thomas Moore*.............	391

CONTENTS.

		PAGE
Departure of Friends	James Montgomery	392
No Sects in Heaven	Mrs. Eliz. H. Jocelyn	393
Heaven	F. W. Faber, D.D.	397
Anticipation of Heaven	Thomas Moore	398
A Home in Heaven	William Hunter	399
Those Mansions Above	Parish Visitor	400
At Home in Heaven	Charles F. Deems, D.D.	402
Meetness for Heaven	United Presbyterian	404
Foretokens of Heaven	R. W. Hamilton	405
Blessed are the Home-Sick	Henrich Stillings	405
Joys of Heaven	Nancy A. W. Priest	406
Unvailed Heaven	Ernst Lange, D.D.	407
What is Heaven?	John Keble	407
Immortality	George D. Prentice	408
Time and Eternity	Horatius Bonar	409
No Night in Heaven	Anonymous	410
No Sorrow There	Daniel March, D.D.	411
Farewell Life, Welcome Life	Thomas Hood	412
The End	Anonymous	412
Benediction	Anonymous	414

MOTHER.

'Tis a mother's large affection
Hears with a mysterious sense,—
Breathings that escape detection
Whisper faint, and fine inflection
Thrill in her with power intense.
Childhood's honeyed words untaught
Hiveth she in loving thought,
Tones that never thence depart.
For she listens—with her heart.
                      LAMAN BLANCHARD.

All that I am or hope to be I owe to my mother.
                      ABRAHAM LINCOLN.

THE MOTHER'S TREASURE.

MOTHER.

[WRITTEN EXPRESSLY FOR THIS WORK.]

By Fanny J. Crosby.

THE light, the spell-word of the heart,
    Our guiding star in weal or woe,
Our talisman—our earthly chart—
    That sweetest name that earth can know.

We breathed it first with lisping tongue
    When cradled in her arms we lay;
Fond memories round that name are hung
    That will not, cannot pass away.

We breathed it then, we breathe it still,
    More dear than sister, friend, or brother;
The gentle power, the magic thrill,
    Awakened at the name of *mother*.

MY MOTHER DEAR.

S. Lover.

THERE was a place in childhood that I remember well,
    And there a voice of sweetest tone bright fairy tales did tell,
And gentle words, and fond embrace, were given with joy to me,
When I was in that happy place upon my mother's knee.

When fairy tales were ended, "Good night," she softly said,
And kissed, and laid me down to sleep, within my tiny bed,
And holy words she taught me then—methinks I yet can see
Her angel eyes, as close I knelt beside my mother's knee.

In the sickness of my childhood, the perils of my prime,
The sorrows of my riper years, the cares of ev'ry time,
When doubt and danger weighed me down, then pleading all for me,
It was a fervent prayer to Heaven that bent my mother's knee.

MOTHER.

Joanna Baillie.

WHEN we are sick, where can we turn for succor,
    When we are wretched, where can we complain?
    And when the world looks cold and surly on us,
Where can we go to meet a warmer eye
With such sure confidence as to a mother?

MOTHER, HOME AND HEAVEN.

Mary J. Muckle.

THERE are three words that sweetly blend,
   That on the heart are graven;
A precious soothing balm they lend—
   They're Mother, Home and Heaven!

They twine a wreath of beauteous flowers,
   Which, placed on memory's urn,
Will e'en the longest, gloomiest hours
   To golden sunlight turn!

They form a chain whose every link
   Is free from base alloy;
A stream where whosoever drinks
   Will find refreshing joy!

They build an altar where each day
   Love's offering is renewed;
And peace illumes with genial ray
   Life's darkened solitude!

If from our side the first has fled,
   And Home be but a name,
Let's strive the narrow path to tread,
   That we the last may gain!

MOTHER.

E. L. Cassanovia.

MID life's commotions—dismal fears—
 Mid cares and woes, and floods of tears,
 How sweetly breaks upon the ear
Some word of comfort or of cheer;
Yet of our friends there's not another
Who speaks as gently as our mother.

Here disappointments crowd each day,
Our brightest hopes soon fade away,
And friends long trusted oft deceive;
We scarcely know whom to believe,
Yet, though we fear to trust each other,
We're not afraid to trust our mother.

Yet here where there's so much deceit,
Some friends we have we love to meet,
There's love we know that will endure.
Not sordid, selfish, but all pure;
But though beloved by sister, brother,
There's none that love us like our mother.

Among the names to mortals given,
There's none like mother, home and heaven;
For home's no home without her care;
And heaven, we know she will be there;
Then let us, while we love each other,
Remember and be kind to mother.

THE MOTHER AT HOME.

ARCHBISHOP LEIGHTON says, "Fill the bushel with good wheat, and there will be no room for chaff and rubbish." This is a good thought for every mother while tending her children, and watching the growth of their power in body and mind.

"As soon as they be born," the Bible says, "children go astray, speaking lies." So soon, therefore, will a Christian mother begin to "train her child in the way he should go," that *good habits* may be formed, ready to carry out *good principles* as the child grows old enough to understand the reason for his conduct.

Good moral habits are essential to the healthfulness of the home; and these may be best taught by the watchful mother's training. One important part of her work is to remove *hindrances* out of her children's way to health and happiness. No dirt, or dirty habits, for example, should be permitted. Washing their hands and faces many times in the day will often remove a sense of discomfort which makes them fretful, as also will giving them food at regular periods. Ragged dress, too, and broken fastenings, add a feeling of degradation, that a careful mother will prevent as far as possible by keeping their clothes whole, neat, and clean. Making their own garments, we may here remark, gives useful employment to girls, and is an important aid in training them up to thrifty habits. Many families go in rags because they never learned to sew; while the same wages in the hands of those who know how to employ that useful "one-eyed servant," the needle, keep the household looking always respectable.

Children also should have time to *play*. Happiness is a great promoter of health. The Bible mentions "boys and girls playing in the streets," as one sign of national prosperity. They do not need expensive toys A little French prince turned from his new year's present of toys from an empress grandmother to watch some peasants making dirt pies, and, it is said, begged the queen his mother to allow him to join in the sport which seemed so charming to his childish eye, as offering some scope to his ingenuity. A few old bits of wood, or scraps of broken crockery, stones, and oyster-shells, afford inexhaustible amusement, cost nothing, and do not spoil; while if the mother will now and then put in a word to show an interest in her little ones' games, her own spirit will be refreshed and cheered by their light-heartedness.

Children are wonderful imitators, so that it is comparatively easy to lead them early into good ways. They are never so happy as when trying to do what they see older people do. Their plays chiefly consist in copying elders. The little cottager "makes believe" to go to market, to plant a garden, to make hay, to wash, to build, to cook, and to teach in school. The boys are never merrier than when playing at horses, or in some other way aspiring to be like their elders. Many of these games bring the bodily organs into excellent exercise, and strengthen and build up the system wonderfully. These amusements, too, often really prepare the children for the actual business of life, so that they the sooner become helpful to their parents. They should be watched and encouraged therefore in their play to habits of thoughtfulness and self-reliance.

Let it be remembered also, that, while by all means it is well to send children to school, the largest portion of their education, whether for good or evil, is carried on at home, often unconsciously, in their amusements, and under the daily influence of what they see and hear about them. It is there that "subtle brains and lissom fingers" find scope, and learn to promote the well-being of the community. We cannot tell what duties our children may be called to perform in after-life; many of England's greatest men were born poor cottagers. But we *can*, in a great measure, preserve their brains and limbs from injury; we can cultivate their faculties, and teach them to exercise all their senses,—to use their hands diligently and skillfully, to observe with their eyes, to listen to good instruction; in short, we can, by God's help, teach them, as the prophet says, "to choose the good and refuse the evil." We can encourage them to be apt to learn, so that they may with readiness set about any duty which God may place before them.

Are the children naughty? Must they be punished? "The Lord loveth the son whom He chasteneth;" "As many as I love I rebuke and chasten," are texts which will mitigate the anger of both father and mother, and teach them to adopt such means of correction as shall improve instead of harden their children's minds. Is a little daughter lame and sickly? Does a son get into a hard place? "Like as a father pitieth his children, so the Lord pitieth them that fear Him;" "As one whom his mother comforteth, so will I comfort you," saith the Lord.

Does work fail and removal among strangers seem inevitable? The children's conclusion that "Father will see about it," "Mother will be with us," are phrases full of deeper meaning to their parents' ears as they raise their hearts to God, and remember, "Thou compassest my path;" "Thou knowest my way;" "Though I walk through the midst of trouble Thou wilt revive me."

"Within Thy circling power I stand,
On every side I find Thine hand;
Awake, asleep, at home, abroad,
I am surrounded still by God."

And when strength fails, and a dear child is languishing into another life beyond the grave, who can tend the dying bed like a mother? In whom is there so much trust as in a father's love? Talk about duty to children, there is no pleasure sweeter than that of training them up in the nurture and admonition of the Lord, repaid as it is by their fervent friendship in after-life, and the hope of presenting them washed in a Saviour's blood and faultless before the great white throne at the last day.—*Mother's Treasury.*

A MOTHER'S LOVE.

(TYPICAL OF GOD'S LOVE.)

Sazs Hulm.

LIKE a cradle rocking, rocking,
   Silent, peaceful, to and fro;
Like a mother's sweet looks dropping
   On the little face below,
Hangs the green earth, swinging, turning,
   Jarless, noiseless, safe and slow;
Falls the light of God's face bending
   Down and watching us below.
And as feeble babes that suffer,
   Toss and cry, and will not rest,
Are the ones the tender mother
   Holds the closest, loves the best:
So, when we are weak and wretched,
   By our sins weighed down, distressed,
Then it is that God's great patience
   Holds us closest, loves us best.

A MOTHER'S HEART.

A LITTLE dreaming, such as mothers know;
   A little lingering over dainty things;
A happy heart, wherein hope all aglow
   Stirs like a bird at dawn that wakes and sings,
      And that is all.

A little clasping to her yearning breast;
   A little musing over future years;
A heart that prays: "Dear Lord, thou knowest best—
   But spare my flower life's bitterest rain of tears"—
      And that is all.

A little spirit speeding through the night;
   A little home grown lonely, dark and chill;
A sad heart groping blindly for the light;
   A little snow-clad grave beneath the hill—
      And that is all.

A little gathering of life's broken thread;
   A little patience keeping back the tears;
A heart that sings, "Thy darling is not dead,
   God keeps her safe through his eternal years"—
      And that is all.—*Macmillan's Magazine.*

The love principle is stronger than the force principle.
                              Dr. A. A. Hodge.

A MOTHER'S INFLUENCE.

J. M. Matthews, D. D.

WE have read history to little purpose if we have not observed that there are periods when corruption seems to acquire a peculiar and fearful sway in our world; and these sad changes are generally attributed to the influence of some distinguished leader or leaders in wickedness, who impress their own corrupt image on the generation in which they live. But if we trace the evils to their true source, we must go farther back than to the men who stand thus prominent in producing them. Had I time, I would here show, that all those great changes from bad to worse which have rendered nations so corrupt as to consign them to ruin, have been effected through the corrupting influence of mothers, acting on those in childhood, who in manhood became the leading men of their day. Such, the holy Scriptures inform us, was the real cause of that awful wickedness which brought the waters of the deluge on the earth. It was not till "the sons of God took to them wives of the daughters of men" (thus contracting unhallowed and forbidden alliances), that "the wickedness of man became so great in the earth, that it repented the Lord that he had made man, and he said, I will destroy man which I created from the face of the earth." And what is so marked as the immediate cause of the wide-spread depravity which called for the destruction of a world, is equally marked in other parts of the Scriptures, as the grand source of ruin to the nations whose history they record. Have you never observed how frequently they allude to the mothers of Israel and of Judah's kings, when in the days of the nation's decline the throne passed in such rapid succession from one king to another, "who did evil in the sight of the Lord"? The career of guilt and declension was sometime checked by the raising up of one good king who walked in the way of the Lord. Such was Josiah, of whom we are told, "his mother's name was Jedediah;" a name which at once announces her piety and worth. But see how the parentage of the wicked and idolatrous kings is noted. We are told of Abijah, the grandson of Solomon, who was perhaps the first who filled the land with idolatry, that his mother's name was Maachah. Of Ahaziah, the son of Ahab, who did evil exceedingly in the sight of the Lord, we are told that his mother was Jezebel, who stirred up his father Ahab to sin. In like manner we are told of Jehoahaz, that his mother's name was Hamutal; of Jehoiakim, that his mother's name was Zebadah; of Jehoiachin, that his mother's name was Nehushta: names which, taken in connection with their history, sufficiently show the evil courses they pursued, and the consequent evil influence they would exert.

Now, why was this all so carefully noted? It was to show that the bane of the nation was found in the *nurseries* of her kings, where their infant minds were tainted and poisoned by their Jezebel mothers; and that being thus early led into sin, when in after-life they gained the throne, their baleful influence was felt in spreading wickedness around them, till their nation was carried away into captivity, and their land left a desolation. It was the corrupt queen-mothers corrupting the minds of their infant sons, who were to be, in future, kings, that primarily and mainly drew down the anger of God; nor was it till this insidious source of evil had been for generations at work, that hope finally perished.

But if maternal influence is thus powerful for evil, it is equally powerful for good, when rightly and wisely employed. Nor do I believe the assertion at all too strong, when I say, that the greatest and best of those whom we count among the great and good of our race, have always derived the elements of their characters from maternal care bestowed on them in childhood. If, in all the annals of the human race, there be an exception to our position, let it be named; let us be told where it is. It cannot be found in the pages of sacred history. The testimony here, respecting those whose names it has embalmed for immortality, is all one way. Such, it tells us, was the training under which the childhood of Moses was passed. The faith and piety of his mother was so strong, that "she did not fear the king's wrath;" thus showing herself a fit mother for a son who was to be the deliverer of Israel from Egyptian bondage, and the lawgiver to the redeemed nation. And who does not see the hand and design of God in that wonderful train of events which secured to the child of such high destiny, the care of a mother so peculiarly fitted for her task? Under a like happy influence was the childhood of David passed, as he acknowledges in his subsequent days of power and fame: "O Lord, truly I am Thy servant; I am Thy servant, and the *son of Thine handmaid:* Thou hast loosed my bonds. I will offer to Thee the sacrifice of thanksgiving, and will call upon the name of the Lord:" thus in the days of his highest prosperity and greatest fame, recognizing his pious mother's influence, not only as having mainly contributed to elevate him to Israel's throne, but as having been the bright star which kept alive his hope in the darkest hour of his previous troubles. To the same cause, as already observed, in the case of Josiah, are we taught to attribute, in great measure, the wisdom and power which distinguished such of Judah's kings as "did that which was right in the sight of the Lord." Again: John, the forerunner of our Saviour, is said to have had none greater than himself of all who had been born of women. But his mother was Elizabeth, a woman who "walked in all the commandments and ordinances of the Lord blameless." Again: among the apostles of our Lord was one distinguished as "a son of thunder;" and another privileged to "lean on his Master's bosom," and to receive very special tokens of His love. But when we are told of the piety and holy ambition of their mother, we may account, at least in part, for their distinction among the twelve (Matt. xx. 20, 21). And not to mention others from the sacred Scriptures, as Timothy, whose "unfeigned faith dwelt first in his grandmother Lois, and his mother Eunice;" on whom, let me ask, has the Saviour's mantle ever fallen, or in whom has His Spirit ever dwelt, with peculiar manifestation, who may not be added to the cloud of witnesses on this point? In far-gone times, look into the biographies of Polycarp, Augustine, Justin, Gregory, and others of the Fathers; and in latter days, look to the childhood of Matthew Henry, Edwards, Dwight, Payson, and the whole army of those, at home and abroad, who are this day owned and hailed as the champions of truth, and you will find them all, without exception, to have been the sons of pious and faithful mothers. Nor is it only from the great and illustrious in the Church that we may collect such facts. Look around you, and see what are the families from which religion derives its most devoted and faithful friends. From what dwellings come the sacramental host who fill the Lord's table when it is spread, and not only there confess His name before men, but are the foremost in efforts to spread His name through the world? Do they come from families where the mother, though she may rule as a queen of fashion, and is perhaps rich in every worldly endowment, yet loves not God, and finds no place for him in her heart and her labors? Far from it. They come, and come almost exclusively, from households where the mother is a Christian; where the nursery for the family is a nursery for the church; where the first lispings of childhood are accents of prayer, and the first thoughts of the heart thoughts of God and of His Christ.

"Just as the twig is bent, the tree's inclined."

But who bends the twig? Who has the mind or character in hand while it is yet so flexible and ductile that it can be turned in any direction, or formed in any shape? It is the mother. From her own nature, and the nature of her child, it results that its first impressions must be taken from her. And she has every advantage for discharging the duty. She is always with her child —if she is where mothers ought to be—sees continually the workings of faculties; where they need to be restrained, and where led and attracted. Early as she may begin her task, let her be assured, that her labor will not be lost because undertaken too soon. Mind, from the first hour of its existence, is ever acting; and soon may a mother see that, carefully as she may study her child, *quite as carefully is her child studying her.* Let her watch the varying expression of its speaking face, as its eyes follow her, and she will perceive its mind is imbibing impressions from everything it sees her do; and thus showing, that, before the lips have begun to utter words, the mind has begun to act, and to form a character. Let her watch on; and when, under her care, the expanding faculties have begun to display themselves in the sportiveness of play, how often will she be surprised to find the elements of character already fixed, when she has least expected it. She has but to watch, and she will find the embryo tyrant or philanthropist, warrior or peace-maker, with her in her nursery; and then, if ever, her constant prayer should be, "How shall I order the child, and what shall I do unto him?" For, what he is to be, and what he is to do, in any of these characters, she must now decide. It is a law of our being that makes it so; a law that I could wish were written on every mother's heart by the finger of God, and on the walls of her nursery in letters of gold, that the mind of childhood is like wax to receive, but like marble to hold, every impression made upon it, be it for good or for evil. Let her then improve her power as she ought, "being steadfast, unmovable, always abounding in the work" which God requires at her hands; and let her know that her labor is not in vain in the Lord. For, even though her own eyes may not be privileged to witness in her child all that is noble and great and good, she may at least save him when her course on earth is finished. It is no picture of the imagination that I hold out, when I ask you to come and see the son of a faithful mother, who has long pursued his course of crime, till he seems hardened against everything good or true; yea, at times "sits in the seat of the scorner," and scoffs at everything holy and good—but yet, hardened and dead as his heart may seem, as to everything else you may urge, there is one point on which, till his dying day, he can be made to feel. You touch it when you remind him of what he saw and felt when a child under the care of a tender mother. His sensibilities there he never utterly loses; and often, often, by that, as the last cord which holds him from utter perdition, is the prodigal drawn back and restored; so that, though "dead, he is alive again," though once "lost, he is found."

Such are some of the illustrations of a mother's power to do good to those most dear to her, and of the responsibility that springs from it. There is no influence so powerful as hers on the coming destinies of the church and the world. She acts a part in forming the ministers of religion and the rulers of the land, without which all subsequent training is comparatively vain. And to her, also, it falls to train those who are to be mothers when she is gone, and to do for their generation what she has done for hers.

A MOTHER'S PRAYER.

THE sweetest sound heard through our earthly home,
　　The brightest ray that gleams from heaven's dome,
　　The loveliest flower that e'er from earth's breast rose,
That purest flame that, quivering, gleams and glows,
Are found alone, where kneels a mother mild,
With heart uplifted, praying for her child.

The stream of tears can never cease to flow
Long as life's sun shall shine on us below;
And many angels have been sent by God
To count the tear-drops wept upon life's road;
But of all the tears that flow, the least defiled
Are when a mother prays beside her child.

Because it is to mortal eyes unseen,
Ye call it foolishness, a childish dream,
In vain, ye cannot rob me of that thought,
That legend with such heavenly sweetness fraught,
That blessed angels have for ages smiled
To see a mother praying for her child.—*Anonymous.*

IT is the mother who moulds the character, and fixes the destiny of the child.

THE MOTHER.

Thomas Campbell.

LO! at the couch where infant beauty sleeps,
  Her silent watch the mournful mother keeps;
  She, while the lovely babe unconscious lies,
Smiles on her slumbering child with pensive eyes,
And weaves a song of melancholy joy,—
"Sleep, image of thy father, sleep, my boy:
No lingering hour of sorrow shall be thine;
No sigh that rends thy father's heart and mine;
Bright as his manly sire the son shall be
In form and soul; but ah! more blest than he!
Thy fame, thy worth, thy filial love, at last,
Shall soothe this aching heart for all the past,
With many a smile my solitude repay,
And chase the world's ungenerous scorn away.

"And say, when summoned from the world and thee,
I lay my head beneath the willow-tree,
Wilt thou, sweet mourner! at my stone appear,
And soothe my parted spirit lingering near?
Oh, wilt thou come, at evening hour, to shed
The tears of memory o'er my narrow bed;
With aching temple on thy hand reclined,
Muse on the last farewell I leave behind,
Breathe a deep sigh to winds that murmur low,
And think on all my love, and all my woe?"

So speaks affection, ere the infant eye
Can look regard, or brighten in reply;

But when the cherub lip hath learnt to claim
A mother's ear by that endearing name;
Soon as the playful innocent can prove
A tear of pity, or a smile of love,
Or cons his murmuring tasks beneath her care,
Or lisps, with holy look, his evening prayer,
Or gazing mutely pensive, sits to hear
The mournful ballad warbled in his ear;
How fondly looks admiring hope the while,
At every artless tear, and every smile!
How glows the joyous parent to descry
A guileless bosom, true to sympathy!

TIRED MOTHERS.

Mrs. May Riley Smith.

A LITTLE elbow leans upon your knee—
    Your tired knee that has so much to bear;
  A child's dear eyes are looking lovingly
    From underneath a thatch of tangled hair.
Perhaps you do not heed the velvet touch
    Of warm, moist fingers holding you so tight;
You do not prize the blessing overmuch—
    You almost are too tired to pray to-night.

But it is blessedness! A year ago
    I did not see it as I do to-day—
We are all so dull and thankless, and too slow
    To catch the sunshine till it slips away.

TIRED MOTHERS.

And now it seems surpassing strange to me
   That while I wore the badge of motherhood
I did not kiss more oft and tenderly
   The little child that brought me only good.

And if, some night, when you sit down to rest,
   You miss the elbow from your tired knee;
This restless curly head from off your breast;
   This lisping tongue that chatters constantly;
If from your own, the dimpled hands had slipped,
   And ne'er would nestle in your palm again;
If the white feet into the grave had tripped—
   I could not blame you for your heartache then.

I wonder so that mothers ever fret
   At their little children clinging to their gowns;
Or that the foot-prints, when the days are wet,
   Are ever black enough to make them frown!
If I could find a little muddy boot,
   Or cap, or jacket, on my chamber floor—
If I could kiss a rosy, restless foot,
   And hear it patter in my house once more;

If I could mend a broken cart to-day,
   To-morrow make a kite to reach the sky—
There is no woman in God's world could say
   She was more blissfully content than I!
But, ah, the dainty pillow next mine own
   Is never rumpled by a shining head,
My singing birdling from its nest has flown—
   The little boy I used to kiss—is dead!

MOTHERS OF DISTINGUISHED MEN.

TIMOTHY, from a child, knew the Scriptures, being taught them by his mother and his grandmother.

Dr. Dodridge's mother taught him the history of the Old and New Testaments before he could read. This was done by means of Dutch tiles in the chimney. Her wise and pious reflections upon the stories there represented, made good impression on his mind; and he never lost them.

Bishop Hall says that he could bless the memory of his mother, who taught him so much divine truth, and gave him so many pious lectures.

J. S. C. Abbott says in his "Mother at Home," that in a college where one hundred and twenty young men were preparing for the ministry, it was found that more than one hundred had been led to Christ by their mothers.

John Randolph, of Roanoke, was deeply attached to his mother, and her death had a melancholy and striking effect upon him ever afterwards. She was but thirty-six years old when she died. Cut off in the bloom of youth and beauty, he always retained a vivid remembrance of her person, her charms, and her virtues. He always kept her portrait hanging before him in his chamber. The loss to him was irreparable. She knew him—she knew the delicacy of his heart, the waywardness and irritability of his temper. "I am a fatalist," said he, "I am all but friendless—only one human being ever knew me. She only knew me—my mother." He always spoke of her in terms of the warmest affection. Many and many a time during his life did he visit the old churchyard at Matoax, in its wasted solitude, and shed tears over the grave of his mother, by whose side it was the last wish of his heart to be buried.

Henry Clay, the pride and honor of his country, always expressed feelings of profound affection and veneration for his mother. A habitual correspondence and enduring affection subsisted between them to the last hour of life. Mr. Clay ever spoke of her as a model of maternal character and female excellence, and it is said that he never met his constituents in Woodford county, after her death, without some allusion to her, which deeply affected both him and his audience. And nearly the last words uttered by this great statesman, when he came to die, were, "Mother, mother, mother." It is natural for us to feel that she must have been a good mother, that was loved and so dutifully served by such a boy, and that neither could have been wanting in rare virtues.

Benjamin Franklin was accustomed to refer to his mother in the tenderest tone of filial affection. His respect and affection for her were manifested, among other ways, in frequent presents, that contributed to her comfort and solace in her advancing years. In one of his letters to her, for example, he sends her a *moidore*, a gold piece of the value of six dollars, "toward chaise hire," said he, "that you may ride warm to meetings during the winter." In another he gives her an account of the growth and improvement of his son and daughter—topics which, as he well understood, are ever as dear to the grandmother as to the mother.

Thomas Gray, author of "Elegy in a Country Churchyard," was most assiduous in his attentions to his mother while she lived, and, after her death, he cherished her memory with sacred sorrow. Mr. Mason informs us that Gray seldom mentioned his mother without a sigh. The inscription which he placed over her remains speaks of her as "the careful, tender mother of many children, one of whom alone had the misfortune to survive her." How touching is this brief tribute of grateful love! Volumes of eulogy could not increase our admiration of the gentle being to whom it was paid—her patient devotion, her meek endurance. Wherever the name and genius of Gray are known, there shall also his mother's virtues be told for a memorial of her. He was buried, according to his directions, by the side of his mother, in the churchyard at Stoke. After his death her gowns and wearing apparel were found in a trunk in his apartments, just as she had left them. It seemed as if he could never take the resolution to open it, in order to distribute them to his female relations, to whom, by his will, he bequeathed them.

Amos Lawrence always spoke of his mother in the strongest terms of veneration and love, and in many letters to his children and grandchildren, are found messages of affectionate regard for his mother, such as could have emanated only from a heart overflowing with filial gratitude. Her form, bending over his bed in silent prayer, at the hour of twilight, when she was about leaving him for the night, was among the earliest and most cherished recollections of his early years and his childhood's home.

SERGEANT S. PRENTISS.—From his mother Mr. Prentiss inherited those more gentle qualities that ever characterized his life—qualities that shed over his eloquence such bewitching sweetness, and gave to his social intercourse such an indescribable charm. A remarkably characteristic anecdote illustrates his filial affection. When on a visit, some years ago, to the North, but after his reputation had become wide-spread, a distinguished lady, of Portland, Me., took pains to obtain an introduction, by visiting the steamboat in which she learned he was to take his departure in a few moments.

"I have wished to see you," said she to Mr. Prentiss, "for my heart has often congratulated the mother who has such a son."

"Rather congratulate the *son* on having such a *mother*," was his instant and heartfelt reply. This is but one of the many instances in which the most distinguished men of all ages have been proud to refer to the early culture of intellect, the promptings of virtue, or the aspirations of piety, and to the influence of the mother's early training.

FRANCIS MARION.—General Marion was once a plodding young farmer, and in no way distinguished as superior to the young men of the neighborhood in which he lived, except for his devoted love and marked respect for his excellent mother, and exemplary honor and truthfulness. In these qualities he was eminent from early childhood, and they marked his character through life. We may remark, in this connection, that it is usual to affect some degree of astonishment when we read of men whose after fame presents a striking contrast to the humility of their origin; yet we must recollect that it is not ancestry and splendid descent, but education and circumstances, which form the man. It is often a matter of surprise that distinguished men have such inferior children, and that a great name is seldom perpetuated. The secret of this is as often evident: the mothers have been inferior—mere ciphers in the scale of existence. All the splendid advantages procured by wealth and the father's position, cannot supply this one deficiency in the mother, who gives character to the child.

Sam Houston's mother was an extraordinary woman. She was distinguished by a full, rather tall and matronly form, a fine carriage, and an impressive and dignified countenance. She was gifted with intellectual and moral qualities, which elevated her, in a still more striking manner, above most of her sex. Her life shone with purity and benevolence, and yet she was nerved with a stern fortitude, which never gave way in the midst of the wild scenes that checkered the history of the frontier settlers. Mrs. Houston was left with the heavy burden of a numerous family. She had six sons and three daughters, but she was not a woman to succumb to misfortune, and she made ample provision, for one in her circumstances, for their future care and education. To bring up a large family of children in a proper manner is, under the most favorable circumstances, a great work; and in this case it rises into sublimity; for there is no finer instance of heroism than that of one parent, especially a mother, laboring for that end alone. The excellent woman, says Goethe, is she who, if her husband dies, can be a father to her children.

As wife and mother, a woman is seen in her most sacred and dignified character, as such she has great influence over the characters of individuals, over the condition of families, and over the destinies of empires. It is a fact that many of our noblest patriots, our most profound scholars, and our holiest ministers, were stimulated to their excellence and usefulness by those holy principles which they derived in early years from pious mothers.

Our mothers are our earliest instructors, and they have an influence over us, the importance of which, for time and eternity, surpasses the power of language to describe.

Every mother should be a Sabbath School teacher. Her own children should be her class; and her home should be her school-house. Then her children will bless her for her tenderness and care; for her pious instructions, her fervent prayers, and the holy example.—*Anonymous.*

MOTHERS AND SONS.

MOST boys go through a period, when they have great need of patient love at home. They are awkward and clumsy, sometimes strangely willful and perverse, and they are desperately conscious of themselves, and very sensitive to the least word of censure or effort at restraint. Authority frets them. They are leaving childhood, but they have not yet reached the sober good sense of manhood. They are an easy prey to the tempter and the sophist. Perhaps they adopt skeptical views, from sheer desire to prove that they are independent, and can do their own thinking. Now is the mother's hour. Her boy needs her now more than when he lay in his cradle. Her finer insight and serener faith may hold him fast, and prevent his drifting into dangerous courses. At all events there is very much that only a mother can do for her son, and that a son can receive only from his mother, in the critical period of which we are thinking. It is well for him, if she have kept the freshness and brightness of her youth, so that she can now be his companion and friend as well as mentor. It is a good thing for a boy to be proud of his mother; to feel complacent when he introduces her to his comrades, knowing that they cannot help seeing what a pretty woman she is, so graceful, winsome, and attractive! There is always hope for a boy when he admires his mother, and mothers should care to be admirable in the eyes of their sons. Not merely to possess characters which are worthy of respect, but to be beautiful and charming, so far as they can, in person and appearance. The neat dress, the becoming ribbon, and smooth hair are all worth thinking about, when regarded as means of retaining influence over a soul, when the world is spreading lures for it on every side.

Above all things, mothers need faith. Genuine, hearty, loving trust in God, a life of meek, glad acquiescence in His will, lived daily through years in the presence of sons, is an immense power. They never can get away from the sweet memory that Christ was their mother's friend. There is a reality in that which no false reasoning can persuade them to regard as a figment of the imagination.
—*Christian Intelligencer.*

THE MOTHER'S PRAYER.

OUT in the wide world, somewhere roaming,
   In the misty chill of this twilight gloaming,
     Homeless and friendless, with only the care
Which Heaven provides for the birds of the air;
Without shelter or bread,
Only sad stars overhead,
And a heart overwhelmed with devouring despair—
Out in the wide world somewhere—somewhere.

With garments all tattered, and filthy, and worn;
With feet that are blistered, and shoes that are torn;
With eyes that are heavy, and drooping, and dim;
And a heart that is vailed in the dust of his sin,
Besmeared with the slime
Of evil and crime,
You would not think it, but down deep within,
A door stands ajar, and you may go in.

In the bygone hours of the old long ago,
Before the winter of vice, with its ice and its snow,
Had chilled that faint heart, I once held the key—
This object of pity once sat on my knee;
I smoothed the fair head,
And kissed the lips, so red;
O, cruel the hand that has taken from me
This gem from my heart-life's sad mystery!

A MOTHER'S LOVE.

O, wide world so mighty, so vast, and so old!
O, wide world so heartless, unfriendly, and cold!
Despise not this wretch, for once he was fair
As the jewel which decks the young maiden's hair.
O, rescue this one,
For he is *my* son,
And God hath forgotten a mother's prayer,
As it wanders world-wide somewhere—somewhere.

Rum, the accursed, which evermore brings
Its withering woe to peasant and kings,
Hath blighted this life, so gifted and rare,
And left it a wreck, unsightly and bare.
While loving hearts must ache,
And sometimes break,
Will Heaven not heed importunate prayer?
And rescue the wandering *sometime—somewhere?*
—*Anonymous.*

A MOTHER'S LOVE.
James Montgomery.

A MOTHER'S love, how sweet the name!
What is a mother's love?
A noble, pure and tender flame,
Enkindled from above,
To bless a heart of earthly mould;
The warmest love that *can* grow cold;
This is a mother's love.

THE MOTHER'S OPPORTUNITY.

MOTHERS, you are the divinely-appointed teachers and guides of your children; and any attempt to free yourselves from your duty is in direct opposition to the will of God. If you neglect them, the consequences are swift and sure, and how fearful they are, let those broken-hearted mothers tell who have bowed in anguish over their lost sons; who, neglecting them in childhood, have at last seen them dead to every manly virtue.

Let me say to you who still have the opportunity to do so, train your children, whether boys or girls, to usefulness. Give them something to do. And as soon as they can walk, teach them to bring any little thing to you, and as they grow older let them do all they can to help you. Spend most of your time with your young children. Sleep near them; attend to washing and dressing them; let them eat at the table with father and mother; read, talk, play, walk with them; be their companion and guide in all things and at all times. When the father can leave his work to take a little recreation, let him take it with the children, making it a special holiday. Don't be in haste to send them to school, but teach them at home. Oral instruction can be given while you are doing your work, and for a while will be of much more benefit than many hours of study. As soon as they want playmates, see that they have those of their own age, who have been well cared for at home, and are truthful. Let them play in or near the house, that you may observe the character of their intercourse. Never send children to school to get rid of the care or trouble of them at home, but when the right time comes, let them see that it is wholly for their good that you part

THE MOTHER'S OPPORTUNITY.

with them. If possible, go often to the school-room yourself—nothing gives children so much encouragement. Always allow them to tell you all that has happened to interest or annoy them while absent from home. Never think anything which affects the happiness of your children too small a matter to claim your attention. Use every means in your power to win and retain their confidence Do not rest satisfied without some account of each day's joys or sorrows. It is a source of great comfort to the innocent child to tell all its troubles to mother, and do you lend a willing ear. For know you, that as soon as they cease to tell you all these things, they have chosen other confidants, and therein lies the danger. O mother! this is the rock on which your son may be wrecked at last. I charge you to set a watch upon it. Be jealous of the first sign that he is not opening all his heart to you.

Boys who are thus cared for and trained find more to please and amuse them at home than away. They are thus saved from temptation. But if they are neglected until they arrive at the age when they would wish to go out evenings, there is small hope that any but arbitrary measures will prevent or secure obedience, and then it hardly can be called obedience. It is much more pleasant to apply the "ounce of prevention" than the "pound of cure" in such cases. When boys know that their society is valued highly at home, and that all its pleasures are marred by their absence, they will willingly stay if they can have something to occupy their time.—*Anonymous.*

SOME hearts, like evening primroses, open most beautifully in the evening of life.

MOTHERS, PUT YOUR CHILDREN TO BED.

THERE may be some mothers who feel it to be a self-denial to leave their parlors, or fire-sides, or work, to put their children to bed. They think that the nurse could do just as well; that it is of no consequence who "hears the children say their prayers." Now, setting aside the pleasure of opening the little bed and tucking the darling up, there are really important reasons why the mother should not yield this privilege to any one. In the first place, it is the time of all times when a child is inclined to show its confidence and affection. All its little secrets come out with more truth and less restraints; its naughtiness through the day can be reproved and talked over with less excitement, and with the tenderness and calmness necessary to make a permanent impression. If the little one has shown a desire to do well and be obedient, its efforts and success can be acknowledged and commended in a manner that need not render it vain or self-satisfied.

We must make it a habit to talk to our children, in order to get from them an expression of their feelings. We cannot understand the character of these little beings committed to our care unless we do. And if we do not know what they are, we shall not be able to govern them wisely, or educate them as their different natures demand. Certainly it would be unwise to excite young children by too much conversation with them just before putting them to bed.

Every mother who carefully studies the temperament of her children will know how to manage them in this respect. But of this all mothers may be assured, that the last words at night are of great importance, even to the babies of the flock; the very tones of the voice they last listened to make an impression upon their sensitive organizations. Mothers, do not think the time and strength wasted, which you spend in reviewing the day with your little boy or girl; do not neglect to teach it how to pray, and pray for it in simple and earnest language, which it can understand. Soothe and quiet its little heart after the experiences of the day. It has had its disappointments and trials as well as its play and pleasures; it is ready to throw its arms around your neck, and take its good-night kiss.—*Mother's Magazine.*

THE GOOD-NIGHT KISS.

ALWAYS send your little child to bed happy. Whatever cares may trouble your mind, give the dear child a warm good-night kiss as it goes to its pillow. The memory of this, in the stormy years which may be in store for the little one, will be like Bethlehem's star to the bewildered shepherds; and welling up in the heart will rise the thought: "My father, my mother—*loved me!*" Lips parched with fever will become dewy again at this thrill of useful memories. Kiss your little child before it goes to sleep.

—*Anonymous.*

A GOOD word is an easy obligation; but not to speak ill, requires only our silence, which costs us nothing.—*Tillotson.*

MOTHER AND CHILD.

Thomas Hood.

LOVE thy mother, little one!
   Kiss and clasp her neck again!
   Hereafter she may have a son
Will kiss and clasp her neck in vain.
   Love thy mother, little one!

Gaze upon her living eyes,
And mirror back her love for thee!
Hereafter thou may'st shudder sighs
To meet them when they cannot see.
   Gaze upon her living eyes!

Press her lips the while they glow
With love that they have often told!
Hereafter thou may'st press in woe,
And kiss them till thine own are cold.
   Press her lips the while they glow!

Oh, revere her raven hair—
Although it be not silver gray!
Too early, death, led on by care,
May snatch save one dear lock away.
   Oh, revere her raven hair!

Pray for her at eve and morn,
That Heaven may long the stroke defer;
For Thou may'st live the hour forlorn,
When thou wilt ask to die with her.
   Pray for her at eve and morn!

OUR MOTHER.

OUR mother's lost her youthfulness,
   Her locks are turning gray,
   And wrinkles take the place of smiles—
   She's fading every day.
We gaze at her in sorrow now,
   For though we've ne'er been told
We can but feel the weary truth—
   Our mother's growing old.

Our mother's lost her youthfulness,
   Her eyes grow dim with tears,
Yet still within her heart there shines
   Some light of other years;
For oft she'll speak in merry tones,
   Smile as in youth she smiled,
As o'er her heart some memory steals
   Of when she was a child.

Our mother's lost her youthfulness,
   The light step has grown slow,
The graceful form has learned to stoop,
   The bright cheek lost its glow.
Her weary hands have grown so thin,
   Her dear hand trembles now;
"Passing away," in sad, deep lines,
   Is traced upon her brow.

OUR MOTHER.

Our mother's lost her youthfulness,
   Her smiles are just as kind,
Her tones to us are soft as erst,—
   Where should we dearer find?
But as we note the trembling tongue,
   And mark the stooping form,
A sad voice whispers to our hearts,—
   "Ye cannot keep her long."

Our mother's lost her youthfulness,
   We see it every day,
And feel more drearily the truth,
   She soon must pass away.
Ah! even now the "boatman pale"
   We fear is hovering nigh;
Waiting with white sails all unfurled,
   He will not heed our cry.

But gently bear the wearied form
   Into the phantom bark,
She will not fear—CHRIST went before,
   The way will not be dark:
And safe beyond the troubled stream,
   Her tired heart's strife o'er,
Our angel mother, glorified,
   Will grow old nevermore.
                  —*Rural New Yorker.*

"COUNT that day lost whose low-descending sun
   Views from thy hand no worthy action done."

PARENTAL AUTHORITY.

THE very height of human wickedness is described in the Holy Book as "lawlessness." Subjection to the holy, just, and good law of the Most High God is the essential condition of well-being here, and the essential element of glory hereafter. In keeping with this, human beings come into this world in a state of dependence and subjection, and for about one-half of the average term of human life that is their proper and natural state.

I cannot doubt that the great idea of the long pupilage of man is just that the principle and habit of *obedience*, of submission to authority, may be wrought into his inmost nature—that, taught to obey an earthly parent, even from infancy, he may pass from subjection to the earthly father to subjection to the heavenly one. *Reverent obedience of the child to parents is the preparation for reverent obedience of the man to God.* The one is the stepping-stone to the other. It is asked in the Epistle of John, "If a man love not his brother whom he hath seen, how can he love God whom he hath not seen?" In the same spirit and with at least equal emphasis it may be asked, "If a child honor not the father whom he hath seen, how shall he honor his Father whom he hath not seen?" There is rebellion against God in our inmost nature. Well, train up a child in willfulness and insubordination, and what must you expect as the result of nature's tendencies and such a training commingled.

Law is everywhere here. There is law in the Bible. There is law in our souls. There are laws written with a pen of iron upon our bodily frames. There are laws upon earth and sky—and to send forth from your home a lawless creature, is to send forth a blind man to walk among pitfalls and precipices, to offer up an immortal nature to the god of misrule.

In a religious point of view it seems to me just of the last importance that the parent should exercise over his children a sovereign authority. There must be no permitted resistance to his will. Obedience must be the primary law of the family. Does this have a sound of harshness? But it is the Bible way! The confidence in regard to Abraham was that he would *command* his children after him. Children are bidden by the apostle to obey their parents. It is the essential requisite of a ruler in God's house that he should be able to rule in his own house, having his children *in subjection*. And authority is not tyranny. As the authority of God is not tyranny, neither is the authority of a parent, rightly used. If it is rightly used, it will be used under the feeling of tender love and affectionate interest. The children themselves will more and more come to feel that; and feeling it, to render a willing and cheerful obedience to it. We parents should rule in love—in Christian love—BUT WE SHOULD RULE.

Parental authority, like all authority, needs a wise hand to wield it. There is needed especially great wisdom in the exercise of it, when the boy is passing into the man. At that stage of human life when you have the feeling of independence beginning to come—when you have so often the passions of manhood to deal with without manhood's checks and sense—no one can tell what the blessing is of having, say, a father to whom a son has been in the habit of looking with submissive reverence, and who has the wisdom to use his influence aright.

But altogether, we may depend on it that there is nothing more ruinous than disobedience allowed in our little ones. I may even venture to say, that it is great cruelty and great sin in us to permit it, out of, it may be, an indolent easiness of mind, or an unwise softness of disposition. The parent is to rule in home, the world of childhood, as the Great Parent rules in the world, the home of manhood.—*Mother's Treasury.*

COURTESIES TO PARENTS.

PARENTS lean upon their children, and especially their sons, much earlier than either of them imagine. Their love is a constant inspiration, a perennial fountain of delight, from which other lips may quaff, and be comforted thereby. It may be that the mother has been left a widow, depending on her only son for support. He gives her a comfortable home, sees that she is well clad, and allows no debts to accumulate, and that is all. It is considerable, more even than many sons do, but there is a lack. He seldom thinks it worth while to give her a caress; he has forgotten all those affectionate ways that kept the wrinkles from her face, and make her look so much younger than her years; he is ready to put his hand in his pocket to gratify her slightest request, but to give of the abundance of his heart is another thing entirely. He loves his mother? Of course he does! Are there not proofs enough of his filial regard? Is he not continually making sacrifices for her benefit? What more could any reasonable woman ask?

Ah, but it is the mother-heart that craves an occasional kiss, the support of your youthful arm, the little attentions and kindly courtesies of life, that smooth down so many of its asperities, and make the journey less wearisome. Material aid is good so far as it goes, but it has not that sustaining power which the loving, sympathetic heart bestows upon its object. You think she has out-grown these weaknesses and follies, and is content with the crust that is left; but you are mistaken. Every little offer of attention,—your escort to church or concert, or for a quiet walk, brings back the youth of her heart; her cheeks glow, and her eyes sparkle with pleasure, and oh! how proud she is of her son!

Even the father, occupied and absorbed as he may be, is not wholly indifferent to these filial expressions of devoted love. He may pretend to care very little for them, but having faith in their sincerity, it would give him serious pain were they entirely withheld. Fathers need their sons quite as much as the sons need the fathers, but in how many deplorable instances do they fail to find in them a staff for their declining years!

My son, are you a sweetener of life? You may disappoint the ambition of your parents; may be unable to distinguish yourself as they fondly hoped; may find your intellectual strength inadequate to your own desires, but let none of these things move you from a determination to be a son of whose moral character they need never be ashamed. Begin early to cultivate a habit of thoughtfulness and consideration for others, especially for those whom you are commanded to honor. Can you begrudge a few extra steps for the mother who never stopped to number those you demanded during your helpless infancy? Have you the heart to slight her requests, or treat her remarks with indifference, when you cannot begin to measure the patient devotion with which she bore with your peculiarities? Anticipate her wants, invite her confidence, be prompt to offer assistance, express your affections as heartily as you did when a child, that the mother may never grieve in secret for the son she has lost.
—*S. S. Times.*

THE MOTHER'S CHARGE.

Mrs L. H. Sigourney.

AND say to mothers what a holy charge
    Is theirs; with what a kingly power their love
    Might rule the fountains of the new-born mind.
Warn them to wake at early dawn and sow
Good seed, before the world has sown its tares.

AUTHORITY OF PARENTS.

Horace Bushnell, D.D.

IT is a great mistake to suppose that what will make a child stare or tremble impresses more authority. The violent emphasis, the hard, stormy voice, the menacing air, only weaken authority. Is it not well understood, that a bawling and violent teamster has no real government of his team? Is it not practically seen that a skillful commander of one of those huge floating cities, moved by steam on our American waters, manages and works every motion by the waving of the hand, or by signs that pass in silence, issuing no order at all, save in the gentlest undertone of voice? So when there is, or is to be, a real order in the house, it will come of no hard and boisterous, or fretful and termagant way of commanding. Gentleness will speak the word of firmness, and firmness will be clothed in that of true gentleness.

THE DYING MOTHER.

LAY the gem upon my bosom,
    Let me feel the sweet, warm breath,
    For a strange chill o'er me passes,
    And I know that it is death.
I would gaze upon the treasure
    Scarcely given ere I go;
Feel her rosy, dimpled fingers
    Wander o'er my cheek of snow.

I am passing through the waters,
    But a blessed shore appears;
Kneel beside me, husband dearest,
    Let me kiss away thy tears.
Wrestle with thy grief, my husband,
    Strive from midnight until day,
It may leave an angel's blessing
    When it vanisheth away.

Lay the gem upon my bosom,
    'Tis not long she can be there;
See! how to my heart she nestles,
    'Tis the pearl I love to wear.
If, in after years, beside thee
    Sits another in my chair,
Though her voice be sweeter music,
    And her face than mine more fair;

If a cherub calls thee "father!"
    Far more beautiful than this;

THE DYING MOTHER.

Love thy first-born, O my husband!
    Turn not from the motherless.
Tell her sometimes of her mother—
    You can call her by my name!
Shield her from the winds of sorrow,
    If she errs, O gently blame!

Lead her sometimes where I'm sleeping.
    I will answer if she calls,
And my breath shall stir her ringlets,
    When my voice in blessing falls;
Her soft black eye will brighten,
    And wonder whence it came;
In her heart, when years pass o'er her,
    She will find her mother's name.

It is said that every mortal
    Walks between two angels here,
One records the ill, but blots it
    If before the midnight drear
Man repenteth—if uncancelled,
    Then he seals it for the skies;
And her right hand angel weepeth,
    Bowing low with veiled eyes.

I will be her right hand angel,
    Sealing up the good for heaven,
Striving that the midnight watches
    Find no misdeed unforgiven.
You will not forget me, husband,
    When I'm sleeping 'neath the sod;
O, love the jewel given us
    As I loved thee—next to God!—*J. A. Dacus.*

RESPONSIBILITY OF PARENTS.

T. F. W.

THE home is the fountain of civilization. Americans are a home-making people. Our laws are made in the home. There are trained the voters who shape the course of our country. The things said there give bias to character far more than do sermons and lectures, newspapers and books. No other audiences are so susceptible and receptive as those gathered about the table and the fireside. No other teachers have the acknowledged divine right to instruct that is granted without challenge to parents. The fountain of our national life is under their hand. They can make it send forth waters bitter or sweet, for the death or the healing of the people.

Intemperance strikes first and most fatally at the home. The evils most dangerous to social order depend upon dram-drinking for their existence. This too is the scene of its most cruel and beastly devilisms. Here it smites, and stabs, and kills. The home must be guarded against its outrages, or the country will be ruined.

The best work against intemperance must be done in this center and seat of power. Parents have it in their power to train their children to abhor that which is evil and cleave to that which is good; and they owe them this duty. They bring their children into existence. They hold them under their hand till the young life has taken a bias that will last through eternity. Usually the tiny, tilting craft has its prow turned toward heaven or hell before the parent's hand lets go the helm. This ought to startle careless people out of their indifference. It ought to drive them to lives of piety; for how can they teach that which they have not learned? How can they impart what they do not possess?

VISIT YOUR PARENTS.

Parents must teach by example. Precept has no authority unless backed by example. For the children's sake all liquors ought to be banished from the home. The story is most pitiful, and quite too common to need repetition: "I learned to drink at my father's table. My mother's hand first passed me the cup that is working my damnation."

In every home there ought to be the right reading on this, as on every by-subject. We are what we read—or we read what we are—as you will. One thing is certain; if we really care much about this horrible traffic, we will see to it that our children have books and papers that will keep them in sympathy with the efforts made for its prohibition.

By personal example, by look, by reading, and by prayer, we may make an atmosphere that shall set and keep our households right on this great question. Only thus can we hope to save ourselves, and those whom God has given to be with us, from the tide that sweeps to destruction so many of the noblest and best.

VISIT YOUR PARENTS.

IF you live in the same place, let your steps be—if possible daily—a familiar one in the old home; if you are miles away—yea many miles away—make it your business to go to your parents. In this matter do not regard time or expense; the one is well spent, and the other will be, even a hundred-fold, repaid. When some day the word reaches you, flashed over the telegraph, that your mother is gone, you will not think them much, those hours of travel which at last bore you to the loved one's side.

—*Anonymous.*

A WORD WITH PARENTS ABOUT THEIR CHILDREN.

WHAT pride is felt by parents in the honest success of their boys. How they like to hear of his good and manly behavior in school, in the counting-house, or on deck, where lives are to be saved or liberty preserved! That parent has lived to some purpose who has his children rooted and grounded in sound principles. Equipping well the son or daughter for the voyage of life, is a duty the neglect of which is sure to entail sorrow and shame. When a minister's boy goes wrong, the whole world is informed of the fact with apparent glee, by those who have no taste for things religious. It is clearly expected, then, that the minister's family, like himself, should be living epistles, known and read of all men. Then again, when the son or daughter of a religious family mingles freely with worldlings, in the ball-room and at the theater, the finger of reproach is justly pointed at Christ's followers, and the majority are held responsible for the acts or neglects of a few. Religion and science unite in positive language, that the defects of the parents are discoverable in the children.

The only cure for this disorder—whatever it may be—is the grace of God, the love and friendship of Jesus. The parent, then—father or mother—who is conscious of dangerous personal proclivities, occupies vantage ground above every other teacher, however qualified, in dealing with his child. He knows the besetting sin, and with heaven's aid, can overcome it. Those parents who leave the education of their children almost altogether to the sacred or secular teacher, have intrusted the most important business of life to hands not fully competent to discharge it. The good housewife bestows much care upon the curtains, the carpets, the pictures, and the statuary within the home; while the sons and daughters, with bad books, impure associates, and misleading plays, are gradually drifting, if not already there, on to dangerous ground. It is proper to remind these drowsy parents that stains on pictures and dirt on curtains are minor evils, unjustifiable as they are, compared with the unmanly act of the boy or the frivolous amusements of the daughter. We are safe in assuming that the parents of Joseph, Samuel, and Timothy, were of superior stock. Grace makes magnificent pictures when it lodges in good, natural soil, in which there are, as we are taught, various degrees. Parents who expect noble children must themselves lead noble lives. In time, and the sooner the better, we will attach more value to the law of heredity. We will then try to do much for posterity by bequeathing blood and habits that will help and not hinder the race.

Nice families! What a comfort and ornament they are to society! There are pleasant homes with the poets and others with orators, but the greatest joy is evening at home with cultured people who know much of Divine things, whose lives are attuned to words that cheer and deeds that ennoble. You are sure to find in such homes grandmotherly and motherly influence modeled after that which made Timothy an example for all the ages. We are not doing enough in the right direction for our children. If we would have more fragrance and fruit we must prune and pray, beginning within and working outward.—*Anonymous.*

CHARMS strike the sight, but merit wins the soul.
Pope.

THE MOTHER'S SORROW.

AS the waters roll in on the shore with incessant throbs, night and day, and always,—not alone when storms prevail, but in calms as well,—so it is with a mother's heart bereaved of her children. There is no grief like unto it,—Rachael weeping for her children, and refusing to be comforted, because they are not! With what long patience, what burden and suffering, does the mother wait until the child of her hope is placed in her arms and under the sight of her eyes! She remembereth no more the anguish, for joy that a man is born into the world.

Who can read, or, if he saw, could utter the thoughts of a mother during all the days and night in which she broods the helpless thing? Every true mother takes home the full meaning of the angel's word; that holy thing which shall be born of thee shall be called the Son of God. The mother does not even whisper what she thinks, and the whole air is full of gentle pictures, every one on the background of the blue heavens.

The child grows,—grows in favor of God and man; and every admiring look cast upon it, even by a stranger, sends light and gladness to the mother's heart. Wonderful child! The sun is brighter for it! The whole earth is blessed by its presence! Sorrows, pains, weariness, self-denials, for its sake, are eagerly sought and delighted in.

But the days come when the little feet are weary; when the night brings no rest; when the cheek is scarlet, the eye changed, and the smile no longer knows how to shine. All day, all night, it is the mother's watch. Her very sleep is but a vailed waking. Joy; the child is coming back to health! Woe; it is drifting out again, away from consciousness and pain. It is far, far out toward—toward darkness. It disappears!

The mother's heart was like a heaven while it lived; now it has ascended to God's heaven, and the mother's heart is as the gloom of midnight. Wild words of self-reproach at length break out, as when a frozen torrent is set loose by spring days. She that has lavished her life-force upon the child turns upon herself with fierce charges of carelessness, of thoughtlessness. She sees a hundred ways in which the child would have lived but for her! All love is turned into self-crimination. Tears come at length to quench the fire of purgatory. But grief takes new shapes every hour, till the nerve has lost its sensibility, and then she coldly hates her unnatural and inhuman heart that will not feel.

A child dying, dies but once; but the mother dies a hundred times. When the sharpness is over, and the dullness of an overspent brain is past, and she must take up the shuttle again, and weave the web of daily life, pity her not that she must work, must join again the discordant voices, and be forced to duties irksome and hateful. These all are kindly medicines. A new thought is slowly preparing. It is that immovable constancy and strength which sorrow gives when it has wrought the Divine intent.—*Methodist.*

SORROWS are often like clouds, which though black when they are passing over us, when they are past become as if they were the garments of God, thrown off in purple and gold along the sky. *H. W. Beecher.*

THE OLD ARM CHAIR.

Eliza Cook.

I LOVE it—I love it, and who shall dare
   To chide me for loving that old arm chair!
   I've treasured it long as a sainted prize—
I've bedewed it with tears, and embalmed it with **sighs**;
'Tis bound by a thousand bands to my heart,
Not a tie will break, not a link will start.
Would you learn the spell? a mother sat there;
And a sacred thing is that old arm chair.

In childhood's hour I lingered near
The hallowed seat with listening ear;
And gentle words that mother would give,
To fit me to die, and teach me to live.
She told me shame would never betide,
With truth for my creed, and God for my **guide**;
She taught me to lisp my earliest prayer,
As I knelt beside that old arm chair.

I sat and watched her many a day,
When her eyes grew dim and her locks were **gray**,
And I almost worshipped her when she smiled
And turned from her Bible to bless her child.
Years rolled on, but the last one sped—
My idol was shattered—my earth star fled:
I learnt how much the heart can bear,
When I saw her die in that old arm chair.

MARY, THE MOTHER OF JESUS.

'Tis past! 'tis past! but I gaze on it now
With quivering breath and throbbing brow:
'Twas there she nursed me— 'twas there she died,
And memory flowed with lava tide—
Say it is folly, and deem me weak,
While the scalding tears run down my cheek.
But I love it—I love it, and cannot tear
My soul from my mother's old arm chair.

MARY, THE MOTHER OF JESUS.

N. P. Willis.

AT God's right hand sits one *who was a child*,
   Born as the humblest, and who here abode
   Till of our sorrow he had suffered all.
They who now weep, remember that he wept.
The tempted, the despised, the sorrowing, feel
That Jesus, too, drank of these cups of woe.
And oh, if our joys he tasted less,—
If all but one passed from his lips away—
That one,—a mother's love—by his partaking,
Is like a thread of heaven spun through our life,
And we in the untiring watch, the tears,
The tenderness and fond trust of a mother,
May feel a heavenly closeness unto God—
For such, all human in its blest excess,
Was Mary's love for Jesus.

MOTHER'S VACANT CHAIR.

T. De Witt Talmage.

I GO a little farther on in your house, and I find the mother's chair. It is very apt to be a rocking-chair. She had so many cares and troubles to soothe, that it must have rockers. I remember it well. It was an old chair, and the rockers were almost worn out, for I was the youngest, and the chair had rocked the whole family. It made a creaking noise as it moved, but there was music in the sound. It was just high enough to allow us children to put our heads into her lap. That was the bank where we deposited all our hurts and worries. Oh, what a chair that was. It was different from the father's chair—it was entirely different. You ask me how? I cannot tell, but we all felt it was different. Perhaps there was about this chair more gentleness, more tenderness, more grief when we had done wrong. When we were wayward, father scolded, but mother cried. It was a very wakeful chair. In the sick day of children, other chairs could not keep awake; that chair always kept awake—kept easily awake. That chair knew all the old lullabies, and all those worldless songs which mothers sing to their sick children—songs in which all pity and compassion and sympathetic influences are combined. That old chair has stopped rocking for a good many years. It may be set up in the loft or the garret, but it holds a queenly power yet. When at midnight you went into that grog-shop to get the intoxicating draught, did you not hear a voice that said, "My son, why go in there?" and a louder than the boisterous encore of the theater, a voice saying, "My son, what do you here?" And when you went into the house of sin, a voice saying, "What would your mother do if she knew you were here?" and you were provoked at yourself, and you charged yourself with superstition and fanaticism, and your head got hot with your own thoughts, and you went home and you went to bed, and no sooner had you touched the bed than a voice said, "What a prayerless pillow!" Man! what is the matter? This! You are too near your mother's rocking-chair. "Oh, pshaw!" you say, "there's nothing in that. I'm five hundred miles off from where I was born—I'm three thousand miles off from the Scotch kirk whose bell was the first music I ever heard." I cannot help that. You are too near your mother's rocking-chair. "Oh!" you say, "there can't be anything in that; that chair has been vacant a great while." I cannot help that. It is all the mightier for that; it is omnipotent, that vacant mother's chair. It whispers. It speaks. It weeps. It carols. It mourns. It prays. It warns. It thunders. A young man went off and broke his mother's heart, and while he was away from home his mother died, and the telegraph brought the son, and he came into the room where she lay, and looked upon her face, and cried out, "O mother, mother, what your life could not do your death shall effect. This moment I give my heart to God." And he kept his promise. Another victory for the vacant chair. With reference to your mother, the words of my text were fulfilled: "Thou shalt be missed because thy seat will be empty."

WONDROUS power! how little understood!
Entrusted to the mother's mind alone,
To fashion genius, form the soul for good.
—*Mrs. Sarah J. Hale.*

RESPECT FOR MOTHERS.

A FEW days ago we heard a stripling of sixteen designate the mother who bore him as the old woman. By coarse husbands we have heard wives so called occasionally, though in the latter case the phrase is more often used endearingly. At all times, as commonly spoken, it jars upon the ears and shocks the sense. An old woman should be an object of reverence above and beyond almost all other phases of humanity. Her very age should be her surest passport to courteous consideration.

The aged mother of a grown-up family needs no other certificate of worth. She is a monument of excellence, approved and warranted. She has fought faithfully "the good fight" and come off conqueror. Upon her venerable face she bears the marks of the conflict in all its furrowed lines. The most grievous of the ills of life have been hers; trials untold, and known only to God and herself, she has borne incessantly, and now, in her old age, her duty done, patiently awaiting her appointed time, she stands more beautiful than ever in her youth, more honorable and deserving than he who has slain his thousands, or stood triumphant upon the proudest field of victory.

Young man, speak kindly to your mother, and ever courteously, tenderly of her. But a little time, and ye shall see her no more forever. Her eye is dim, her form bent, and her shadow falls graveward. Others may love you when she has passed away—a kind-hearted sister, perhaps, or she whom of all the world you choose for a partner—she may love you warmly, passionately; children may love you fondly, but never again, never, while time is yours, shall the love of woman be to you as that of your old, trembling mother has been.—*Anonymous.*

TO MY MOTHER.

Henry Kirke White.

...d send a happy
   birthday, dear,
...d bless thee through
   the coming year.

...st thou, mother, for a moment think
...t we, thy children, when old age shall shed
...blanching honors on thy weary head,
...our best of duties ever shrink?
...un from his high sphere should sink,
...e, ungrateful, leave thee in that day,
... in solitude thy life away,
...e, tottering on the grave's cold brink.
...hought!—where'er our steps may roam,
...iling plains, or wastes without a tree,
...ll fond memory point our hearts to thee,
...he pleasures of thy peaceful home;
...duty bids us all thy griefs assuage,
...ooth the pillow of thy sinking age.

...eak a shade more kindly
Than the year before;
...y a little oftener;
Love a little more;
...g a little closer
To the Father's love;
...below shall liker grow
To the life above.

MY MOTHER.

George P. Morris.

...ther, at that holy name
...thin my bosom there's a gush
...feeling which no time can tame,
...hich, for years of fame,
..., could not crush.

A FEW days ago we heard a stripling of sixt[een?]
mother who bore him as the old woman. B[ut?]
we have heard wives so called occasionall[y?]
latter case the phrase is more often used endearing[ly?]
as commonly spoken, it jars upon the ears and s[ense?]
An old woman should be an object of reverence a[nd?]
almost all other phases of humanity. Her very ag[e is the?]
surest passport to courteous consideration.

The aged mother of a grown-up family needs no [proof?]
of worth. She is a monument of excellence, app[reciated? war-?]
ranted. She has fought faithfully "the good fight[" and is a?]
conqueror. Upon her venerable face she bears th[e marks of?]
conflict in all its furrowed lines. The most grievou[s trials of?]
life have been hers; trials untold, and known only t[o her-?]
self, she has borne incessantly, and now, in her ol[d age, work?]
done, patiently awaiting her appointed time, she stan[ds more beauti-?]
ful than ever in her youth, more honorable and des[erving than he?]
who has slain his thousands, or stood triumphant upo[n the gory?]
field of victory.

Young man, speak kindly to your mother, and e[ver think?]
tenderly of her. But a little time, and ye shall see h[er no more for-?]
ever. Her eye is dim, her form bent, and her shad[ow points grave-?]
ward. Others may love you when she has passed [away; a true-?]
hearted sister, perhaps, or she whom of all the world [you choose as?]
a partner—she may love you warmly, passionately; [children may?]
love you fondly, but never again, never, while time [lasts, shall?]
the love of woman be to you as that of your old, tre[mbling mother?]
has been.—*Anonymous.*

TO MY MOTHER.

Henry Kirke White.

AND canst thou, mother, for a moment think
    That we, thy children, when old age shall shed
    Its blanching honors on thy weary head,
Could from our best of duties ever shrink?
Sooner the sun from his high sphere should sink,
    Than we, ungrateful, leave thee in that day,
    To pine in solitude thy life away,
Or shun thee, tottering on the grave's cold brink.
Banish the thought!—where'er our steps may roam,
    O'er smiling plains, or wastes without a tree,
    Still will fond memory point our hearts to thee,
And paint the pleasures of thy peaceful home;
    While duty bids us all thy griefs assuage,
    And smooth the pillow of thy sinking age.

MY MOTHER.

George P. Morris.

MY mother, at that holy name
    Within my bosom there's a gush
    Of feeling which no time can tame,
A feeling which, for years of fame,
I would not, could not crush.

TRIBUTE TO A MOTHER

Lord Macaulay.

CHILDREN, look in those eyes, listen to that dear voice, notice the feeling of even a single touch that is bestowed upon you by that gentle hand. Make much of it while yet you have that most precious of all good gifts, a loving mother. Read the unfathomable love of those eyes; the kind anxiety of that tone and look, however slight your pain. In after-life you may have friends, fond, dear, kind friends; but never will you have again the inexpressible love and gentleness lavished upon you which none but a mother bestows. Often do I sigh in my struggles with the hard, uncaring world, for the sweet, deep security I felt when, of an evening, nestling in her bosom, I listened to some quiet tale, suitable to my age, read in her tender and untiring voice. Never can I forget her sweet glances cast upon me when I appeared asleep; never her kiss of peace at night. Years have passed away since we laid her beside my father in the old churchyard; yet still her voice whispers from the grave, and her eye watches over me, as I visit spots long since hallowed to the memory of my mother.

THE MOTHER'S MISSION.

THE mother in her office holds the key
   Of the soul; and she it is who stamps the coin
   Of character, and makes the being who would be a savage
But for her gentle care, a Christian man.—*Anonymous.*

GRANDPAPA'S PETS.

OLD AGE.

M. W. B.

"ALL the days of my appointed time will I wait, till my change come." Yes, patiently wait. It is God's will. Jesus said, "My time is not yet come, but your time is always ready." Old age is honorable, and a multitude of years teach wisdom. How pleasant to converse with the aged of the times fifty, three-score, or even threescore and ten years since. Some young people, children and grandchildren, are impatient of old age, while others have a filial delight in their company, and love to care for them, and tenderly lessen their burdens. Old age, however serene the conscience and well spent the life, has its sadness. And after all their care and toil the provision they have made for themselves, and children on whom they wish to learn in the decline of life, they have a dread and fear of being a burden. Now is needed the grace to wait. Job's reverses of fortune were great, and having passed through the most extreme suffering and sorrow with integrity, he has handed down to future generations a character renowed for patience and fidelity. He had all the temptations to end his own life, but no, he would wait. For, says he, "I know that my Redeemer liveth, and though after my skin, worms destroy this body, yet in my flesh I shall see God." Thus Methuselah waited 969 years, and then had an eternity before him. And Enoch walked with God, waiting 365 years, and was not, for God took him. Abraham waited and died 175 years of age. Isaac lived till he was 180, having been blind and nearly helpless, 62 years. Jacob waited till the change came at the age of 147. But he said, "Evil and few have been the days of my pilgrimage, and have not attained to the years of my fathers." When dying he blessed both of the sons of Joseph through faith, and worshiped leaning on the top of his staff. Thus may we wait and die.

MY MOTHER'S HANDS.

SUCH beautiful, beautiful hands!
    They're neither white nor small,
    And you, I know, would scarcely think
That they were fair at all.
I've looked on hands whose form and hue
A sculptor's dream might be,
Yet are these aged, wrinkled hands,
More beautiful to me.

Such beautiful, beautiful hands!
Though heart were weary and sad,
These patient hands kept toiling on
That children might be glad.
I almost weep, as looking back
To childhood's distant day,
I think how these hands rested not
When mine were at their play.

Such beautiful, beautiful hands!
They're growing feeble now;
For time and pain have left their work
On hand, and heart, and brow.
Alas! alas! the wearing time,
And the sad, sad day to me,
When 'neath the daisies, out of sight,
These hands will folded be.

But O, beyond this shadowy damp,
Where all is bright and fair,

MY MOTHER'S PICTURE.

I know full well these dear old hands
Will palms of victory bear;
Where crystal streams, thro' endless years,
Flow over golden sands,
And where the old grow young again,
I'll clasp my mother's hands.
—*Anonymous.*

MY MOTHER'S PICTURE.
Wm. Cowper.

THAT those lips had language! Life has pass'd
With me but roughly since I heard thee last,
Those lips are thine,—thy own sweet smile I see,
The same, that oft in childhood solac'd me;
Voice only fails, else how distinct they say,
"Grieve not, my child, chase all thy fears away!"
The meek intelligence of those dear eyes,
(Bless'd be the art that can immortalize,
The art that baffles Time's tyrannic claim
To quench it,) here shines on me still the same.

Faithful remembrancer of one so dear,
O welcome guest, though unexpected here!
Who bid'st me honor with an artless song,
Affectionate, a mother lost so long.
I will obey, not willingly alone,
But gladly, as the precept were her own;
And, while that face renews my filial grief,
Fancy shall weave a charm for my relief,
Shall steep me in Elysian reverie,
A momentary dream, that thou art she.

THE MOTHER AS TEACHER.

A. W. K.

THE mother is the luminary that shines and reigns alone in the early child-life; as years advance, the scepter is divided and the teacher shares the sway.

We often think, as we meet the earnest gaze of the interested pupil, and watch the mind working and the young thought shaping to the will, "Why is it that mothers so willingly yield to others this broad sphere of their domain, and are content to foster the physical and external life of their children, leaving the intellectual and spiritual to grow without their aid?"

One would suppose that capable mothers would jealously keep to themselves the high privilege of training the mind, and so bind their children to themselves by ties which are stronger than the mere physical tie can be.

We who have grown to realize to whom we are debtors, are thrilled with delight as we think of those who have been the parents of our intellectual life—who seem nearer to us than our familiar friends, though we never have and never may look upon their living faces,—Bryant, Longfellow, Ruskin, Emerson and Carlyle, and many another. How they have covered our lives with a rich broidery of beautiful and inspiring thought, so that to live in the same world, and at the same time, seems a benison of blessing.

So may the mother weave into the life of her children thoughts and feelings, rich, beautiful, grand and noble, which will make all after-life brighter and better.

Many a good mother may think she has no time for this mind

and soul culture, but we find no lack of robes and ruffles, and except in cases where the daily bread of the family must be earned by daily work, away from home, as is done by many a weary mother, we must feel that there is not one who cannot command one half hour each morning, when the mind is fresh and vigorous, to collect her children around her, and minister for a little to their higher wants.

If each mother, according to her several ability, seeks to develop the higher and better faculties of her children, the reward will be as great as the aim is noble.

HOW MAMMA PLAYS.

Ella Farman.

JUST the sweetest thing that the children do
   Is to play with mamma, a-playing too;
   And "Baby is lost," they think is the best,
For mamma plays that with a merry zest.

"My baby's lost!" up and down mamma goes,
A-peering about and following her nose;
Inside the papers, and under the books,
And all in between the covers she looks,
    "Baby! Baby!" calling.
But though in her way is papa's tall hat,
She never once thinks to look under that.

She listens, she stops, she hears the wee laugh,
And around she flies, the faster by half,
"Why, where can he be?" and she opens the clock,
She tumbles her basket, she shakes papa's sock,
    "Baby! Baby!" calling.

HOW MAMMA PLAYS.

While the children all smile at papa's tall hat,
Though none of them go and look under that.

A sweet coo calls. Mamma darts everywhere,
She feels in her pockets to see if he's there,
In every vase on the mantel shelf,
She searches sharp for the little elf,
    "Baby! Baby!" calling.
Another coo comes from papa's tall hat,
Yet none of them stir an inch toward that.

Somewhere he certainly must be, she knows,
So up to the China cupboard she goes;
The covers she lifts from the sugar-bowls,
The sweet, white lumps she rattles and rolls,
    "Baby! Baby!" calling.
But though there's a stir near papa's tall hat,
They will not so much as look toward that.

She moves the dishes, but baby is not
In the cream-pitcher nor in the tea-pot;
And she wrings her hands and stamps on the floor.
She shakes the rugs, and she opens the door,
    "Baby! Baby!" calling.
They stand with their backs to papa's tall hat,
Though the sweetest murmurs come from that.

The children join in the funny distress,
Till mamma, all sudden, with swift caress,
Makes a pounce right down on the old, tall black hat,
And brings out the baby from under that,
    "Baby! Baby!" calling.
And this is the end of the little play,
The children would like to try every day.

MOTHER'S EMPIRE.

Rev. H. H. Birkins.

THE queen that sits upon the throne of home, crowned and sceptred as none other ever can be, is—mother. Her enthronement is complete, her reign unrivalled, and the moral issues of her empire are eternal. "Her children arise up, and call her blessed."

Rebellious, at times, as the subjects of her government may be, she rules them with marvelous patience, winning tenderness and undying love. She so presents and exemplifies divine truth, that it re-produces itself in the happiest development of childhood—character and life.

Her memory is sacred while she lives, and becomes a perpetual inspiration, even when the bright flowers bloom above her sleeping dust. She is an incarnation of goodness to the child, and hence her immense power. Scotland, with her well-known reverence for motherhood, insists that "An ounce of mother is worth more than a pound of clergy."

Napoleon cherished a high conception of a mother's power, and believed that the mothers of the land could shape the destinies of his beloved France. Hence he said in his sententious, laconic style: "The great need of France is mothers."

The ancient orator bestowed a flattering compliment upon the homes of Roman mothers when he said, "The empire is at the fireside." Who can think of the influence that a mother wields in the home, and not be impressed with its far-reaching results! What revolutions would take place in our families and communities if that strange, magnetic power were fully consecrated to the welfare of the child and the glory of God.

Mohammed expressed a great truth when he said that "Paradise is at the feet of mothers."

There is one vision that never fades from the soul, and that is the vision of mother and of home. No man in all his weary wanderings ever goes out beyond the overshadowing arch of home.

Let him stand on the surf-beaten coast of the Atlantic, or roam over western wilds, and every dash of the wave and murmur of the breeze will whisper *home*, sweet home.

Set him down amid the glaciers of the North, and even there thoughts of home, too warm to be chilled by the eternal frosts, will float in upon him.

Let him rove through the green, waving groves, and over the sunny slopes of the South, and in the smile of the soft skies, and in the kiss of the balmy breeze, home will live again.

John Randolph was once heard to say that only one thing saved him from atheism, and that was the tender remembrance of the hour when a devout mother, kneeling by his side, took his little hand in hers, and taught him to say "Our Father, who art in Heaven."

God hasten the time when our families, everywhere, shall catch the cry of childhood as it swells up over all the land, like the voice of God's own sweet evangel, calling the *home*—the home to enter the children's temple, and crowd its altars with the best offerings of sympathy and service.

Fathers, mothers, let the home go with your children to Jesus,—let it go with them at every step, to cheer them in every struggle, until from the very crest of the cold wave that bears them from you forever, they shout back their joy over a home on earth, that helped them rise to a home in Heaven.

FOR HIS MOTHER'S SAKE.

A YOUNG man, who had left his home, ruddy and vigorous, was seized with the yellow fever in New Orleans; and, though nursed with devoted care by friendly strangers, he died. When the coffin was being closed, "*Stop,*" said an aged woman who was present, "*Let me kiss him for his mother!*"

"LET me kiss him for his mother!
　Ere ye lay him with the dead,
　Far away from home, another
Sure may kiss him in her stead.
How that mother's lips would kiss him
Till her heart should nearly break!
How in days to come she'll miss him!
Let me kiss him for her sake.

"Let me kiss him for his mother!
Let me kiss the wandering boy;
It may be there is no other
Left behind to give her joy.
When the news of woe, the morrow,
Burns the bosom like a coal,
She may feel this kiss of sorrow
Fall as balm upon her soul.

"Let me kiss him for his mother!
Heroes, ye, who by his side,
Waited on him as a brother
Till the Northern stranger died,—

BE KIND UNTO THE OLD.

Heeding not the foul infection,
Breathing in the fever-breath,—
Let me, of my own election,
Give the mother's kiss in death.

"Let me kiss him for his mother!"
Loving thought and loving deed!
Seek nor fear nor sigh to smother,
Gentle matrons, while ye read.
Thank the God who made ye human,
Gave ye pitying tears to shed;
Honor ye the Christian woman
Bending o'er another's dead.—*Anonymous.*

HAIL, woman! Hail, thou faithful wife and mother,
The latest, choicest part of Heaven's great plan!
None fills thy peerless place at home; no other
Helpmeet is found for laboring, suffering man.
                           Rev. Mark Trafton.

BE KIND UNTO THE OLD.

BE kind unto the old, my friend;
   They're worn with this world's strife,
Though bravely once perchance they fought
   The stern, fierce battle of life.

They taught our youthful feet to climb
   Upwards life's rugged steep;
Then let us lead them gently down,
   To where the weary sleep.—*Anonymous.*

THE OLD FOLKS.

IF you would make the aged happy, lead them to feel that there is still a place for them where they can be useful. When you see their powers failing, do not notice it. It is enough for them to feel it, without a reminder. Do not humiliate them by doing things after them. Accept their offered services, and do not let them *see you* taking off the dust their poor eye-sight has left undisturbed, or wiping up the liquid their trembling hands have spilled; rather let the dust remain, and the liquid stain the carpet, than rob them of their self-respect by *seeing you* cover their deficiencies. You may give them the best room in your house, you may garnish it with pictures, and flowers, you may yield them the best seat in your church-pew, the easiest chair in your parlor, the highest seat of honor at your table; but if you *lead*, or *leave*, them to feel that they have passed their usefulness, you plant a thorn in their bosom that will rankle there while life lasts. If they are capable of doing nothing but preparing your kindlings, or darning your stockings, indulge them in those things, but never let them feel that it is because they can do nothing else; rather that they do this so well.

Do not ignore their taste and judgment. It may be that in their early days, and in the circle where they moved, they were as much sought and honored as you are now; and until you arrive at that place, you can ill imagine your feelings should you be considered entirely void of these qualities, be regarded as essential to no one, and your opinions be unsought, or discarded if given. They *may* have been active and successful in the training of children and youth in the way they should go; and will they not feel it keenly, if no attempt is made to draw from this rich experience?

Indulge them as far as possible in their old habits. The various forms of society in which they were educated may be as dear to them as yours are now to you; and can they see them slighted or disowned without a pang? If they relish their meals better by turning their tea into the saucer, having their butter on the same plate with their food, or eating with both knife and fork, do not in word or deed imply to them that the customs of their days are obnoxious in good society; and that they are stepping down from respectability as they *descend* the hill-side of life. Always bear in mind that the customs of which you are now so tenacious may be equally repugnant to the next generation.

In this connection I would say, do not notice the pronunciation of the aged. They speak as they were taught, and yours may be just as uncourtly to the generations following. I was once taught a lesson on this subject, whice I shall never forget while memory holds its sway. I was dining, when a father brought his son to take charge of a literary institution. He was intelligent, but had not received the early advantages which he had labored hard to procure for his son; and his language was quite a contrast to that of the cultivated youth. But the attention and deference he gave to his father's quaint though wise remarks, placed him on a higher pinnacle in my mind, than he was ever placed by his world-wide reputation as a scholar and writer.—*Congregationalist.*

ALONE

She moves, the queen of her own quiet home.

Rev. Mark Trafton.

MY MOTHER'S BIBLE.

George P. Morris.

THIS book is all that's left me now,—
Tears will unbidden start,—
With faltering lip and throbbing brow
I press it to my heart.
For many generations past
Here is our family tree;
My mother's hands this Bible clasped,
She, dying, gave it me.

Ah! well do I remember those
Whose names these records bear;
Who round the hearthstone used to close
After the evening prayer,
And speak of what these pages said,
In tones my heart would thrill!
Though they are with the silent dead,
Here are they living still!

My father read this holy book
To brothers, sisters, dear;
How calm was my poor mother's look
Who loved God's word to hear!
Her angel face—I see it yet!
What thronging memories come!
Again that little group is met
Within the halls of home!

Thou truest friend man ever knew,
Thy constancy I've tried;
When all were false, I found thee true,
My counselor and guide.
The mines of earth no treasures give
That could this volume buy;
In teaching me the way to live,
It taught me how to die!

MY MOTHER'S BIBLE.

Bishop Gilbert Haven.

ON one of the shelves in my library, surrounded by volumes of all kinds, on various subjects, and in various languages, stands an old book, in its plain covering of brown paper, unprepossessing to the eye, and apparently out of place among the more pretentious volumes that stand by its side. To the eye of a stranger it has certainly neither beauty nor comeliness. Its covers are worn; its leaves marred by long use; its pages, once white, have become yellow with age; yet, old and worn as it is, to me it is the most beautiful and most valuable book on my shelves. No other awakens such associations, or so appeals to all that is best and noblest within me. It is, or rather it *was*, my mother's Bible—companion of her best and holiest hours, source of her unspeakable joy and consolation. From it she derived the principles of a truly Christian life and character. It was the light to her feet and the lamp to her path. It was constantly by her side; and, as her steps tottered in the advancing pilgrimage of life, and her eyes grew dim with age, more and more precious to her became the well-worn pages.

One morning, just as the stars were fading into the dawn of the coming Sabbath, the aged pilgrim passed on beyond the stars and beyond the morning, and entered into the rest of the eternal Sabbath—to look upon the face of Him of whom the law and the prophets had spoken, and whom, not having seen, she had loved. And now, no legacy is to me more precious than that old Bible. Years have passed; but it stands there on its shelf, eloquent as ever, witness of a beautiful life that is finished, and a silent monitor to the living. In hours of trial and sorrow it says, "Be not cast down, my son; for thou shalt yet praise Him who is the health of thy countenance and thy God." In moments of weakness and fear it says, "Be strong now, my son, and quit yourself manfully." When sometimes, from the cares and conflicts of external life, I come back to the study, weary of the world and tired of men—of men that are so hard and selfish, and a world that is so unfeeling—and the strings of the soul have become untuned and discordant, I seem to hear that Book saying, as with the well-remembered tones of a voice long silent, "Let not your heart be troubled. For what is your life? It is even as a vapor." Then my troubled spirit becomes calm; and the little world, that had grown so great and so formidable, sinks into its true place again. I am peaceful, I am strong.

There is no need to take down the volume from the shelf, or open it. A glance of the eye is sufficient. Memory and the law of association supply the rest. Yet there are occasions when it is otherwise; hours in life when some deeper grief has troubled the heart, some darker, heavier cloud is over the spirit and over the dwelling, and when it is a comfort to take down that old Bible and search its pages. Then, for a time, the latest editions, the original languages, the notes and commentaries, and all the critical apparatus which the scholar gathers around him for the study of the Scriptures are laid aside; and the plain old English Bible that was my mother's is taken from the shelf.

MY MOTHER'S GRAVE.

Rev. M. C. Henderson.

THE grave of my mother is on an elevation that overlooks a beautiful village where many an hour was spent in study and recreation, in days of boyhood. A marble slab marks the place where we laid her to rest, nearly a score of years ago. Occasionally, during these years have we stood by her grave, while precious remembrances have crowded upon our mind, and the sweet hope of meeting again cheered our sad heart. Our hands may be full of labor, our hearts burdened with care and the responsibilities of life, and our home far away, but a mother's grave, with all the hallowed associations clustering around, can never be forgotten.

The grave of a mother is indeed a sacred spot. It may be retired from the noise of business, and unnoticed by the stranger, but to *our hearts* how dear. The love we bear to a mother, is not measured by years, is not annihilated by distance, nor forgotten when she sleeps in dust. Marks of age may appear in our homes, and on our persons, but the memory of a mother is more enduring than time itself. Who has stood by the grave of a mother and not remembered her pleasant smiles, kind words, earnest prayer, and assurance expressed in a dying hour. Many years may have passed, memory may be treacherous in other things, but will reproduce with freshness the impressions once made by a mother's influence. Why may we not linger where rests all that was earthly of a sainted mother? It may have a restraining influence upon the wayward, prove a valuable incentive to increased faithfulness, encourage hope in the hour of depression, and give fresh inspiration in Christian life.

MOTHERS, SPARE YOURSELVES.

MANY a mother grows old, faded, and feeble long before her time, because her boys and girls are not thoughtfully considerate and helpful. When they become old enough to be of service in a household, mother has become so used to doing all herself, to taking upon her shoulders all the care, that she forgets to lay off the burden little by little, on those who are so well able to bear it. It is partly her own fault, to be sure, but a fault committed out of love and mistaken kindness for her children.

—Anonymous.

MY MOTHER'S GRAVE.

George D. Prentice.

THE trembling dewdrops fell
   Upon the shutting flowers; like star-set rest
    The stars shine gloriously, and all,
       Save me, are blest.

Mother, I love thy grave;
   The violet with its blossoms, blue and mild
    Waves o'er thy head; when shall it wave
       Above thy child?

'Tis a sweet flower, yet must
   Its bright leaves to the coming tempest bow!
    Dear mother, 'tis thine emblem; dust
       Is on thy brow.

MY MOTHER'S GRAVE.

And I could love to die;
To leave untasted life's dark, bitter streams—
   By thee, as erst in childhood, lie
                  And sear thy dreams.

But I must linger here
To stain the plumage of my sinless years,
   And mourn the hopes to childhood dear,
                  With bitter tears.

Aye, I must linger here,
A lonely branch upon a withered tree,
   Whose last frail leaf, untimely sere,
                  Went down with thee.

Oft from life's withered bower,
In still communion with the past, I turn
   And muse on thee, the only flower
                  In memory's urn.

And when the evening pale
Bows, like a mourner on the dim blue wave,
   I stay to hear the night winds wail
                  Around thy grave.

HOME.

*Home of our childhood! how affection clings
And hovers round thee with her seraph wings!
Dearer thy hills, though clad in autumn brown,
Than fairest summits which the cedars crown.*
OLIVER WENDELL HOLMES.

Whenever we step out of domestic life in search of felicity, we come back again, disappointed, tired, and chagrined. One day passed under our own roof, with our friends and our family, is worth a thousand in another place.
EARL OF ORRERY

THE OLD HOMESTEAD.

HOME.

[WRITTEN EXPRESSLY FOR THIS WORK.]

By Fanny J Crosby.

'TIS whispered in the ear of God,
    'Tis murmured through our tears;
'Tis linked with happy childhood days,
    And blessed in riper years.

That hallowed word is ne'er forgot,
    No matter where we roam,
The purest feelings of the heart,
    Still cluster round our home.

Dear resting-place, where weary thought
    May dream away its care,
Love's gentle star unvails her light,
    And shines in beauty there.

HOME.

James Montgomery.

THERE is a land of every land the pride,
   Beloved by heaven o'er all the world beside;
   Where brighter suns dispense serener light,
And milder moons emparadise the night;
A land of beauty, virtue, valor, truth,
Time-tortured age, and love-exalted youth.

The wandering mariner, whose eye explores
The wealthiest isles, the most enchanting shores,
Views not a realm so bountiful and fair,
Nor breathes the spirit of a purer air;
In every clime the magnet of his soul,
Touched by remembrance, trembles to that pole;
For in this land of heaven's peculiar grace,
The heritage of nature's noblest race,
There is a spot of earth supremely blest.
A dearer, sweeter spot than all the rest,
Where man, creation's tyrant, casts aside
His sword and sceptre, pageantry and pride,
While in his softened looks benignly blend
The sire, the son, the husband, brother, friend.

Here woman reigns; the mother, daughter, wife,
Strew with fresh flowers the narrow way of life!
In the clear heaven of her delightful eye
An angel-guard of loves and graces lie;

Around her knees domestic duties meet,
And fireside pleasures gambol at her feet.
Where shall that land, that spot of earth be found?
Art thou a man?—a patriot?—look around;
Oh, thou shalt find, howe'er thy footsteps roam,
That land *thy* country, and that spot *thy* home.

HOME DEFINED.
Charles Swain.

HOME'S not merely four square walls,
    Though with pictures hung and gilded:
    Home is where affection calls,
    Filled with shrines the heart hath builded!
Home! go watch the faithful dove,
  Sailing 'neath the heaven above us;
Home is where there's one to love!
  Home is where there's one to love us!

Home's not merely roof and room,
  It needs something to endear it;
Home is where the heart can bloom,
  Where there's some kind lip to cheer it!
What is home with none to meet,
  None to welcome, none to greet us?
Home is sweet,—and only sweet—
  When there's one we love to meet us!

THE HOME OF CHILDHOOD.

Samuel D. Burchard, D.D.

THE most impressive series of pictures I have ever seen are by Thomas Cole, an American artist, and termed "The Voyage of Life."

The first represents a child seated in a boat amid varied and beautiful flowers, and his guardian angel standing by to guard and protect the little voyager.

The second represents the youth, still on his voyage, guiding his own bark down the stream, his finger pointing upward to a beautiful castle painted in the clouds.

The third represents the man, still in the boat, going down the rapids; the water rough, the sky threatening, and the guardian angel looking on from a distance, anxiously.

The fourth represents an old man, still in his boat, the sun going down amid floating clouds tinged with gold, purple, and vermilion, the castle or House Beautiful in full view, and the guardian angel with an escort of shining celestials waiting to attend him to his home in glory.

The pictures have suggested to me a series of articles on Life's Great Mission and work for the grander life beyond. And on this sublime voyage to the land of immortals, to the Palace Beautiful in the skies, let us start from the dear old home of childhood, that home which, though it may be desolate, is still imperishable in memory.

> Home of my childhood, thou shalt ever be dear
> To the heart that so fondly revisits thee now;

THE HOME OF CHILDHOOD.

Though thy beauty be gone, thy leaf in the sere,
The wreaths of the past still cling to thy brow.

Spirit of mine, why linger ye here;
Why cling to those hopes so futile and vain ?
Go, seek ye a home in that radiant sphere,
Which through change and time thou shalt ever retain.

Let our destined port be the home of the blessed—the city which hath foundations, whose builder and maker is God !

"And thou shalt bring thy father, and thy mother, and thy brethren, and thy father's household home unto thee."—Joshua ii. 18.

The Christian home, implying marriage, mutual affection, piety, gentleness, refinement, meekness, forbearance, is our ideal of earthly happiness—a beautiful and impressive type of heaven.

It is more than a residence, a place of abode, however attractive in its surroundings, however richly adorned with art and beauty.

It is where the heart is, where the loved ones are—husband, wife, father, mother, brothers, sisters, all united in sympathy, fellowship and worship. It may be humble, unpretentious, exhibiting no signs of material wealth; but there is the wealth of mutual affection, which fire cannot consume, and no commercial disaster alienate or destroy, and this is home—the home of the heart, the home of childhood, the elysium of riper years, the refuge of age.

That we may the better appreciate the Christian homes that God has given us—the homes of comfort and refinement, that rocked the cradle of our infancy—let us consider, first, the vast multitudes of our fallen race that really have no home; none in the Christian sense, none that antidate heaven in peace, refinement and mutual love. How many children are born to the heritage of vice, poverty and crime, left to drift upon the tide of circumstances, to be buffeted in the wild and angry storm, to be chilled on the desolate moor of life—to wander amid the voids of human sympathy—the solitude and estrangement of human society—the children of dire misfortune—victims of vice and crime, polluted and polluting from the first.

How many fall, like blossoms prematurely blown, nipped by the lingering frosts of winter and sinking into the shadowed stream, or the sobbing soil of earth to be seen no more.

Think of the dwellings of hard-handed, wearied, ill-requited labor, where ignorance and discontent reign supreme,—where there is no recognition of God, who, in his all-wise Sovereignty, raiseth up one and casteth down another. Such homes, or rather places of abode, there are all over the land, all over the dark and wide realm of heathendom, the children of which must be devoted to sacrifice to the horrors of the Ganges or the Nile.

Look now to the other extreme of society, to the habitations of the millionaires, adorned with all the luxuries of wealth, the appliances of art, taste, beauty, whose children are trained up to worship at the shrine of Mammon, to exclude from their minds all thoughts of God and the hereafter, to live only for this world, to feel that there is no society worth cultivating except that of the rich, the *elite*, the would-be fashionable; that all enjoyments are material, sensuous, worldly; that the chief end of man is to eat, drink, and be merry. Such households do not furnish the best schools in which to educate children to wrestle with misfortune and to do the great work of life. They are liable to grow up effeminate, lacking executive strength, cold, proud, misanthropic, alienated in sympathy from the toiling masses.

There can be no well-regulated home without piety, without the fear and love of God. And such homes are usually found in the middle walks of life, not among the extreme poor, nor the proudly affluent, but among the mutually loving—the reverently worshipful.

It is to such homes that the world owes its highest interests. The old patriarchs understood the secret, even under the former dispensation, long before the dawn of the Christian era. God testified of Abraham, of Moses, of Samuel and Job how truly they comprehended the nature of that family institution, around which cluster all the associations of the first period of human life.

And it has only been in the line and in the light of the Christian revelation, that the highest type of the household has been produced and preserved. And it is upon the application of Christian principles alone, that the structure of the Christian family and the Christian home can stand.

The family in its origin is divine, and God has instituted laws for its regulation and perpetuity, and these laws must be scrupulously observed and obeyed or it ceases to be an ornament and a blessing—the great training-school for the Church and the State—the safeguard of society and a type of heaven.

HOME SONGS.

OH, sing once more those joy-provoking strains,
    Which, half forgotten, in my memory dwell!
They send the life blood bounding through my veins,
    And circle round me like an airy spell.
The songs of home are to the human heart
    Far dearer than the notes that song birds pour,
And of our inner nature seem a part;
    Then sing those dear, familiar lays once more—
Those cheerful lays of other days —
    Oh, sing those cheerful lays once more!—*Anonymous.*

THE OLD HOME.

Alfred Tennyson.

WE love the well-beloved place
    Where first we gazed upon the sky;
    The roofs that heard our earliest cry,
Will shelter one of stranger race.

We go, but ere we go from home,
    As down the garden-walks I move,
    Two spirits of a diverse love
Contend for loving masterdom.

One whispers, "Here thy boyhood sung
    Long since, its matin song, and heard
    The low love-language of the bird,
In native hazels tassel-hung."

The other answers, "Yea, but here
    Thy feet have strayed in after hours,
    With thy best friend among the bowers,
And this hath made them trebly dear."

These two have striven half a day;
    And each prefers his separate claim,
    Poor rivals in a losing game,
That will not yield each other way.

I turn to go: my feet have set
    To leave the pleasant fields and forms;
    They mix in one another's arms
To one pure image of regret.

HOME SHADOWS.

Robert Collyer, D.D.

FRIENDS, I wonder whether we have any deep consciousness of the shadows we are weaving about our children in the home; whether we ever ask ourselves, if, in the far future, when we are dead and gone, the shadow our home casts now will stretch over them for bane or blessing. It is possible we are full of anxiety to do our best, and to make our homes sacred to the children. We want them to come up right, to turn out good men and women, to be an honor and praise to the home out of which they sprang. But this is the pity and the danger, that, while we we may not come short in any real duty of father and mother, we may yet cast no healing and sacramental shadow over the child. Believe me, friends, it was not in the words he said, in the pressure of the hand, in the kiss, that the blessing lay Jesus gave to the little ones, when he took them in his arms. So it is not in these, but in the shadow of my innermost, holiest self; in that which is to us what the perfume is to the flower, a soul within the soul,—it is that which, to the child, and in the home, is more than the tongue of men or angels, or prophecy or knowledge, or faith that will move mountains, or devotion that will give the body to be burned. I look back with wonder on that old time, and ask myself how it is that most of the things, I suppose my father and mother built on especially to mould me to a right manhood are forgotten and lost out of my life. But the thing they hardly ever thought of,—the shadow of blessing cast by the home; the tender unspoken, love; the sacrifices made, and never thought of, it was so natural to make them; ten thousand little things, so simple as to attract no notice, and yet so sublime as I look back at them,—they fill my heart still and always with tenderness, when I remember them, and my eyes with tears. All these things, and all that belong to them, still come over me, and cast the shadow that forty years, many of them lived in a new world, cannot destroy.

I fear, few parents know what a supreme and holy thing is this shadow cast by the home, over, especially, the first seven years of this life of the child. I think the influence that comes in this way is the very breath and bread of life. I may do other things for duty or principle or religious training; they are all, by comparison, as when I cut and trim and train a vine; and, when I let the sun shine and the rain fall on it, the one may aid the life; the other *is* the life. Steel and string are each good in their place; but what are they to sunshine? It is said that a child, hearing once of heaven, and that his father would be there, replied, "Oh! then, I dinna want to gang." He did but express the holy instinct of a child, to whom the father may be all that is good, except just goodness,—be all any child can want, except what is indispensable—that gracious atmosphere of blessing in the healing shadow it casts, without which even heaven would come to be intolerable.

HOME ADORNMENTS.

Rev. Dr. Downing.

A ROOM without pictures is like a room without windows. Pictures are loop-holes of escape to the soul, leading to other scenes and other spheres. Pictures are consolers of loneliness; they are books, they are histories and sermons, which we can read without the trouble of turning over the leaves.

HAPPY CHILDHOOD.

THE SCENES OF MY CHILDHOOD.

(THE OLD OAKEN BUCKET.)

Samuel Woodworth.

HOW dear to this heart are the scenes of my childhood,
When fond recollection presents them to view!
The orchard, the meadow, the deep-tangled wildwood,
And every loved spot which my infancy knew!
The wide-spreading pond and the mill that stood by it,
The bridge and the rock where the cataract fell,
The cot of my father, the dairy-house nigh it,
And e'en the rude bucket that hung in the well,
The old oaken bucket, the iron-bound bucket,
The moss-covered bucket which hung in the well.

That moss-covered vessel I hailed as a treasure,
For often at noon, when returned from the field,
I found it the source of an exquisite pleasure,
The purest and sweetest that nature can yield.
How ardent I seized it with hands that were glowing,
And quick to the white pebbled bottom it fell;
Then soon, with the emblem of truth overflowing
And dripping with coolness, it rose from the well;
The old oaken bucket, the iron-bound bucket,
The moss-covered bucket, arose from the well.

How sweet from the green, mossy brim to receive it,
As poised on the curb it inclined to my lips!

Not a full, blushing goblet could tempt me to leave it,
The brightest that beauty or revelry sips.
And now, far removed from the loved habitation,
The tear of regret will intrusively swell,
As fancy reverts to my father's plantation,
And sighs for the bucket that hangs in the well;
The old oaken bucket, the iron-bound bucket,
The moss-covered bucket, that hangs in the well!

LONGINGS FOR HOME.

Oliver Goldsmith.

IN all my wanderings round this world of care,
  In all my griefs—and God has given my share—
  I still had hopes my latest hours to crown,
Amidst these humble bowers to lay me down;
To husband out life's taper at the close,
And keep the flame from wasting, by repose;
I still had hopes, for pride attends us still,
Amidst the swains to show my book-learned skill;
Around my fire an evening group to draw,
And tell of all I felt, and all I saw;
And as a hare, whom hounds and horns pursue,
Pants to the place from whence at first she flew,
I still had hopes, my long vexations past,
Here to return—and die at home at last.

HOME GOVERNMENT—WHAT IS IT?

IT is not to watch children with a suspicious eye, to frown at the merry outbursts of innocent hilarity, to suppress their joyous laughter, and to mould them into melancholy little models of octogenarian gravity. And when they have been in fault, it is not simply to punish them on account of the personal injury that you have chanced to suffer in consequence of their fault, while disobedience, unattended by inconvenience to yourself, passes without rebuke.

Nor is it to overwhelm the little culprit with angry words; to stun him with a deafening noise; to call him by hard names, which do not express his misdeeds; to load him with epithets which would be extravagant if applied to a fault of tenfold enormity; or to declare, with passionate vehemence, that he is the worst child in the world, and destined for the gallows.

But it is to watch anxiously for the *first* risings of sin, and to repress them; to counteract the *earliest* workings of selfishness; to repress the *first* beginnings of rebellion against rightful authority; to teach an implicit and unquestioning and cheerful obedience to the will of the parent, as the best preparation for a future allegiance to the requirements of the civil magistrate, and the laws of the great Ruler and Father in heaven.

It is to punish a fault because it is a fault, because it it sinful, and contrary to the command of God, without reference to whether it may or may not have been productive of immediate injury to the parent or others.

It is to reprove with calmness and composure, and not with angry irritation,—in a few words, fitly chosen, and not with a torrent of abuse; to punish as often as you threaten, and threaten only when you intend and can remember to perform; to say what you mean, and infallibly do as you say.

It is to govern your family as in the sight of Him who gave you authority, and who will reward your strict fidelity with such blessings as he bestowed on Abraham, or punish your criminal neglect with such curses as He visited on Eli.—*Mother's Treasury.*

HOME GOVERNMENT—ITS IMPORTANCE.

Rev. B. F. Booth.

THE importance of sacredly guarding the family relation can not well be overestimated. It is the foundation-stone of all that is good and pure both in civilization and religion. Take this away, and the whole fabric must topple and fall. The first government on earth was patriarchal, and in it was contained the inception of all civil authority; and, indeed, all rightful civil government to the present day is only an enlarged form of family government in a representative form, taking into consideration the wants and necessities of each individual family within its jurisdiction. The unity and perpetuity of the family tie in purity and peace is the only safeguard to national perpetuity, peace, and honor. Demoralize the family and you thereby destroy both domestic and national happiness, and undermine completely the temple of virtue and hope, and prepare the way of moral and civil desolation. The first impulse of patriotism and morality is germinated, nurtured, and largely if not entirely developed in the family circle. It is here that the first fruits of everything which is good and pure are brought forth. Hence the nations that disregard the sacredness of this relation have no permanent forms of government, and anything like common morality is nowhere to be found among them. And it is also worthy of careful note that just so far as any people depart from the true form of the family tie, just in that same ratio do they give evidence of it in their civility and morality. It is therefore within the family circle that the star of hope, of religion and civil rights is to be seen, and let it go down and all would be turned into the dismal darkness of midnight without moon or star to guide the weary pilgrim on his way. This spot is to be guarded as the tree of life, with the flaming sword turning either way, perpetually guarantying thus the most sacred bond of union and strength and the only remaining institution of man's primeval state. There may be, and doubtless are, numerous abuses of the marriage state; but that does not argue against its importance, neither does it detract from its absolute value and necessity.

The family circle may be—ought to be—the most charming and delightful place on earth, the center of the purest affections and most desirable associations as well as the most attractive and exalted beauties to be found this side of paradise. Nothing can exceed in beauty and sublimity the quietude, peace, harmony, affection, and happiness of a well-ordered family, where virtue is nurtured and every good principle fostered and sustained. From the well-ordered homes in this great, broad land of religious and civil liberty not only are great and good statesmen to come, and eminently pious and intelligent divines; but what is equally important, from these homes must come the more common populace of the land, upon whose intelligence, patriotism, and purity depends the continuance of the rich blessings which are now common to all. If freedom is kept and sanctified by the people; if the true spirit of Christianity is to be continued, in all its sacred purity, on to our children's children, even to the latest generations of men, they must be kept inviolate in our families and impressed in our homes. They are both dependent upon the family circle and the training and order administered therein. Then they who would dissolve the marriage rite, with all its hallowed and binding influences, would overthrow everything that is worth living for, and turn society into a bedlam of confusion and moral degradation; for it is the chain that binds the entire network of human society together, in all of its highest prospects, both for time and eternity. There is no civilization equal to it; in fact, there is none without it to the Christian, and there is no Christian civilization without the marriage ceremony, in all of its binding and uniting force. In fact, domestic happiness is wholly dependent upon the sanctity of the marriage relation; is an exclusive trait of Christianity; and Christianity is the only system in the world calculated to advance the interests of common humanity, and insure to all equal rights, earthly bliss, and a sweet home forever beyond the narrow limits of the quiet tomb.

What was said concerning Abraham may be said of every true Christian father: "For I know him, that he will command his children and his household after him; and they shall keep the way of the Lord, to do justice and judgment, that the Lord may bring upon Abraham that which he hath spoken of him." Happy is that nation whose children are brought up in families like this. There purity, virtue, and true manhood in every principle of justice and mercy will be permanently secured. What an important place, therefore, does the family occupy in the social, moral, and political worlds! Take this away, and the bond of sacred union is forever dissolved, and the most distressing and deplorable results must follow. Break asunder these centers of holy affections of truth, honor, and purity, and you will fill the land with every enormity, and desolation, the most far-reaching and dreadful, will fill its entire breadth. It is highly important and necessary not only to continue the validity of the marriage rite, upon which the true idea of the family is based, but great care should be exercised to make these homes all that they can and should be made,—the most delightful and enticing places on earth, where everything that is good is encouraged, and everything evil pointed out and discountenanced; for as children leave the parental home they are, to a large extent, molded for life. Orders and correct morals should here receive the proper stamp upon the opening mind. Yes, everything we wish our children to be, in time and eternity, should here be taught and enforced. Then "all thy children shall be taught of the Lord, and great shall be the peace of thy children."

HOME TRAINING OF CHILDREN.

D. L. Moody.

I HAVE no doubt some parents have got discouraged and disheartened that they have not seen their children brought to the Saviour as early as they expected. I do not know any thing that has encouraged me more in laboring for children than my experience in the inquiry room. In working there I have found that those who had religious training, whose parents strove early to lead them to Christ, have been the easiest to lead toward Him. I always feel as if I had a lever to work with when I know that a man has been taught by a godly father and mother; even if his parents died when he was young, the impression that they died praying for him has always a great effect through life. I find that such men are always so much easier reached, and though we may not live to see all our prayers answered, and all our children brought into the fold, yet we should teach them diligently, and do it in love. There is where a good many make a mistake, by not teaching their children in love—by doing it coldly or harshly. Many send them off to read the Bible by themselves for punishment. Why, I would put my hand in the fire before I would try to teach them in that way. If we teach our children as we ought to do, instead of Sunday being the dreariest, dullest, tiresomest day of the week to them, it will be the brightest, happiest day of the whole seven. What we want to do is to put religious truths before our children in such an attractive form that the Bible will be the most attractive of books to them. Children want the same kind of food and truth that we do, only we must cut it up a little finer, so that they can eat it. I have great respect for a father and mother who have brought up a large family and trained them so that they have come out on the Lord's side. Sometimes mothers are discouraged and do not think they have so large a sphere to do good in as we have, but a mother who has brought up a large family to Christ need not consider her life a failure. I know one who has brought up ten sons, all Christians; do you think her life has been a failure? Let us teach our children diligently, in season and out of season. We might train them that they shall be converted so early they can't tell when they were converted. I do not believe, as some people seem to think, that they have got to wander off into sin first, so that they may be brought back to Christ. Those who have been brought up in that way from their earliest childhood, do not have to spend their whole life in forgetting some old habit. Let us be encouraged in bringing our children to Christ.

HOME AFFECTION.

H. C. Dane.

AFFECTION does not beget weakness, nor is it effeminate for a brother to be tenderly attached to his sisters. That boy will make the noblest, the bravest man. On the battle-field, in many terrible battles during our late horrible war, I always noticed that those boys who had been reared under the tenderest home culture always made the best soldiers. They were always brave, always endured the severe hardships of camp, the march, or on the bloody field most silently, and were most dutiful at every call. More, much more, they resisted the frightful temptations that so often surrounded them, and seldom returned to their loved ones stained with the sins incident to war. Another point, they were always kind and polite to those whom they met in the enemy's country. Under their protection, woman was always safe. How often I have heard one regiment compared with another, when the cause of the difference was not comprehended by those who drew the comparison! I knew the cause, it was the home education.

We see the same every day in the busy life of the city. Call together one hundred young men in our city, and spend an evening with them, and we will tell you their home education. Watch them as they approach young ladies, and converse with them, and we will show you who have been trained under the influence of home affection and politeness, and those who have not.

That young man who was accustomed to kiss his sweet, innocent, loving sister night and morning as they met, shows its influence upon him, and he will never forget it, and when he shall take some one to his heart as his wife, she shall reap the golden fruit thereof. The young man who was in the habit of giving his arm to his sister as they walked to and from church, will never leave his wife to find her way as best she can. The young man who has been taught to see that his sister had a seat before he sought his, will never mortify a neglected wife in the presence of strangers. And that young man who always handed his sister to her chair at the table, will never have cause to blush as he sees some gentleman extend to his wife the courtesy she knows is due from him.

Mothers and daughters, wives and sisters, remember that, and remember that you have the making of the future of this great country, and rise at once to your high and holy duty. Remember that you must make that future, whether you will or not. We are all what you make us. Ah! throw away your weakening follies of fashion, and soul-famine, and rise to the level where God intended you should be, and make every one of your homes, from this day, schools of true politeness and tender affection. Take those little curly-headed boys, and teach them all you would have men to be, and my word for it, they will be just such men, and will go forth to bless the world, and crown you with a glory such as queens and empresses never dreamed of. Wield your power now, and you shall reap the fruit in your ripe age.

HOME TEACHING.

James Thomson.

DELIGHTFUL task! to rear the tender thought,
  To teach the young idea how to shoot,
    To pour the fresh instruction o'er the mind,
To breathe the enliv'ning spirit, and to fix
The generous purpose in the glowing breast.

HOME INSTRUCTION.

Hon. Schuyler Colfax.

ABOVE all things, teach children what their life is. It is not breathing, moving, playing, sleeping, simply. Life is a battle. All thoughtful people see it so. A battle between good and evil, from childhood. Good influences, drawing us up, toward the divine; bad influences, drawing us down to the brute. Midway we stand, between the divine and the brute. How to cultivate the good side of the nature is the greatest lesson of life to teach. Teach children that they lead these two lives: the life without, and the life within; and that the inside must be pure in the sight of God, as well as the outside in the sight of men.

There are five means of learning. These are:

Observation, reading, conversation, memory, reflection.

Educators sometimes, in their anxiety to secure a wide range of studies, don't sufficiently impress upon their scholars the value of memory. Now, our memory is one of the most wonderful gifts God has bestowed upon us; and one of the most mysterious. Take a tumbler and pour water into it; by-and-by you can pour no more; it is full. It is not so with the mind. You cannot fill it full of knowledge in a whole life-time. Pour in all you please, and it still thirsts for more.

Remember this:

Knowledge is not what you learn, but what you remember.

It is not what you eat, but what you digest, that makes you grow.

It is not the money you handle, but that you keep, that makes you rich.

It is not what you study, but what you remember and reflect upon, that makes you learned.

One more suggestion:

Above all things else, strive to fit the children in your charge, to be useful men and women; men and women you may be proud of in after-life. While they are young, teach them that far above physical courage—which will lead them to face the cannon's mouth —above wealth—which would give them farms and houses, and bank stocks and gold—is moral courage. That courage by which they will stand fearlessly, frankly, firmly, for the right. Every man or woman who dares to stand for the right when evil has its legions, is the true moral victor in this life, and in the land beyond the stars.

HOME INFLUENCES.

THERE is music in the word home. To the old it brings a bewitching strain from the harp of memory; to the young it is a reminder of all that is near and dear to them. Among the many songs we are wont to listen to, there is not one more cherished than the touching melody of "Home, Sweet Home."

Will you go back with me a few years, dear reader, in the history of the past, and traverse in imagination the gay streets and gilded saloons of Paris, that once bright center of the world's follies and pleasures? Passing through its splendid thoroughfares is one (an Englishman) who has left his home and native land to view the splendors and enjoy the pleasures of a foreign country. He has beheld with delight its paintings, its sculpture, and the grand yet graceful proportions of its buildings, and has yielded to the spell of the sweetest muse. Yet, in the midst of his keenest happiness, when he was rejoicing most over the privileges he possessed, temptations assailed him. Sin was presented to him in one of its most bewitching garbs. He drank wildly and deeply of the intoxicating cup, and his draught brought madness. Reason was overwhelmed, and he rushed out, all his scruples overcome, careless of what he did or how deeply he became immersed in the hitherto unknown sea of guilt.

The cool night air lifted the damp locks from his heated brow, and swept with soothing touch over his flushed cheeks. Walking on, calmer, but no less determined, strains of music from a distance met his ear. Following in the direction the sound indicated, he at length distinguished the words and air. The song was well remembered. It was "Home, Sweet Home." Clear and sweet the voice of some English singer rose and fell on the air, in the soft cadences of that beloved melody.

Motionless, the wanderer listened till the last note floated away and he could hear nothing but the ceaseless murmur of a great city. Then he turned slowly, with no feeling that his manhood was shamed by the tear which fell as a bright evidence of the power of song.

The demon that dwells in the wine had fled; and reason once more asserted her right to control. As the soft strains of "Sweet Home" had floated to his ear, memory brought up before him his own "sweet home." He saw his gentle mother, and heard her speak, while honest pride beamed from her eye, of her son, in whose nobleness and honor she could always trust; and his heart smote him as he thought how little he deserved such confidence. He remembered her last words of love and counsel, and the tearful farewell of all those dear ones who gladdened that far-away home with their presence. Well he knew their pride in his integrity, and the tide of remorse swept over his spirit as he felt what their sorrow would be could they have seen him an hour before. Subdued and repentant, he retraced his steps, and with this vow never to taste of the terrible draught that could so excite him to madness was mingled a deep sense of thankfulness for his escape from further degradation. The influence of home had protected him, though the sea rolled between.

None can tell how often the commission of crime is prevented by such memories. If, then, the spell of home is so powerful, how important it is to make it pleasant and lovable! Many a time a cheerful home and smiling face does more to make good men and women, than all the learning and eloquence that can be used. It has been said that the sweetest words in our language are " Mother, Home and Heaven ;" and one might almost say the word home included them all; for who can think of home without remembering the gentle mother who sanctified it by her presence? And is not home the dearest name for heaven? We think of that better land as a home where brightness will never end in night. Oh, then, may our homes on earth be the centers of all our joys; may they be as green spots in the desert, to which we can retire when weary of the cares and perplexities of life, and drink the clear waters of a love which we know to be sincere and always unfailing.—*Saturday Evening Post.*

THE SMILES OF HOME.

John Keble

SWEET is the smile of home; the mutual look
Where hearts are of each other sure;
Sweet all the joys that crowd the household nook,
The haunt of all affections pure.

HOME COURTESY.

NO pleasanter sight is there, than a family of young folks who are quick to perform little acts of attention toward their elders. The placing of the big arm-chair for mamma, running for a footstool for aunty, hunting up papa's spectacles, and scores of little deeds, show the tender sympathy of gentle loving hearts; but if mamma never returns a smiling "Thank you, dear;" if papa's "Just what I was wanting, Susie," does not indicate that the little attention is appreciated, the children soon drop the habit. Little people are imitative creatures, and quickly catch the spirit surrounding them. So if, when the mother's spool of cotton roll from her lap, the father stoops to pick it up, bright eyes will see the act, and quick minds make a note of it. By example, a thousand times more quickly than by precept, can children be taught to speak kindly to each other, to acknowledge favors, to be gentle and unselfish, to be thoughtful and considerate of the comfort of the family. The boys, with inward pride of their father's courteous demeanor, will be chivalrous and helpful to their own young sisters;. the girls, imitating their mother, will be patient and gentle, even when big brothers are noisy and heedless. In the homes where true courtesy prevails, it seems to meet you on the threshold. You feel the kindly welcome on entering. No angry voices are heard upstairs. No sullen children are sent from the room. No peremptory orders are given to cover the delinquencies of house-keeping or servants. A delightful atmosphere pervades the house—unmistakable, yet indescribable.

Such a house, filled by the spirit of love, is a home indeed to all:

who enter within its consecrated walls. And it is of such a home that the Master said, "And into whatsoever house ye enter, first say, Peace be to this house. And if the *Son of Peace* be there, your peace shall rest upon it." Luke x. 5, 6.

> " Blest are the sons of peace,
>   Whose hearts and hopes are one;
> Whose kind designs to serve and please,
>   Through all their actions run.
>
> " Thus on the heavenly hills,
>   The saints are blessed above;
> Where joy like morning dew distills,
>   And all the air is love."
>
> —*Anonymous.*

THE HAPPY HOME.

Martin F. Tupper.

A HAPPY home! O, bright and cheerful hearth!
Look round with me, my lover, friend, and wife,
On these fair faces we have lit with life,
And in the perfect blessing of their birth,
Help me to live our thanks for so much heaven on earth.

HOME OF OUR CHILDHOOD.

Oliver Wendell Holmes.

HOME of our childhood! How affection clings
And hovers round thee with her seraph wings!
Dearer thy hills, though clad in autumn brown,
Than fairest summits which the cedars crown;
Sweeter the fragrance of thy summer breeze,
Than all Arabia breathes along the seas!
The stranger's gale wafts home the exile's sigh,
For the heart's temple is its own blue sky.

HOME BY THE LAKE SIDE.

AN IDEAL HOME.
Samuel Rogers.

MINE be a cot beside the hill;
  A bee-hive's hum shall soothe my ear;
  A willowy brook, that turns a mill,
  With many a fall, shall linger near.

The swallow oft, beneath my thatch,
  Shall twitter near her clay-built nest;
Oft shall the pilgrim lift the latch,
  And share my meal, a welcome guest.

Around my ivied porch shall spring
  Each fragrant flower that drinks the dew;
And Lucy, at her wheel, shall sing,
  In russet gown and apron blue.

The village church beneath the trees,
  Where first our marriage vows were given,
With merry peals shall swell the breeze,
  And point with taper spire to heaven.

HOME.
James Thomson.

HOME is the resort
  Of love, of joy, of peace, and plenty, where
  Supporting and supported, polish'd friends,
  And dear relations mingle into bliss.

HOME RELIGION.

A HOUSE may be full of persons who are very dear to each other, very kind to each other; full of precious things,— affections, hopes, living interests; but if God is not there as the Ruler and Father of the house, the original and true idea of home will not be realized; vacancy and need will still be at the heart of all. Good things will grow feebly and uncertainly, like flowers in winter, trying to peep out into sunshine, yet shrinking from the blast. Evil things will grow with strange persistency, notwithstanding protests of the affections and efforts of the will. Mysterious gulfs will open at times where it was thought strong foundations had been laid. Little things will produce great distress. Great things, when attained, will shrink to littleness. Flickerings of uncertainty and fear will run along the days. Joys will not satisfy. Sorrow will surprise.

In the very heart of the godless home there will be sickness, arising from need unsatisfied and "hope deferred." It will be as when a man of ingenuity tries in vain to put together the separated parts of a complicated piece of mechanism. He tries in this way and that, puts the pieces into every conceivable mode of arrangement, then at last stops, and says: "There must be a piece wanting."

Home without Divine presence is at best a moral structure with the central element wanting. The other elements may be arranged and re-arranged; they will never exactly fit, nor be "compact together," until it is obtained. We have heard of haunted houses. That house will be haunted with the ghost of an unrealized idea. It will seem to its most thoughtful inmates at best but "the shadow of some good thing to come;" and the longing for the substance will be the more intense, because the shadow, as a providential prophecy, is always there.

In many a house there is going on, by means of those quick spiritual sighs by which One above can read, what we may call a dialogue of souls, composed chiefly of unspoken questions, which, if articulate, might be something like the following :—" How is it that we cannot be to each other as we wish, that we cannot do for each other what we try, even when it seems to be quite within the range of possibility ? Why is there such a sorrow in our affection ? such a trembling in our joys ? so great a fear of change, and so profound a sense of incompleteness in connection with the very best we can do and be ? "

And what is the answer to such mute yet eager questionings ? And who can speak that answer ? That One above who hears the dialogue must take part in it; and all must listen while He speaks, and tells of another fatherhood, under which the parents must become little children, of another brotherhood which, when attained, will make the circle complete. When the members of such a household, who have been looking so much to each other, shall agree to give one earnest look above, and say, "Our Father, which art in heaven!" "our elder Brother, and Advocate with the Father!" then will come back, sweet as music, into the heart of that house, these fulfilling words from the everlasting Father, "Ye shall be my sons and daughters;" from the eternal Son, "Behold my mother and sister and brother!" Then the one thing that was lacking will be present. The missing element will be in its place, and all the other elements will be assembled around it. It is a haunted house no more. The ghost has been chased away. The house is wholesome. Mornings are welcome. Nights are restful. The aching sorrow has passed away now from the heart of that home. The long-sought secret is revealed. Soul whispers to soul, "Emmanuel. God with us." Home is home at last.—*Mother's Treasury.*

KIND WORDS AT HOME.

SPEAK kindly in the morning; it lightens the cares of the day, and makes the household and all other affairs move along more smoothly.

Speak kindly at night, for it may be that before the dawn some loved one may finish his or her space of life, and it will be too late to ask forgiveness.

Speak kindly at all times; it encourages the downcast, cheers the sorrowing, and very likely awakens the erring to earnest resolves to do better, with strength to keep them.

Kind words are balm to the soul. They oil up the entire machinery of life, and keep it in good running order.—*Anonymous*

A HAPPY HOME DEFINED.

Rev. Dr. Hamilton.

SIX things are requisite to create a happy home. Integrity must be the architect, and tidiness the upholsterer. It must be warmed by affection, and lightened up with cheerfulness, and industry must be the ventilator, renewing the atmosphere and bringing in fresh salubrity day by day; while over all, as a protecting canopy and glory, nothing will suffice except the blessings of God.

FAMILY PRAYERS.

WE are far from thinking that the good old custom of having family prayers is being dropped from Christian households. It is a custom held in honor wherever there is real Christian life, and it is the one thing which, more than any other, knits together the loose threads of a home and unites its various members before God. The short religious service in which parents, children and friends daily join in praise and prayer, is at once an acknowledgment of dependence on the heavenly Father and a renewal of consecration to his work in the world. The Bible is read, the hymn is sung, the petition is offered, and unless all has been done as a mere formality and without hearty assent, those who have gathered at the family altar leave it helped, soothed, strengthened, and armored, as they were not before they met there. The sick and the absent are remembered. The tempted and the tried are commended to God, and, as the Israelites in the desert were attended by the pillar and the cloud, so in life's wilderness the family who inquire of the Lord are constantly overshadowed by his presence and love.

There are many reasons which are allowed to interfere with and thrust aside the privilege of family prayer in homes where father and mother mean to have it daily.

Whatever comes in the way of a plain duty ought, however, to be set aside. If there be any among our readers who recognize the need there is in their house to have a daily open worship of God, let them begin it at once. They must find the time, choose the place, and appoint the way. The actual time spent in worship may be a few minutes only. A brief service which cannot tire the youngest child, if held unvaryingly as the sun, in the morning when the day begins, and in the evening when its active labors close, is far more useful and edifying than a long one which fatigues attention.

It is possible to have a daily worship which shall be earnest, vivifying, tender and reverential, and yet a weariness to nobody. Only let the one who conducts it *mean* toward the Father the sweet obedience of the grateful child, and maintain the attitude of one who goes about earthly affairs with a soul looking beyond and above them to the rest that remaineth in heaven. It is not every one who is able to pray in the hearing of others with ease. The timid tongue falters, and the thoughts struggle in vain for utterance. But who is there who cannot read a Psalm, or a chapter, or a cluster of verses, and, kneeling, repeat in accents of tender trust the Lord's prayer? When we think of it, that includes everything.—*Christian at Work.*

FREQUENT PRAYER.

Bishop Taylor.

PRAYER is the key to open the day, and the bolt to shut in the night. But as the clouds drop the early dew, and the evening dew upon the grass, yet it would not spring and grow green by that constant and double falling of the dew, unless some great shower at certain seasons did supply the rest; so the customary devotion of prayer twice a day, is the falling of the early and latter dew. But if you will increase and flourish in works of grace, empty the great clouds sometimes, and let them fall in a full shower of prayer. Choose out seasons when prayer shall over flow like Jordan in time of harvest.

NO TIME TO PRAY.

NO time to pray!
  Oh, who so fraught with earthly care
  As not to give to humble prayer
    Some part of day?

No time to pray!
What heart so clean, so pure within,
That needeth not some check from sin,
    Needs not to pray?

No time to pray!
'Mid each day's danger, what retreat
More needful than the mercy-seat?
    Who need not pray?

No time to pray!
Then sure your record falleth short;
Excuse will fail you as resort,
    On that last day.

What thought more drear,
Than that our God his face should hide,
And say through all life's swelling tide,
    No time to hear!—*Anonymous.*

ALWAYS leave the home with loving words, for they may be the last.

THE CHILDREN.

Dickenson.

WHEN the lessons and tasks are all ended,
    And the school for the day is dismissed,
    And the little ones gather around me,
To bid me good-night and be kissed;
Oh, the little white arms that encircle
    My neck in a tender embrace!
Oh, the smiles that are halos of heaven,
    Shedding sunshine of love on my face!

And when they are gone I sit dreaming
    Of my childhood too lovely to last;
Of love that my heart will remember,
    When it wakes to the pulse of the past,
Ere the world and its wickedness made me
    A partner of sorrow and sin;
When the glory of God was about me,
    And the glory of gladness within.

Oh! my heart grows weak as a woman's,
    And the fountain of feeling will flow,
When I think of the paths steep and stony,
    Where the feet of the dear ones must go;
Of the mountains of sin hanging o'er them,
    Of the tempest of fate blowing wild!
Oh! there is nothing on earth half so holy
    As the innocent heart of a child.

THE CHILDREN.

They are idols of hearts and of households;
   They are angels of God in disguise;
His sunlight still sleeps in their tresses,
   His glory still gleams in their eyes;
Oh! these truants from home and from heaven
   They have made me more manly and mild,
And I know how Jesus could liken
   The kingdom of God to a child.

I ask not a life for the dear ones,
   All radiant, as others have done,
But that life may have enough shadow
   To temper the glare of the sun;
I would pray God to guard them from evil,
   But my prayer would come back to myself;
Ah, a seraph may pray for a sinner,
   But a sinner must pray for himself.

The twig is so easily bended,
   I have banished the rule and the rod;
I have taught them the goodness of knowledge,
   They have taught me the goodness of God;
My heart is a dungeon of darkness,
   Where I shut them from breaking a rule;
My frown is sufficient correction;
   My love is the law of the school.

I shall leave the old house in the autumn,
   To traverse its threshold no more;
Ah, how I shall sigh for the dear ones,
   That meet me each morn at the door,

THE CHILDREN.

I shall miss the " good-nights " and the kisses,
   And the gush of their innocent glee,
The group on the green, and the flowers
   That are brought every morning to me.

I shall miss them at morn and evening,
   Their song in the school and the street;
I shall miss the low hum of their voices,
   And the tramp of their delicate feet.
When the lessons and tasks are all ended,
   And death says: " The school is dismissed,"
May the little ones gather around me,
   To bid me good-night and be kissed.

THE CHILDREN.
H. W. Longfellow.

AH! what would the world be to us
   If the children were no more?
We should dread the desert behind us
   Worse than the dark before.

What the leaves are to the forest,
   With light and air for food,
Ere their sweet and tender juices
   Have been hardened into wood—

That, to the world, are children;
   Through them it feels the glow
Of a brighter and sunnier climate
   Than reaches the trunks below.

THE RIGHTS OF CHILDREN.

THE child has a right to ask questions and to be fairly answered; not to be snubbed as if he were guilty of an impertinence, nor ignored as though his desire for information were of no consequence, nor misled as if it did not signify whether true or false impressions were made upon his mind.

The child has a right to his individuality, to be himself and no other; to maintain against the world the divine fact for which he stands. And before this fact father, mother, instructor should stand reverently; seeking rather to understand and interpret its significance than to wrest it from its original purpose. It is not necessarily to be inscribed with the family name, nor written over with family traditions. Nature delights in surprise and will not guarantee that the children of her poets shall sing, nor that every Quaker baby shall take kindly to drab color, or have an inherent longing for a scoop-bonnet or a broad-brimmed hat.

In the very naming of a child his individuality should be recognized. He should not be invested with the cast-off cognomen of some dead ancestor or historical celebrity, a name musty as the grave-clothes of the original wearer—dolefully redolent of old associations—a ghostly index-finger forever pointing to the past. Let it be something fresh; a new name standing for a new fact, the suggestion of a history yet to be written, a prophecy to be fulfilled. The ass was well enough clothed in his own russet; but when he would put on the skin of the lion, every attribute became contemptible. Commonplace people slip easily through the world; but when we would find them heralded by great names, we resent the incon gruity, and insist upon making them less than they are. George Washington selling peanuts, Julius Cæsar as a bootblack, and Virgil a vender of old clothes, make but a sorry figure.

We are indebted to our children for constant incentives to noble living; for the perpetual reminder that we do not live to ourselves alone; for their sakes we are admonished to put from us the debasing appetite, the unworthy impulse; to gather into our lives every noble and heroic quality, every tender and attractive grace.

We owe them gratitude for the dark hours which their presence has brightened, for the helplessness and dependence which have won us from ourselves; for the faith and trust which it is evermore their mission to renew; for their kisses on cheeks wet with tears, and on brows that but for that caressing had furrowed into frowns.—*Littell's Living Age.*

SUFFERINGS OF CHILDHOOD.

THE sufferings of a bashful boy! Can torture chamber be more dreadful than the juvenile party, the necessary parade of the Christmas-dinner, to a shy boy? I have sometimes taken the hand of such a one, and have found it cold and clammy; desperate was the struggle of that young soul, afraid of he knew not what, caught by the machinery of society, which mangled him at every point, crushed every nerve, and filled him with faintness and fear. How happy he might have been with that brood of young puppies in the barn, or the soft rabbits in their nest of hay! How grand he was, paddling his poor leaky boat down the rapids, jumping into the river, and dragging it with his splendid strength over the rocks! Nature and he were friends; he was not afraid of her;

SUFFERINGS OF CHILDHOOD.

she recognized her child and greeted him with smiles. The young animals loved him, and his dog looked up into his fair blue eyes, and recognized his king. But this creature must be tamed; he must be brought into prim parlors, and dine with propriety; he must dress himself in garments which scratch, and pull, and hurt him; boots must be put on his feet which pinch; he must be clean,—terrible injustice to a faun who loves to roll down-hill, to grub for roots, to follow young squirrels to their lair, and to polish old guns rather than his manner.

And then the sensitive boy, who has a finer grain than the majority of his fellows, suddenly thrown into the pandemonium of a public school! Nails driven into the flesh could not inflict such pain as such a one suffers; and the scars remain. One gentleman told me, in mature life, that the loss of a toy stolen from him in childhood still rankled. How much of the infirmity of human character may be traced to the anger, the sense of wounded feeling, engendered by a wrong done in childhood when one is helpless to avenge!

All this may be called the necessary hardening process, but I do not believe in it. We have learned how to temper iron and steel, but we have not learned how to treat children. Could it be made a money-making process, like the Bessemer, I believe one could learn how to temper the human character. Our instincts of intense love for our children are not enough; we should study it as a science. The human race is very busy; it has to take care of itself, and to feed its young; it must conquer the earth—perhaps it has not time to study Jim and Jack and Charley, and Mary and Emily and Jane, as problems. But, if it had, would it not perhaps pay? There would be fewer criminals.

Many observers recommend a wise neglect—not too much inquiry, but a judicious surrounding of the best influences, and then

—let your young plant grow up. Yes; but it should be a very wise neglect—it should be a neglect which is always on the watch lest some inisdious parasite, some unnoticed but strong bias of character, take possession of the child and mould or ruin him. Of the ten boys running up yonder hill, five will be failures, two will be moderate successes, two will do better, one will be great, good and distinguished. If such are the terrible statistics—and I am told that they are so—who is to blame? Certainly the parent or guardian, or circumstance—and what is circumstance?—*Appleton's Journal.*

———•———

GOVERNMENT OF CHILDREN.

THERE were many ideas entertained by the Puritan settlers of New England that happily were not bequeathed to those who came after them, but in fixing proper relations between parents and children, and in parental government generally it would have been better to have preserved some of the inflexibility of discipline that distinguished them. The youth of the present have their own way too much. No obedience or respect is exacted from them by father or mother in many instances, and they grow up selfish, overbearing, and sometimes dangerous. The case of the boy in Maine who a year or so ago killed his father because he was angry with him, is probably familiar to all. The other day a father in New York was obliged to complain of his son on account of the boy's repeated thefts. When the youth had been sentenced, he turned to his father, and told him that as soon as he got out of jail he would "blow the top of his head off." A few days since a young man in high station in Brooklyn tried to murder his wife. He was neither intoxicated nor insane. The only trouble was that he had always been permitted to have his own way, and the groove of selfishness and petty tyranny to which he had been allowed to shape himself led but in one direction, and he considered any means—even shot-guns and bowie-knives—justifiable in revenging himself upon those who opposed in the slightest his wishes or course of life. Children need checks, direction and good influences. A well-governed child is in the grand majority of cases sure to grow into a respectable man or woman, but the noblest natures may be blighted unless the weeds of untrained propensity are kept down.—*Boston Post.*

KIND WORDS.

AS the breath of the dew on the tender plant, they gently fall upon the drooping heart, refreshing its withered tendrils and soothing its burning woes. Bright oases they are in life's great desert. Who can estimate the pangs they have alleviated, or the good works they have accomplished? Long after they are uttered do they reverberate in the soul's inner chamber, and sing low, sweet, liquid strains, that quell all the raging storms that may have before existed. And oh! when the heart is sad, and like a broken harp, the sweetest chords of pleasure cease to vibrate, who can tell the power of one kind word? One little word of tenderness gushing in upon the soul, will sweep the long-neglected chords, and awaken the most pleasant strains. Kind words are like jewels in the heart, never to be forgotten, but perhaps to cheer by their memory a long, sad life. While words of cruelty are like darts in the bosom, wounding and leaving scars that will be borne to the grave by their victim.—*Saturday Evening Post.*

NOT ONE CHILD TO SPARE.*

Mrs. Ethel L. Beers.

"WHICH shall it be? Which shall it be?"
  I looked at John—John looked at me,
  (Dear, patient John, who loves me yet,
As well as though my locks were jet),
And when I found that I must speak,
My voice seemed strangely low and weak :
"Tell me again what Robert said !"
And then I listening bent my head.
"This is his letter :—' I will give
A house and land while you shall live,
If, in return, from out your seven,
One child to me for aye is given.' "
I looked at John's old garments worn,
I thought of all that John had borne
Of poverty, and work, and care,
Which I, though willing, could not share ;
I thought of seven mouths to feed,
Of seven little children's need,
And then of this.—" Come, John," said I,
" We'll choose among them as they lie
Asleep ;" so, walking hand in hand,
Dear John and I surveyed our band—

---

* A father and mother in straitened circumstances, with seven children, were offered by a wealthy, but childless neighbor, a comfortable provision, on condition that they would give him one of their children. This beautiful poem tells the result.

NOT ONE CHILD TO SPARE.

First to the cradle lightly stepped,
Where Lilian the baby slept.
A glory 'gainst the pillow white;
Softly the father stooped to lay
His rough hand down in loving way,
When dream or whisper made her stir,
And huskily he said: "Not her, not her."
We stooped beside the trundle-bed,
And one long ray of lamplight shed
Athwart the boyish faces there,
In sleep so pitiful and fair;
I saw on Jamie's rough, red cheek,
A tear undried. Ere John could speak,
"He's but a baby, too," said I,
And kissed him as we hurried by.
Pale patient Robbie's angel face
Still in his sleep bore suffering's trace.
"No, for a thousand crowns, not him,"
He whispered, while our eyes were dim.
Poor Dick! bad Dick! our wayward son,
Turbulent, reckless, idle one—
Could he be spared? "Nay, He who gave
Bid us befriend him to his grave;
Only a mother's heart can be
Patient enough for such as he;
And so," said John, "I would not dare
To send him from her bedside prayer."
Then stole we softly up above
And knelt by Mary, child of love.
"Perhaps for her 'twould better be,"
I said to John. Quite silently,

He lifted up a curl that lay
Across her cheek in willful way,
And shook his head, "Nay, love, not thee,"
The while my heart beat audibly.
Only one more, our eldest lad,
Trusty and truthful, good and glad—
So like his father. "No, John no—
I can not, will not, let him go."
And so we wrote, in courteous way,
We could not drive one child away;
And afterward toil lighter seemed,
Thinking of that of which we dreamed,
Happy in truth that not one face
Was missed from its accustomed place;
Thankful to work for all the seven,
Trusting the rest to One in heaven!

BABIES AND THEIR RIGHTS.

M. E. Sangster.

A BABY has a right, too frequently denied it, *to be let alone*. It ought to be a rule in the nursery never to disturb the infant when it is happy and quiet. Older children, too, two, three, and four years of age, who are amusing themselves in a peaceful, contented way, ought not to be wantonly interfered with. I have often seen a little creature lying in its crib cooing, laughing, crooning to itself in the sweetest baby fashion, without a care in the world to vex its composure, when in would come mamma or nurse, seize it, cover it with endearments, and effectually break up its tranquillity. Then, the next time, when these thoughtless people wanted it to be quiet, they were surprised that it refused to be so. It is habit and training which make little children restless and fretful, rather than natural disposition, in a multitude of cases. A healthy babe, coolly and loosely dressed, judiciously fed, and frequently bathed, will be good and comfortable if it have not too much attention. But when it is liable a dozen times a day to be caught wildly up, bounced and jumped about, smothered with kisses, poked by facetious fingers, and petted till it is thoroughly out of sorts, what can be expected of it? How would fathers and mothers endure the martyrdom to which they allow the babies to be subjected?

Another right which every baby has is to its own mother's care and supervision. The mother may not be strong enough to hold her child and carry it about, to go with it on its outings, and to personally attend to all its wants. Very often it is really better for both mother and child that the strong arms of an able-bodied woman should bear it through its months of helplessness. Still, no matter how apparently worthy of trust a nurse or servant may be, unless she have been tried and proved by long and faithful service and friendship, a babe is too precious to be given unreservedly to her care. The mother herself, or an elder sister or auntie, should hover protectingly near the tiny creature, whose life-long happiness may depend on the way its babyhood is passed. Who has not seen in the city parks the beautifully-dressed infants, darlings evidently of homes of wealth and refinement, left to bear the beams of the sun and stings of gnats and flies, while the nurses gossiped together, oblivious of the flight of time? Mothers are often quick to resent stories of the neglect or cruelty of their employees, and cannot be made to believe that their own children are sufferers. And the children are too young to speak.

The lover of little ones can almost always see the subtle difference which exists between the babies whom mothers care for, and the babies who are left to hirelings. The former have a sweeter, shyer, gladder look than the latter. Perhaps the babies who are born, so to speak, with silver spoons in their mouths, are better off than those who came to the heritage of a gold spoon. The gold spooners have lovely cradles and vassinets. They wear Valenciennes lace and embroidery, and fashion dicates the cut of their bibs, and the length of their flowing robes. They are waited upon by bonnes in picturesque aprons and caps, and the doctor is sent for whenever they have the colic. The little silver-spooners, on the other hand, are arrayed in simple slips, which the mother made herself in dear, delicious hours, the sweetest in their mystic joy which happy womanhood knows. They lie on the sofa, or on two chairs with a pillow placed carefully to hold them, while she sings at her work, spreads the snowy linen on the grass, moulds the bread, and shells the peas. The mother's hands wash and dress them, the father rocks them to sleep, the proud brothers and sisters carry them to walk, or wheel their little wagons along the pavement. Fortunate babies of the silver spoon!

Alas and alack! for the babies who have never a spoon at all, not even a horn or a leaden one. Their poor parents love them, amid the squalid circumstances which hem them in, but they can do little for their well-being, and they die by hundreds in garrets and cellars and close tenement rooms. When the rich and charitable shall devise some way to care for the babies of the poor, when New York shall imitate Paris in founding an institution akin to La Creche, we shall have taken a long step forward in the direction of social and moral elevation.

THE CHILDREN'S BED-TIME.

Jane Ellis Hopkins.

THE clock strikes seven in the hall,
    The curfew of the children's day,
    That calls each little pattering foot
        From dance and song and lively play;
Their day that in a wider light
Floats like a silver day-moon white,
Nor in our darkness sinks to rest,
But sets within a golden west.

Ah, tender hour that sends a drift
    Of children's kisses though the house,
And cuckoo notes of sweet "Good night,"
    That thoughts of heaven and home arouse,
And a soft stir to sense and heart,
As when the bee and blossom part;
And little feet that patter slower,
Like the last droppings of a shower.

And in the children's room aloft,
    What blossom shapes do gaily slip
Their daily sheaths, and rosy run
    From clasping hand and kissing lip,
A naked sweetness to the eye—
Blossom and babe and butterfly
In witching one, so dear a sight!
An ecstasy of life and light.

THE CHILDREN'S BED-TIME.

Then lily-drest, in angel white,
   To mother's knee they trooping come.
The soft palms fold like kissing shells,
   And they and we go singing home—
Their bright heads bowed and worshiping,
As though some glory of the spring,
Some daffodil that mocks the day,
Should fold his golden palms and pray.

The gates of paradise swing wide
   A moment's space in soft accord,
And those dread angels, Life and Death,
   A moment vail the flaming sword,
As o'er this weary world forlorn
From Eden's secret heart is borne
That breath of Paradise most fair,
Which mothers call "the children's prayer."

Then kissed, on beds we lay them down,
   As fragrant white as clover'd sod,
And all the upper floors grow hushed
   With children's sleep, and dews of God.
And as our stars their beams do hide,
The stars of twilight, opening wide,
Take up the heavenly tale at even,
And light us on to God and heaven.

NEVER wish for anything for which you dare not pray.

THE EVENING PRAYER.

ALL day the children's busy feet
    Had pattered to and fro;
And all the day their little hands
    Had been in mischief so,—

That oft my patience had been tried;
    But tender, loving care
Had kept them through the day from harm,
    And safe from ev'ry snare.

But when the even-tide had come,
    The children went up-stairs,
And knelt beside their little beds,
    To say their wonted prayers.

With folded hands and rev'rent mien,
    "Our Father," first they say,
Then, "Now I lay me down to sleep,"
    With childlike faith they pray.

With cheeks upon the pillow pressed,
    They give a kiss, and say,—
"Good-night; we love you, dear mamma,
    You've been so kind to-day."

"Dood-night; I love oo, too, mamma."
    And baby's eyelids close;
And tired feet and restless hands
    Enjoy the sweet repose.

The trouble and the weariness
  To me indeed seemed light,
Since love had thus my efforts crowned
  To guide their steps aright.

And as I picked the playthings up,
  And put the books away,
My heart gave grateful thanks to God,
  For His kind care all day.—*Anonymous.*

HOME AND ITS QUEEN.

THERE is probably not an unperverted man or woman living, who does not feel that the sweetest consolations and best rewards of life are found in the loves and delights of home. There are very few who do not feel themselves indebted to the influences that clustered around their cradles for whatever good there may be in their characters and condition. Home, based upon Christian marriage, is so evident an institution of God, that a man must become profane before he can deny it. Wherever it is pure and true to the Christian idea, there lives an institution conservative of all the nobler instincts of society.

Of this realm woman is the queen. It takes the cue and hue from her. If she is in the best sense womanly—if she is true and tender, loving and heroic, patient and self-devoted—she consciously and unconsciously organizes and puts in operation a set of influences that do more to mould the destiny of the nation than any man, uncrowned by power of eloquence, can possibly effect. The men of the nation are what mothers make them, as a rule; and the voice that those men speak in the expression of power, is the voice of the woman who bore and bred them. There can be no substitute for this. There is no other possible way in which the women of the nation can organize their influence and power that will tell so beneficially upon society and the state.—*Scribner's Monthly.*

GIRLS' INFLUENCE.

GIRLS, and especially those who are members of large families, have much influence at home, where brothers delight in their sisters, and where parents look fondly down on their dear daughters, and pray that their example may influence the boys for good. Girls have much in their power with regard to those boys; they have it in their power to make them gentler, purer, truer, to give them higher opinions of women; to soften their manners and ways; to tone down rough places, and shape sharp, angular corners.

All this, to be done well, must be done by imperceptibly influencing them, and giving them an example of the gentleness, the purity, the politeness and tenderness we wish them to emluate. When we see boys careless to their elders, rude in manner and coarse in speech, and we know that they have sisters, we often, and I think with reason, conclude that there must be something wrong, and that the sisters are not trying to make them better boys, but leaving things alone, letting them go their own course. Perhaps their excuse would be that they were too much occupied themselves and that their own studies and pursuits prevent them from being able to pay much attention to their brothers; and "boys will be boys," you know. By all means let boys be boys. I, for one, regard boys far too highly to wish them to be otherwise; but the roughness, and coarseness, and rudeness, of which I speak, are not necessary ingredients of boyhood; and it is you, their sisters, who must prove that they are not. Interest yourselves in their pursuits, show them, by every means in your power, that you do not consider them and their doings beneath your notice; spare an hour from your practicing, from your drawing, from your languages, for their boating or sports, and don't turn contemptuously away from the books and amusements in which they delight, as if, though good enough for them, they are immeasurably below you. Try this behavior, girls, for a short time; it will not harm you, and will benefit them greatly. You will soon find how a gentle word will turn off a sharp answer; how a grieved look will effectually reprove an unfitting expression; how gratefully a small kindness will be received; and how unbounded will be the power for good you will obtain by a continuance of this conduct.

Equally great will a girl's influence be on her younger sisters, in whose eyes she is the perfection of grace and goodness, in whose thoughts she is ever present. Beautiful, exceedingly beautiful, is the close friendship between an elder and a younger sister; but let the elder beware of the influence she exerts. If she herself be careless, frivolous, undutiful, and irreligious, the child will inevitably be so too, unless the fatal influence be counteracted by some other holier one. If she gives sharp answers, or shows but little regard for truth, let her not be astonished if the little one be ill-tempered and untruthful; and sorrowful will be the conviction that she has had not a little to do with making her so.

In school, too, a girl of determined, resolute character will soon take the lead and acquire a certain influence. School-girls are gregarious, and follow naturally anyone who is stronger-minded and more decided. When the influence is exercised to elevate the .

young minds, and give them higher and noble aspirations, it is a salutary and beneficial effect of school life; but when it is otherwise, it is a very sad one. Two or three older girls in a school, having a noble object in view, steadily endeavoring to do right, acting quietly and without ostentation, but seeking humbly to follow in the footsteps Christ has marked out for us, may do an immense amount of good. "A little leaven leaveneth the whole lump."

> We know not half the power for good or ill,
> Our daily lives possess o'er one another;
> A careless word may help a soul to kill,
> Or by one look we may redeem our brother.
>
> 'Tis not the great things that we do or say,
> But idle words forget as soon as spoken;
> And little, thoughtless deeds of every day
> Are stumbling blocks on which the weak are broken.
> —*Anonymous.*

TO OUR GIRLS.

Mary F. Lathrop.

THE pastor of a church in one of our large cities said to me not long ago: "I have officiated at forty weddings since I came here, and in every case, save one, I felt that the bride was running an awful risk." Young men of bad habits and fast tendencies never marry girls of their own sort, but demand a wife above suspicion. So pure, sweet women, kept from the touch of evil through the years of their girlhood, give themselves, with all their costly dower of womanhood, into the keeping of men who, in base associations, have learned to undervalue all that belongs to them, and then find no time for repentance in the sad after years. There is but one way out of this that I can see, and that is for you

—the young women of the country—to require in association and marriage, purity for purity, sobriety for sobriety, and honor for honor. There is no reason why the young men of this Christian land should not be just as virtuous as its young women, and if the loss of your society and love be the price they are forced to pay for vice, they will not pay it. I admit with sadness that not all of our young women are capable of this high standard for themselves or others; too often from the hand of reckless beauty has the temptation to drink come to men; but I believe there are enough of earnest, thoughtful girls in the society of our country to work wonders in the temperance reform, if fully aroused. Dear girls, will you help us in the name of Christ? Will you, first of all, be so true to yourselves and God, so pure in your inner and outer life, that you shall have a right to ask that the young men with whom you associate, and especially those you marry, shall be the same? The awful gulf of dishonor is close beside your feet, and in it fathers, brothers, lovers, and sons are going down. Will you not help us in our great work?

A PLEA FOR THE BOY.

THE boy is an offense in himself. He must have something to do, and as his hands are idle the proverbial provider of occupation for idle hands is always ready with instructions for him. A boy makes noise in utter defiance of the laws of acoustics. Shoe him in velvet, and carpet your house as you will, your boy shall make such a hubbub with his heels as no watchman's rattle ever gave forth. Doors in his hands always shut with a violence which jars the whole house, and he is certain to acquire each day the art of screaming or whistling in some wholly new and excruciating way. Loving his mother so violently that his caresses derange her attire and seriously endanger her bones, ready to die in her defense if need be, he nevertheless torments her from morning to night, and allows her no possible peace until slumber closes his throat and eyelids, and deprives his hands and feet of their demoniac cunning.

In public your boy is equally a nuisance. Collectively or individually he offends the public in the streets. Whatever he does is sure to be wrong. He monopolizes space and takes to himself all the air there is for acoustical purposes. Your personal peculiarities interest him, and with all the frankness of his soul he comments upon your appearance, addressing his remarks to his fellow on the next block.

Nevertheless the boy has his uses. He is the material out of which men are to be made for the next generation. He is not a bad fellow,—that is to say, he is not intentionally or consciously bad. There are springs in his limbs which keep him in perpetual motion, and the devil of uproar of which he is possessed utters the ear-piercing sounds which annoy his elders, but the utterances of which he can no more restrain than he can keep his boots or trousers from wearing out. In a ten-acre lot, well away from the house, the boy is a picturesque and agreeable person; it is only when one must come into closer contact with him that his presence causes suffering and suggests a statue to King Herod. It is in cities that the boy makes himself felt most disagreeably, and we fancy that the fault is not altogether his. As the steam which bursts boilers would be a perfectly harmless vapor but for the sharp restraint that is put upon it, so the effervescent boy becomes dangerous to social order only when he is confined, when an effort is made to compress him into smaller space than the law of his expansive being absolutely requires. We send him upon the war-path by encroaching upon his hunting-grounds; we drive him into hostility by treating him as a public enemy. In most of our dealings with him in cities, our effort is to suppress him, and it is an unwise system. If his ball-playing in the streets becomes an annoyance, we simply forbid ball-playing in the streets, and it is an inevitable consequence that, deprived of his ball, he will throw stones at street lamps or at policemen. What else is he to do?

In Brooklyn, for example, whose streets are long and wide, there was thought to be room enough for boys, and the inspiring rumble of the velocipede was heard there until somebody objected, when straightway the policemen were directed to arrest all machines of that character, whether with two, three, or four wheels, found upon sidewalks. Now this order we held was not only cruel, but it was unwise as well. Without a doubt the velocipedes were a source of serious annoyance in crowded thoroughfares, but they are not so in streets in which pedestrians are few, as they are in fully one-half of Brooklyn's thoroughfares. Velocipede riding might have been forbidden in the main thoroughfares, and permitted in less frequented ones, and the boy would have been content; to forbid it where it offends nobody—merely for the sake of preventing it where it does offend—is illogical and unjust, and, worse still, it is unwise. The boy cannot be banished or confined, and, lacking his velocipede he will resort to something more annoying still. What it will be we do not pretend to guess, but for its capacity to annoy we may safely trust to the boy's ingenuity.

Speaking in all seriousness, it is not well to suppress the sports of boys from which they derive strength and health and manly vigor of body. We may and must regulate these things; but mere suppression is a crude and tyrannical method of dealing with them. In Boston, a city of notions, whose notions are sometimes surprisingly wise and good, care is taken to give the boys room. A sport which becomes annoying is not suppressed, but is given ample room in places where it will annoy least; and when, for example, certain streets are publicly set apart for coasting, as they are in Boston every winter, the police have no difficulty in preventing coasting elsewhere. The boy who may ride his sled or his velocipede to his heart's content in one street will not care to intrude upon another. We need to adopt a like system in our larger cities. The boys must have room in which to exercise and grow. If we do not give it to them in one place they will take it in another, to our sore inconvenience.—*New York Evening Post.*

BOYHOOD.

Rev. W. H. H. Murray.

PARENTS should remember that the children of to-day, and especially those born in cities, are peculiarly exposed to temptation. The opportunities which came to many of us from the old home life in the country, with its crisp atmosphere of Puritan government, its habits of honesty and honorable industry, its conservative customs, and its simple reverent faith in God, all centered around one spot, all hallowing one locality, will not come to our children, because the causes and incentives which operated to establish them in us, do not operate to establish them in the rising generation. A boyhood passed in the city is a far different thing from one passed in the country. The sights and sounds and surroundings of metropolitan life force the growth of the young, and at a time, too, when the physical and the sensuous preponderate in the nature. These beget a looseness of thought and freedom of conduct before the judgment is sufficiently matured by experience to check them. These educate one into necessities faster than individual effort can earn the means of supplying them; and foster that worst of all habits of the young man—eating, and wearing, and spending, what he has not earned. We do not say, parents, that these evil tendencies cannot be lessened or wholly counterbalanced, but we do say that they call for the utmost effort on your part, and make anxiety reasonable. They may achieve what the world calls success, although even this will be hazarded. But they will never lead that life of piety and holiness which can alone commend them in their character and conduct to the favor of God. They will live and labor as those whose lives end at the grave. The line of pure selfishness will circumscribe their lives, and shame and confusion of face will cover them when they appear to render their account before God.

MY BOY.

Frank T. Marzials.

O LITTLE face, little, loved, tender face,
   Set, like a saint's, in curls for aureole—
   Little, loved face, in which the clear child soul
Is mirror'd with a changeful, perfect grace;
Where sudden ripples of light laughter chase
   The dimples round the dainty mouth; where roll
   Cloud shadows of great questionings, and dole
For human ills half realized, where race,
In restless sequence, gloom, gleam, shade, and shine—
   A thousand feelings, sorrow, love, and joy,
A thousand thoughts, of folly half divine,
   And bold imaginings, and fancies coy,
   And reasonings dream-like!—
        O my boy, my boy,
How I do love that little face of thine!

CHILDREN OF THE RICH AND POOR CONTRASTED.

James Russell Lowell.

THE rich man's son inherits lands,
And piles of brick, and stone and gold,
And he inherits soft white hands,
And tender flesh that fears the cold,
Nor dares to wear a garment old:
A heritage, it seems to me,
One scarce would wish to hold in fee.

The rich man's son inherits cares,—
The bank may break, the factory burn,
A breath may burst his bubble shares;
And soft white hands could hardly earn
A living that would serve his turn:
A heritage, it seems to me,
One scarce would wish to hold in fee.

What doth the poor man's son inherit?
Stout muscles and a sinewy heart,
A hardy frame, a hardier spirit;
King of two hands he does his part
In every useful toil and art:
A heritage, it seems to me,
A king might wish to hold in fee.

What doth the poor man's son inherit?
A patience learned of being poor,

Courage, if sorrow comes, to bear it,
A fellow feeling that is sure
To make the outcast bless his door:
A heritage, it seems to me,
A king might wish to hold in fee.

Both, heirs to some six feet of sod,
Are equal in the earth at last,
Both, children of the same dear God,
Prove title to your heirship vast
By records of a well-fill'd past:
A heritage it seems to me,
Well worth a life to hold in fee.

BE KIND, BOYS.

Horace Mann.

YOU are made to be kind, boys, generous, magnanimous. If there is a boy in school who has a club foot, don't let him know you ever saw it. If there is a poor boy with ragged clothes, don't talk about rags in his hearing. If there is a lame boy, assign him some part of the game which does not require running. If there is a hungry one, give him part of your dinner. If there is a dull one, help him to get his lesson. If there is a bright one, be not envious of him; for if one boy is proud of his talents, and another is envious of them, there are two great wrongs, and no more talent than before. If a larger or stronger boy has injured you, and is sorry for it, forgive him. All the school will show by their countenances how much better it is than to have a great fist.

GOOD MANNERS.

IT has been said, that a "man's manners form his fortune." Whether this be really so or not, it is certain that his manners form his reputation—stamp upon him, as it were, his current worth in the circles where he moves. If his manners are the products of a kind heart, they will please, though they be destitute of graceful polish. There is scarcely anything of more importance to a child of either sex, than good breeding. If parents and teachers perform their duties to the young faithfully, there will be comparatively few destitute of good manners.

Visit a family where the parents are civil and courteous toward all within their household, whether as dwellers or as guests, and your children will learn good manners, just as they learn to talk, from imitation. But reverse the order of things concerning parents, and the children learn ill manners, just as in the former case they learn good manners, by imitation.

Train children to behave at home as you would have them act abroad. It is almost certain, that they, while children, conduct themselves abroad as they would have been in the habit of doing under like circumstances when at home. "Be courteous," is an apostolical injunction, which all should ever remember and obey.

Finally, "be ye all of one mind, having compassion one of another, love as brethren, be pitiful, be courteous." 1 Peter, iii. 8.
—*Anonymous.*

KIND MANNERS AT HOME.

THERE are many families, the members of which are, without doubt, dear to each other. If sickness or sudden trouble falls on one, all are afflicted, and make haste to sympathize, help and comfort. But in their daily life and ordinary intercourse there is not only no expression of affection, none of the pleasant and fond behavior that has, perhaps, little dignity, but which more than makes up for that in its sweetness; but there is an absolute hardness of language and actions which is shocking to every sensitive and tender feeling. Between father and mother, and brother and sister, pass rough and hasty words; yes, and angry words, far more frequently than words of endearment. To see and hear them, one would think that they hated, instead of loved each other. It does not seem to have entered into their heads that it is their duty, as it should be their best pleasure, to do and say all that they possibly can for each other's good and happiness. "Each one for himself, and bad luck take the hindermost." The father orders and growls, the mother frets, complains, and scolds, the children snap, snarl, and whine, and so goes the day. Alas! for it, if this is a type of heaven!—as "the family" is said to be—at least, it is said to be the nearest thing to heaven of anything on earth. But the spirit of selfishness, of violence, render it more like the other place—yes, and this too often, even when all the members of the household are members of the Church. Where you see—when you know it—one family where love and gentleness reign, you see ten where they only make visits, and this among Christian families as well as others.

HOME.

...ing to "sit solitary" in life,
..., give me a lodge in any
...r face of human being ever
...ts, friends, or kindred, in
...ch causes pain, or where I
...ove. No wealth, no advan-
...ve with people whose inter-
... they were to me, the less
...did not do all they could to
...rangers one might endure,
... for a time; for what they
...e's feelings; but how mem-
... same parents, can remain
...y they hear quarreling, if
...ords fly on all sides of them,
... their house are rendered
...ry.

... will last
...ace is o'er;
...joys are past,
...hter shore."
—*Anonymous.*

... home that is well ordered,
...us heavenly by the agency
...and. No school can teach
...us.

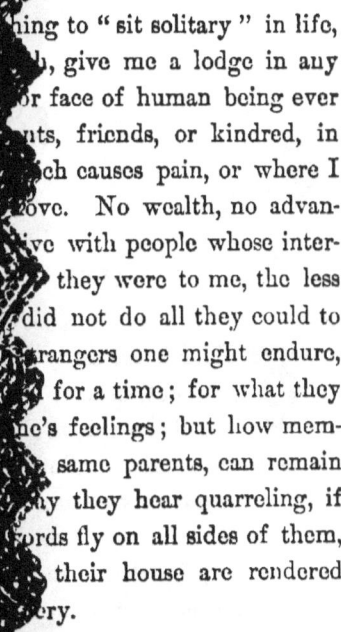

KIND

THERE are many
doubt, dear to
falls on one, a
help and comfort. But
there is not only no ex
fond behavior that ha
makes up for that in its
of language and actio
tender feeling. Betw
pass rough and hasty w
quently than words
would think that they
not seem to have entere
should be their best p
for each other's good a
bad luck take the hind
mother frets, compla
whine, and so goes t
heaven!—as "the fami
nearest thing to heav
selfishness, of violence,
this too often, even
members of the Chur
family where love and
make visits, and this

KIND MANNERS AT HOME.

Now, it is a sad and melancholy thing to "sit solitary" in life, but give me a cave in the bowels of earth, give me a lodge in any waste, howling wilderness, where foot nor face of human being ever came, rather than an abode with parents, friends, or kindred, in which I must hear or utter language which causes pain, or where I must see conduct which is not born of love. No wealth, no advantage of any kind, would induce me to live with people whose intercourse was of such a nature. The dearer they were to me, the less would I remain among them, if they did not do all they could to make each other happy. With mere strangers one might endure, even under such circumstances, to remain for a time; for what they say or do has but limited effect upon one's feelings; but how members of the same family, children of the same parents, can remain together, year after year, when every day they hear quarreling, if they do not join in it, and when hard words fly on all sides of them, thick as hail, and the very visitors in their house are rendered uncomfortable by them, is indeed a mystery.

> "Count life by virtues; these will last
> When life's lame, foiled, race is o'er;
> And these, when earthly joys are past,
> Shall cheer us on a brighter shore."
>
> —*Anonymous.*

HOME is next to heaven. And the home that is well ordered, comely, pure, and bright is thus heavenly by the agency of woman's heart and woman's hand. No school can teach the science of housekeeping.—*Anonymous.*

HOME AMUSEMENTS.

W. H. H. Murray.

A CLOSE observer of American life said to us the other day that a great change had come in the last ten years to the home life of the country. And in answer to our interrogation, he proceeded to point out the character of this change. One point which he made was that a great many games of skill and chance were being played in New England homes, to-day, which were not known, or if known, were forbidden by parents ten years ago. Our own observation coincides with his on this point. We know that chess within the last ten years has captured for itself a high place in popular regard. It speaks well for a people when such an intellectual game can become popular. For it takes brains to play chess even moderately well, and none but clever and thoughtful people would ever like it. We noticed also that cards are no longer abjured as they once were in households. Whist and euchre are domiciled, to-day, in homes where, a decade ago, their names could not have been spoken safely save in a whisper. Checkers are not perhaps more universal, but they are more fashionable. They have fought their way into high life; and whereas they once found their friends in the village tavern and in the farmer's kitchen, they are now admitted into the parlors of the wealthy and refined. The games played with historical cards are also numerous and many of them pleasantly exciting. And you find them in almost every household. Now all this is very pleasant and hopeful. It reveals to the thinker the fact that home life is more vivacious and happy than it used to be; that the long dull evenings are being enlivened with sprightly and stimulating amusements, and that the home circle is charged with attractions which it once sadly lacked. These games are helping to make the homes of the country happier, helping to make the children more contented with their homes, and in doing this they are helping to make the country more intelligent and more virtuous. By wise parents these games are looked upon as God-sends. They help solve the problem of home amusements and recreation; and this, as all parents know, is one of the gravest problems they have to solve. Parents, make your homes as happy as you possibly can for your children and their mates. Fill them with fun and frolic and the cheerfulness of spirited social life. Play these games with your children yourselves, and thus share their joys with them; and feed your happiness on the spectacle of theirs. A great many homes are like the frame of a harp that stands without strings. In form and outline they suggest music; but no melody rises from the empty spaces; and thus it happens that home is unattractive, dreary and dull. Let us hope that this introduction of pleasant games—which will try both the wit and patience of the children, and of the older ones for that matter,—may become the fashion of the times, until every home in the land shall be perfectly furnished with these accessories of profit and pleasure. For the children's sake, let the reformation go on until every child shall have, in his father's house, be it humble or costly, such appliances and helps for his entertainment that he shall find his joy under his father's roof and in his father's presence.

"Home, home, sweet, sweet home,
Be it ever so humble, there is no place like home."

A CHEERFUL HOME.

A SINGLE bitter word may disquiet an entire family for a whole day. One surly glance casts a gloom over the household, while a smile, like a gleam of sunshine, may light up the darkest and weariest hours. Like unexpected flowers, which spring up along our path, full of freshness, fragrance and beauty, do kind words and gentle acts and sweet dispositions, make glad the home where peace and blessing dwell. No matter how humble the abode, if it be thus garnished with grace and sweetened with kindness and smiles, the heart will turn lovingly toward it from all the tumult of the world, will be the dearest spot beneath the circuit of the sun.

And the influences of home perpetuate themselves. The gentle grace of the mother lives in the daughter long after her head is pillowed in the dust of death; and the fatherly kindness finds its echo in the nobility and courtesy of sons, who come to wear his mantle and to fill his place; while on the other hand, from an unhappy, misgoverned and disordered home, go forth persons who shall make other homes miserable, and perpetuate the sourness and sadness, the contentions and strifes and railings which have made their own early lives so wretched and distorted.

Toward the cheerful home, the children gather "as clouds and as doves to their windows," while from the home which is the abode of discontent and strife and trouble, they fly forth as vultures to rend their prey.

The class of men who disturb and distress the world, are not those born and nurtured amid the hallowed influences of Christian homes; but rather those whose early life has been a scene of trouble and vexation,—who have started wrong in the pilgrimage, and whose course is one of disaster to themselves, and trouble to those around them.—*Friend's Intelligencer.*

THE FARMER'S HOME.

William H. Yeomans.

WEBSTER defines home as a "dwelling-place," but it admits of a broader meaning. There are brilliant and elegant homes. Some are wise, thrifty and careful, and others are warm and genial, by whose glowing hearths any one, at any time, may find enough and to spare. There are bright homes and gloomy homes. There are homes that hurry and bustle through years of incessant labor, until one and another of the inmates fall, like the falling leaves, and the homes turn to dust. We do not say the dairymaid's home compares with this last view. Science has done much to remove the drudgery in our homes, introducing ease and comfort. An ideal home must first have a government, but love must be the dictator. All the members should unite to make home happy. We should have light in our homes, heaven's own pure, transparent light. It matters not whether home is clothed in blue and purple, if it is only brimful of love, smiles, and gladness.

Our boards should be spread with everything good and enjoyable. We should have birds, flowers, pets, everything suggestive of sociability. Flowers are as indispensable to the perfections of a home as to the perfections of a plant. Do not give them all the sunniest windows and pleasantest corners, crowding out the children.

If you cannot have a large conservatory, have a small one. Give your children pets, so that by the care and attention bestowed upon them they may learn the habits of animals.

Of the ornamentation about a house, although a broad lake lends a charm to the scenery, it cannot compare with the babbling brook. As the little streamlet goes tumbling over the rocks and along the shallow, pebbly bed, it may be a marvelous teacher to the children, giving them lessons of enterprise and perseverance.

In our homes we must have industry and sympathy. In choosing amusements for the children, the latter element must be brought in. To fully understand the little ones, you must sympathize with them. When a child asks questions don't meet it with, "Oh, don't bother me." Tell it all it wants to know. Never let your angry passions rise, no matter how much you may be tried. For full and intelligent happiness in the home circle, a library of the best works is necessary. Do not introduce the milk and water fiction of the present day, but books of character. Our homes should have their Sabbaths and their family altars. Around these observances cling many of the softest and most sacred memories of our lives.

HOME MEMORIES.

Thomas Hood.

I REMEMBER, I remember,
The house where I was born,
The little window where the sun
Came peeping in at morn.
He never came a wink too soon,
Nor brought too long a day;

But now I often wish the night
Had borne my breath away!

I remember, I remember,
The roses, red and white,
The violets and the lily-cups,—
Those flowers made of light!
The lilacs where the robin built,
And where my brother set
The laburnum on his birthday —
The tree is living yet!

I remember, I remember,
Where I was used to swing,
And thought the air must rush as fresh
To swallows on the wing;
My spirit flew in feathers then,
That is so heavy now,
And summer pools could hardly cool
The fever on my brow!

I remember, I remember,
The fir-trees dark and high;
I used to think their slender tops
Were close against the sky.
It was a childish ignorance,
But now 'tis little joy
To know I'm farther off from heaven
Than when I was a boy.

SINGING IN THE FAMILY.

CULTIVATE singing in your family. Begin when the child is not yet three years old. The songs and hymns your childhood sang, bring them all back to your memory, and teach them to your little ones; mix them all together to meet the varying moods as in after life they come over us so mysteriously at times. Many a time, in the very whirl of business, in the sunshine and gayety of the avenue, amid the splendor of the drive in the park, some little thing wakes up the memories of early youth—the old mill, the cool spring, the shady tree by the little school-house—and the next instant we almost see again the ruddy cheeks, the smiling faces, and the merry eyes of schoolmates, some of whom are gray-headed now, while most have passed from amid earth's weary noises. And, anon, "the song my mother sang" springs unbidden to the lips, and soothes and sweetens all these memories. At other times, amid the crushing mishaps of business, a merry ditty of the olden time breaks in upon the ugly train of thought, and throws the mind in another channel; light breaks from behind the cloud in the sky, and new courage is given us. The honest man goes gladly to his work; and when, the day's labor done, his tools are laid aside and he is on his way home, where wife and child and the tidy table and cheery fireside await him, how can he but have music in his heart to break forth so often into the merry whistle or the jocund song? Moody silence, not the merry song, weighs down the dishonest tradesman, the perfidious clerk, the unfaithful servant, the perjured partner.

"We accord," says a gentleman who has written much, "our unqualified indorsement of the above; and even now, although we have passed our three-score years, the songs of our youth are often resurrected, and we love to hum them over again, and often do so, in the lone hours of the night, when there are none to hear save ourself and the drowsy 'gray spiders on the wall;' and while doing so, we feel less inclined toward 'treason, stratagem and spoils,' than at any other hour within the twenty-four. We fondly look back to the days when we were as musical as a hand organ—and perhaps as 'cracked' as many of them, too—those days when we so lightly touched the keys to the measure of the songs we sang. We often regret time, circumstance and advancing years have so effectually quieted our vocal muse; still we revert to the ballads of yore, and mentally exclaim,

> "'Sing me the songs that to me were so dear,
> Long, long ago; long, long ago.'"
>
> —*Anonymous.*

ART IN THE FAMILY.

IT has been said that there is sure to be contentment in a home, in the windows of which can be seen birds or flowers, and it may also be added that there will be the same conditions wherever there are pictures on the walls. It is, of course, not every one who is a judge of art, but even a contemplation of art will educate, and it is safe to say that a man cannot have a painting in his room and see it day after day without sooner or later beginning to be able to tell its merits or defects, and thus being better fitted to judge of others in the future. The engravings and chromos seen in the homes of the poor may, if measured by the critical rules of art, be wretched daubs, but they at least show a longing and an aspiration after beauty, while their presence helps to produce a repose of mind, and brings nothing with it but good. The loving manner in which children linger over pictures tells how deeply this feeling is implanted in the heart, and long before they can read, their dawning powers are gradually being strengthened by these silent educators.

Nor is the influence which flowers have, any less than that of paintings. At all seasons of the year they are gladly welcomed. They are emblematic of both, the joys and sorrows of life, and religion has associated them with the highest spiritual verities. Faded although they sometimes may be, they have the power to wake the chords of memory and make us children again. At the sick bed and the marriage feast, on the altar and the cathedral walls, they have a meaning, and the humblest home looks brighter where they bloom. A few years ago, at horticultural societies in England, prizes were offered to villagers for the best efforts in cottage gardening, and the result was that a great change came over the home-life of the people. Instead of gardens filled with rank grass and weeds, there could be seen flaming hollyhocks, blood-red roses and purple geraniums, and a spirit of friendly rivalry and emulation was created, leading to improvements in households, and aiding habits of cleanliness and industry. Let any one walk through our markets on these bright spring mornings and watch how tenderly some poor seamstress will linger over a tiny flower and bear it away proudly to cheer the loneliness of her scantily furnished room, and he will admit that if such a little thing can bring pleasure or satisfaction, every effort made to improve the taste of the masses and lead them to make home pleasant is to be commended as weakening the influence of evil and diffusing a power which will prove a potent factor for good.—*Baltimore American.*

CONVERSATION.

AMONG home amusements the best is the good old habit of conversation, the talking over the events of the day, in bright and quick play of wit and fancy, the story which brings the laugh, and the speaking the good and kind and true things, which all have in their hearts. It is not so much by dwelling upon what members of the family have in common, as bringing each to the other something interesting and amusing, that home life is to be made cheerful and joyous. Each one must do his part to make conversation genial and happy. We are too ready to converse with newspapers and books, to seek some companion at the store, hotel, or club-room, and to forget that home is anything more than a place to sleep and eat in. The revival of conversation, the entertainment of one another, as a roomful of people will entertain themselves, is one secret of a happy home. Wherever it is wanting, disease has struck into the root of the tree; there is a want which is felt with increasing force as time goes on. Conversation, in many cases, is just what prevents many people from relapsing into utter selfishness at their firesides. This conversation should not simply occupy husband and wife, and other older members of the family, but extend itself to the children. Parents should be careful to talk with them, to enter into their life, to share their trifles, to assist in their studies, to meet them in the thoughts and feelings of their childhood. It is a great step in education, when around the evening lamp are gathered the different members of a family, sharing their occupation with one another—the older assisting the younger, each one contributing to the entertainment of the other, and all feeling that the evening has passed only too rapidly away. This is the truest and best amusement. It is the healthy education of great and noble characters. There is the freedom, the breadth, the joyousness of natural life. The time spent thus by parents, in the higher entertainment of their children, bears a harvest of eternal blessings, and these long evenings furnish just the time.—*Churchman.*

SPEAK CHEERFUL WORDS.

WHY is it that so many people keep all their pleasant thoughts and kind words about a man bottled and sealed until he is dead, when they come and break the bottle over his coffin, and bathe his shroud in fragrance? Many a man goes through life with scarcely one bright, cheerful, encouraging, hopeful word. He toils hard and in lowly obscurity. He gives out his life freely and unstintedly for others. I remember such a man. He was not brilliant; he was not great; but he was faithful. He had many things to discourage him. Troubles thickened about his life. He was misrepresented and misunderstood. Everybody believed that he was a good man, but no one ever said a kindly word or pleasant thing to him. He never heard a compliment, scarcely ever a good wish. No one ever took any pains to encourage him, to strengthen his feeble knees, to lighten his burdens, or to lift up his heart by a gentle deed of love, or by a cheerful word. He was neglected. Unkind things were often said of him.

I stood at his coffin, and then there were many tongues to speak his praise. There was not a breath of aspersion in the air. Men spoke of self denial—of his work among the poor, of his quietness, modesty, his humility, his pureness of heart, his faith and prayer.

There were many who spoke indignantly of the charges that falsehood had forged against him in past years, and of the treatment he had received. There were enough kind things said during the two or three days that he lay in his coffin, and while the company stood around his open grave, to have blessed him and made him happy all his fifty years, and to have thrown sweetness and joy about his soul during all his painful and weary journey. There was enough sunshine wasted about the black coffin and dark grave to have made his whole life-path bright as the clearest day.

But his ears were closed then, and could not hear a word that was spoken. His heart was still then, and could not be thrilled by the grateful sounds. He cared nothing then for the sweet flowers that were piled upon his coffin. The love blossomed out too late. The kindness came when the life could not receive its blessings.—*Anonymous.*

NONE LIVETH TO HIMSELF.

GOD has written upon the flower that sweetens the air, upon the breeze that rocks the flower upon its stem, upon the rain-drops that swell the mighty river, upon the dew-drops that refresh the smallest sprig of moss that rears its head in the desert, upon the ocean that rocks every swimmer in its channel, upon every penciled shell that sleeps in the caverns of the deep, as well as upon the mighty sun which warms and cheers the millions of creatures that live in his light—upon all he has written, "None of us liveth to himself."—*Anonymous.*

SPEAK A GOOD WORD.

IF you say anything about a neighbor or friend, or even a stranger, say no ill. It is a Christian and brotherly charity to suppress our knowledge of evil of one another, unless our higher public duty compels us to bear accusing witness. And if it be true charity to keep our *knowledge* of such evils to ourselves, much more should we refuse to spread *evil report* of one another. Discreditable as the fact is, it is by far the commonest tendency to suppress the good we know of our neighbors and friends. We act in this matter as though we felt that by pushing our fellows down or back a peg we were putting ourselves up and forward. We are jealous of commendation unless we get the larger share. Social conversation, as known to every observer, is largely made up of what is best understood by the term *scandal*. It would be difficult to find a talkative group, of either sex, who could spend an evening or an hour together without evil speech of somebody. "Blessed are the peace-makers," is not the maxim by which we are chiefly governed in our treatment of personalities. Better a thousand times, stand or sit dumb than to open our lips never so eloquently in the disparagement of others. What we should do in this, as in all our human relations, is to practice the Golden Rule. If we do unto others as we would that others should do unto us, we shall be exceedingly careful not to volunteer ill words about them. When other than a good word is to be spoken, let it be spoken to the person concerned, that he may know your motive is not idle, cowardly and sinister, and that he may have a chance to defend himself.—*Anonymous.*

SMILES.

Mrs. Burr.

IF people will only notice, they will be amazed to find how much a really enjoyable evening owes to smiles. But few consider what an important symbol of fine intellect and fine feeling they are. Yet all smiles, after childhood, are things of education. Savages do not smile; coarse, brutal, cruel men may laugh, but they seldom smile. The affluence, the benediction, the radiance, which

> Fills the silence like a speech,

is the smile of a full appreciative heart.

The face that grows finer as it listens, and then breaks into sunshine instead of words, has a subtle, charming influence, universally felt, though very seldom understood or acknowledged. Personal and sarcastic remarks show not only a bad heart and a bad head, but bad taste also.

Now, society may tolerate a bad heart and a bad head, but it will not endure bad taste; and it is in just such points as this that the conventional laws which they have made, represent and enforce real obligations. There are many who would not cease from evil speaking because it is wrong, who yet restrain themselves because it is vulgar. Lord Bacon tells of a nobleman whom he knew—a man who gave lordly entertainments, but always suffered some sarcastic personality to "mar a good dinner," adding, "Discretion of speech is more than eloquence; and to speak agreeably to him with whom we deal is more than to speak in good words; for he that hath a satirical vein, making others afraid of his wit, hath need to be afraid of another's memory."

JOY BRINGERS.

SOME men move through life as a band of music moves down the street, flinging out pleasure on every side through the air to every one, far and near, that can listen. Some men fill the air with their presence and sweetness, as orchards in October days fill the air with the perfume of ripe fruit. Some women cling to their own houses, like the honeysuckle over the door, yet, like it, sweeten all the region with the subtle fragrance of their goodness. There are trees of righteousness, which are ever dropping precious fruit around them. There are lives that shine like star-beams, or charm the heart like songs sung upon a holy day.

How great a bounty and blessing it is to hold the royal gifts of the soul, so that they shall be music to some and fragrance to others, and life to all! It would be no unworthy thing to live for, to make the power which we have within us the breath of other men's joy; to scatter sunshine where only clouds and shadows reign; to fill the atmosphere where earth's weary toilers must stand, with a brightness which they can not create for themselves, and which they long for, enjoy and appreciate.—*Anonymous.*

GRUMBLERS.

THERE are persons who are not satisfied in circumstances that to all but themselves seem to be the most favorable to their interests. Leigh Hunt—in one of his letters, we think—speaks of a day that could not make any creature happy but a vendor of umbrellas. Yet a friend of ours, remembering this utterance, availed himself of a day "of never-tiring rain" to congratulate his umbrella merchant, and he secured this reply: "It's all very well, sir, so far as my umbrellas are concerned, but you see I'm not selling a single parasol!" He would have had it wet on one side of the street, and stormy upon the other, and since it was not, he was dissatisfied—a natural grumbler.—*Anonymous.*

LOVE TO OUR FELLOW MEN.

(ABOU BEN ADHEM.)

Leigh Hunt.

ABOU BEN ADHEM, may his tribe increase,
   Awoke one night from a deep dream of peace,
   And saw within the moonlight in his room,
Making it rich, and like a lily in bloom,
An angel, writing in a book of gold.
Exceeding peace had made Ben Adhem bold,
And to the presence in his room he said:
"What writest thou?" The vision raised its head,
And with a look, made all of sweet accord,
Answered, "The names of those that love the Lord."
"And is mine one?" said Abou. "Nay, not so,"
Replied the angel. Abou spoke more low,
But cheerly still, and said, "I pray thee, then,
Write me as one that loves his fellow men."
The angel wrote and vanished. The next night
He came again with a great waking light,
And showed the names whom love of God had blest,
And, lo! Ben Adhem's name led all the rest.

WORDS TO BOYS.

James T. Fields.

I WOULD keep "better hours," if I were a boy again; that is, I would go to bed earlier than most boys do. Nothing gives more mental and bodily vigor than sound rest when properly applied. Sleep is our great replenisher, and if we neglect to take it regularly in childhood, all the worse for us when we grow up. If we go to bed early, we ripen; if we sit up late, we decay; and sooner or later we contract a disease called insomnia, allowing it to be permanently fixed upon us, and then we begin to decay, even in youth. Late hours are shadows from the grave.

If I were a boy again, I would practise perseverance oftener, and never give up a thing because it was hard or inconvenient to do it. If we want light, we must conquer darkness. When I think of mathematics I blush at the recollection of how often I "gave in" years ago. There is no trait more valuable than a determination to persevere when the right thing is to be accomplished. We are inclined to give up too easily in difficult or unpleasant situations, and the point I would establish with myself, if the choice was again within my grasp, would be never to relinquish my hold on a possible success if mortal strength or brains in my case were adequate to the occasion. That was a capital lesson which a learned Professor taught one of his students in the lecture-room after some chemical experiment. The lights had been put out in the hall, and by accident some small article dropped on the floor from the Professor's hand. The Professor lingered behind, endeavoring to pick it up. "Never mind," said the student, "it is of no consequence to-night, sir, whether we find it or no." "That is true," replied the Professor; "but it is of grave consequence to me, as a principle, that I am not foiled in my determination to find it." Perseverance can sometimes equal genius in its results. "There are only two creatures," says the Eastern proverb, "who can surmount the pyramids —the eagle and the snail."

THE LIGHT OF A CHEERFUL FACE.

THERE is no greater every-day virtue than cheerfulness. This quality in man, among men, is like sunshine to the day, of gentle renewing moisture to parched hearts. The light of a cheerful face diffuses itself, and communicates the happy spirit that inspires it. The sourest temper must sweeten in the atmosphere of continuous good humor. As well might fog and cloud, and vapor, hope to cling to the sun-illuminated landscape, as the blues and moroseness to combat jovial speech and exhilarating laughter. Be cheerful always. There is no path but will be easier traveled, no load but will be lighter, no shadow on heart or brain, but will lift sooner in presence of a determined cheerfulness. It may sometimes seem difficult for the happiest temper to keep the countenance of peace and content; but the difficulty will vanish when we truly consider that sullen gloom and passionate despair do nothing but multiply thorns and thicken sorrows. Ill comes to us as providentially as good, and is a good, if we rightfully apply its lessons. Who will not then cheerfully accept the ill, and thus blunt its apparent sting? Cheerfulness ought to be the fruit of philosophy and of Christianity. What is gained by peevishness and fretfulness, by perverse sadness and sullenness? If we are ill, let us be cheered by the trust that we shall soon be in health; if misfortune befall us, let us be cheered by hopeful visions of better fortune; if death robs us of dear ones, let us be cheered by the thought that they are only gone before to the blissful bowers where we shall all meet to part no more forever. Cultivate cheerfulness if only for personal profit. You will do and bear every duty and burden better by being cheerful. It will be your consoler in solitude, your passport and commendator in society. You will be more sought after, more trusted and esteemed for your steady cheerfulness. The bad, the vicious, may be boisterously gay and vulgarly humorous, but seldom or never truly cheerful. Genuine cheerfulness is an almost certain index of a happy and a pure heart.—*Anonymous.*

DOMESTIC BLISS.

James Thomson.

HAPPY they, the happiest of their kind,
   Whom gentler stars unite, and in one fate
   Their hearts, their fortunes, and their beings blend.
'Tis not the coarser tie of human laws,
Unnatural oft and foreign to the mind,
That binds their peace, but harmony itself,
Attuning all their passions into love;
Where friendship full exerts her softest power,
Perfect esteem, enliven'd by desire
Ineffable, and sympathy of soul;
Thought meeting thought, and will preventing will,
With boundless confidence.

THE BRIGHT SIDE.

LOOK on the bright side. It is the right side. The times may be hard, but it will make them no easier to wear a gloomy and sad countenance. It is the sunshine and not the cloud that gives beauty to the flower. There is always before or around us that which should cheer and fill the heart with warmth and gladness. The sky is blue ten times where it is black once. You have troubles, it may be. So have others. None are free from them; and perhaps it is as well that none should be. They give sinew and tone to life, fortitude and courage to man. That would be a dull sea, and the sailor would never acquire skill, where there is nothing to disturb its surface. It is the duty of every one to extract all the happiness and enjoyment he can within and without him; and above all, he should look on the bright side. What though things do look a little dark? The lane will turn, and the night will end in broad day. In the long run the great balance rights itself. What appears ill becomes well—that which appears wrong, right. Men are not always to hang down their heads or lips, and those who do, only show that they are departing from the paths of true common sense and right. There is more virtue in one sunbeam than in a whole hemisphere of clouds and gloom. Therefore we repeat, look on the bright side. Cultivate all that is warm and genial—not the cold and repulsive, the dark and morose.—*The Interior*.

IT is worth a thousand pounds a year to have the habit of looking on the bright side of things.—*Dr. Johnson*.

THE EVENING HEARTHSTONE.

GLADLY now we gather round it,
    For the toiling day is done,
  And the gay and solemn twilight
    Follows down the golden sun,
Shadows lengthen on the pavement,
  Stalk like giants through the gloom,
Wander past the dusky casement,
  Creep around the fire-lit room.
    Draw the curtain, close the shutters,
      Place the slippers by the fire;
    Though the rude wind loudly mutters,
      What care we for wind sprite's ire !

What care we for outward seeming?
  Fickle fortune's frown or smile ?
If around us love is beaming,
  Love can human ills beguile.
'Neath the cottage roof and palace,
  From the peasant to the king,
All are quaffing from life's chalice
  Bubbles that enchantment bring.
    Grates are glowing, music flowing
      From the lips we love the best;
    Oh, the joy, the bliss of knowing
      There are hearts whereon to rest !

CHEERFULNESS.

Hearts that throb with eager gladness—
Hearts that echo to our own—
While grim care and haunting sadness
Mingle ne'er in look or tone.
Care may tread the halls of daylight,
Sadness haunt the midnight hour,
But the weird and witching twilight
Brings the glowing hearthstone's dower.
Altar of our holiest feelings!
Childhood's well-remembered shrine!
Spirit yearnings—soul revealings—
Wreaths immortal round thee twine!
—*Anonymous.*

CHEERFULNESS.

LET your cheerfulness be felt for good wherever you are, and let your smiles be scattered like sunbeams "on the just as well as on the unjust." Such a disposition will yield a rich reward, for its happy effects will come home to you and brighten your moments of thought. Cheerfulness makes the mind clear, gives tone to thought, adds grace and beauty to the countenance. Joubert says, "When you give, give with joy, smiling." Smiles are little things, cheap articles to be fraught with so many blessings, both to the giver and the receiver—pleasant little ripples to watch as we stand on the shore of every-day life. These are the higher and better responses of nature to the emotion of the soul. Let the children have the benefit of them—those little ones who need the sunshine of the heart to educate them, and would find a level for their buoyant nature in the cheerful, loving faces of those who need them. Let them not be kept from the middle aged, who need the encouragement they bring. Give your smiles also to the aged. They come to them like the quiet rain of summer, making fresh and verdant the long, weary path of life. They look for them from you, who are rejoicing in the fullness of life.

If your seat is hard to sit upon, stand up. If a rock rises up before you, roll it away, or climb over it. If you want money, earn it. It takes longer to skin an elephant than a mouse, but the skin is worth something. If you want confidence, prove yourself worthy of it. Do not be content with doing what another has done—surpass it. Deserve success, and it will come. The boy was not born a man. The sun does not rise like a rocket, or go down like a bullet fired from a gun; slowly and surely it makes its round, and never tires. It is as easy to be a lead horse as a wheel horse. If the job be long, the pay will be greater ; if the task be hard, the more competent you must be to do it.—*Anonymous.*

COURTESY AT HOME.

COURTESY is the perfume of Christian grace. Its luster should be an expression of the best emotions of the soul. The word is derived from the French, and is closely allied therefore, in origin, with "courtier," which has an equivocal meaning. A courtier is supposed to possess elegant manners, cultivated however and used mainly for selfish ends. Politeness, which is the synonym of courtesy, is of nobler birth. It comes from a Greek term, signifying citizenship. As the divine kingdom is distinct in its laws, spirit, and purpose, from the kingdoms of this earth, so too are its members held together by a supernatural life. They compose one body, ruled by one Supreme Head. Christian politeness is therefore the product of regeneration. Its roots are in the heart. They are watered from above. All, then, who are subjects of Divine grace, should be gracious, kind, considerate, courteous, and polite in their deportment, and show forth the savor of the precious anointing they have received.

How much a sincere and hearty politeness may do for others is readily tested and measured by all who have learned to appreciate it for themselves. While it is comparatively easy to be courteous toward strangers, or toward people of distinction, whom one meets in society or on public occasions, still it should be remembered that it is at home, in the family, and among kindred, that an every-day politeness of manners is really most to be prized. There it confers substantial benefits and brings the sweetest returns. The little attentions which members of the same household may show towards one another day by day belong, in fact, to what is styled "good breeding." There cannot be any ingrained gentility which does not exhibit itself first at home. There, of all places in the world, it will be able to demonstrate how much genuine politeness there is in the heart. A well-ordered family cannot afford to dispense with the observance of the good rules of mutual intercourse which are enforced in good society. A churlish, sour, morose deportment at home is simply cruel, for it cuts into the tenderest sensibilities and hurts love just where love is strongest and most loyal. Parents and children, brothers and sisters, husbands and wives, never lose anything by mutual politeness; on the contrary, by maintaining not only its forms, but by the inward cultivation of its spirit, they become contributors to that domestic felicity which is, in itself, a foretaste of heaven.—*Christian Weekly.*

CHRISTIAN COURTESY.

I SAW somewhere the other day a sentence like this: "The truest courtesy is the truest Christianity." This is not simply saying, I take it, that a Christian will be a gentleman; it teaches that the spirit of self-denial, of foregoing personal advantages for the sake of favoring another, is the root and substance of the regenerated life. Now, here is a practical test, brought near to us in all the scenes of our intercourse with our fellows, showing what manner of spirit we are of. If we are truly—that is sincerely—courteous and polite, we are serving Christ, showing his example, and exhibiting his spirit. If in the collisions of personal interests through the day we are more careful to favor ourselves, to secure the best, to be served first, to gratify our own wishes and tastes, than to gratify and serve others, I care not what names we bear, or what professions we make, or what religious exercises we engage in, the spirit of the Master is not in us.—*Anonymous.*

NO man can possibly improve in any company, for which he has not respect enough to be under some degree of restraint.—*Lord Chesterfield.*

PEOPLE seldom improve when they have no other model but themselves to copy after.—*Oliver Goldsmith.*

MORALITY OF MANNERS.

Horace Mann.

easily and rapidly mature into morals. As child-
ances to manhood, the transition from bad manners
orals is almost imperceptible. Vulgar and obscene
e mind, engender impure images in the imagination
ful desires prurient. From the prevalent state of
s proceed as water rises from a fountain. Hence
lly only a word or phrase becomes a thought, is
nbellished by the imagination, is inflamed into a
ins strength and boldness by always being welcome,
er some urgent temptation, it dares, for once, to put
rm of action; it is then ventured upon again and
uently and less warily, until repetition forges the
and then language, imagination, desire and habit
n to the prison house of sin. In this way profane
way the reverence for things sacred and holy; and
been allowed to follow, and mock and hoot at an
in the streets is far more likely to become intem-
han if he has been accustomed to regard him with
brother, and with sacred abhorrence, as one self-
onized. So, on the other hand, purity and chaste-
tend to preserve purity and chasteness of thought
ey repel licentious imaginings; they delight in the
e untainted, and all their tendencies are on the side

CHRISTIAN COURTESY.

SAW somewhere the other day a sentence truest courtesy is the truest Christianity." T saying, I take it, that a Christian will be teaches that the spirit of self-denial, of foregoing tages for the sake of favoring another, is the root a the regenerated life. Now, here is a practical test, us in all the scenes of our intercourse with our what manner of spirit we are of. If we are truly— —courteous and polite, we are serving Christ, show and exhibiting his spirit. If in the collisions of p through the day we are more careful to favor our the best, to be served first, to gratify our own w than to gratify and serve others, I care not what or what professions we make, or what religious exe in, the spirit of the Master is not in us.—*Anonymor*

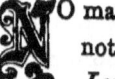

O man can possibly improve in any company, not respect enough to be under some degre *Lord Chesterfield.*

PEOPLE seldom improve when they have no themselves to copy after.—*Oliver Goldsmith.*

THE MORALITY OF MANNERS.

Horace Mann.

MANNERS easily and rapidly mature into morals. As childhood advances to manhood, the transition from bad manners to bad morals is almost imperceptible. Vulgar and obscene objects before the mind, engender impure images in the imagination and make unlawful desires prurient. From the prevalent state of the mind, actions proceed as water rises from a fountain. Hence what was originally only a word or phrase becomes a thought, is meretriciously embellished by the imagination, is inflamed into a vicious desire, gains strength and boldness by always being welcome, until at last, under some urgent temptation, it dares, for once, to put on the visible form of action; it is then ventured upon again and again, more frequently and less warily, until repetition forges the chains of habit; and then language, imagination, desire and habit bind their victim to the prison house of sin. In this way profane language wears away the reverence for things sacred and holy; and a child who has been allowed to follow, and mock and hoot at an intemperate man in the streets is far more likely to become intemperate himself than if he has been accustomed to regard him with pity, as a fallen brother, and with sacred abhorrence, as one self-brutified or demonized. So, on the other hand, purity and chasteness of language tend to preserve purity and chasteness of thought and of taste; they repel licentious imaginings; they delight in the unsullied and the untainted, and all their tendencies are on the side of virtue.

THE WITCHERY OF MANNER.

ALMOST every man can recall scores of cases within his knowledge where pleasing manners have made the fortunes of lawyers, doctors, divines, merchants, and, in short, men in every walk of life. Raleigh flung down his laced coat into the mud for Elizabeth to walk on, and got for his reward a proud queen's favor. The politician who has this advantage easily distances all rival candidates, for every voter he speaks with becomes instantly his friend. The very tones in which he asks for a pinch of snuff are often more potent than the logic of a Webster or a Clay. Polished manners have often made a scoundrel successful, while the best of men, by their hardness and coldness, have done themselves incalculable injury; the shell being so rough that the world could not believe there was a precious kernel within. Civility is to a man what beauty is to a woman. It creates an instantaneous impression in his behalf, while the opposite quality excites as quick a prejudice against him. It is a real ornament, the most beautiful dress that man or woman can wear, and worth more as a means of winning favor than the finest clothes and jewels ever worn. The gruffest man loves to be appreciated; and it is oftener the sweet smile of a woman, which we think intended for us alone, than a pair of Juno-like eyes, or "lips that seem on roses fed," that bewitches our heart, and lays us low at the feet of her whom we afterward marry.—*Anonymous.*

———◆———

Best men are moulded out of faults.—*Shakespeare.*

A Sister's Sympathy—Taking out the Thorn.

CULTIVATE PATIENCE.

BE patient with your friends. They are neither omniscient nor omnipotent. They can not see your heart, and may misunderstand you. They do not know what is best for you, and may select what is worst. Their arms are short, and they may not be able to reach what you ask. What if also they lack purity of purpose of tenacity of affection; do not you also lack these graces? Patience is your refuge. Endure, and in enduring conquer them, and if not them, then at least yourself. Above all, be patient with your beloved. Love is the best thing on the earth, but it is to be handled tenderly, and impatience is a nurse that kills it.

Be patient with your pains and cares. We know it is easy to say and hard to do. But, dear child, you must be patient. These things are killed by enduring them, and made strong to bite and sting by feeding them with your frets and fears. There is no pain or care that can last long. None of them shall enter the city of God. A little while and you shall leave behind you the whole troop of howling troubles, and forget in your first sweet hour of rest that such things were on earth.—*Anonymous.*

THE greater the difficulty, the more the glory in surmounting it. Skillful pilots gain their reputation from storms and tempests.—*Anonymous.*

BEWARE the fury of a patient man.—*Dryden.*

A WOMAN'S CARES.

T. De Witt Talmage.

THE reason I have preached ten sermons to men and none to women, is that the women are better than men. I do not say this out of compliment or in gallantry; although when women are bad they are dreadful. Statistics prove this. They have fewer temptations, are naturally reverential and loving, and it is easier for them to become Christians. "They are the majority in Church on earth, and I suppose they will be three-fourths of the population in Heaven." In a beautiful homestead in Bethany, a widow was left to take charge of the premises. The pet of the house was Mary, a younger sister, who, with a book under her arm, has no appearance of anxiety or perturbation. Christ and several of his friends arrived at the house. They did not keep him waiting till they adjusted their dress, and after two or three knockings, hasten to the door and say, "Why! is that you?" No. They were ladies, and always presentable, though they might not have on their best. If we always had on our best, our best would not be worth putting on. They threw open the door and greeted Christ with "Good morning. Be seated." Martha went off to the kitchen; while Mary, believing in division of labor, said, "Martha, you go and cook, and I'll be good." Something went wrong in the kitchen. Perhaps the fire wouldn't burn, or the bread wouldn't bake, or Martha scalded her hand. At any rate she lost her patience; and with besweated brow, and possibly with pitcher in one hand and the tongs in the other, rushed into the presence of Christ, saying, "Lord, dost thou not care that my sister has left me to serve alone?"

But Christ scolded not a word. He seemed to say, "My dear woman, don't worry. Let the dinner go. Sit down on the ottoman beside Mary, your humble sister." When a man comes home from business and sees his wife worn out, he thinks she ought to have been in Wall street, and then she would have something to worry her. He does not know that she conducts a university, a clothing establishment, a restaurant, a laundry and a library; while she is health officer, police and president of her residence.

They have to contend with severe economy. Ninety-nine out of a hundred are subjected to it. If a man smokes very expensive cigars and eats costly dinners in New York, he is exceedingly desirous of making five dollars do the work of seven at home. The wife is banker in the household; she is president, cashier, teller and discount clerk; and there is a panic every few weeks. This severe discipline will make heaven very attractive to you.

EVE was made of a rib out of the side of Adam,—not made out of his head to top him, nor out of his feet to be trampled upon by him, but out of his side to be equal with him, under his arm to be protected, and near his heart to be beloved.

Matthew Henry.

WOMAN! in our hours of ease,
Uncertain, coy, and hard to please,
And variable as the shade
By the light of quivering aspen made;
When pain and anguish wring the brow,
A ministering angel thou!

Sir Walter Scott.

TELL YOUR WIFE.

IF you are in any trouble or quandary, tell your wife—that is if you have one—all about it at once. Ten to one her invention will solve your difficulty sooner than all your logic. The wit of woman has been praised, but her instincts are quicker and keener than her reason. Counsel with your wife, or mother or sister, and be assured, light will flash upon your darkness. Women are too commonly adjudged as verdant in all but purely womanish affairs. No philosophical students of the sex thus judge them. Their intuitions, or insights, are the most subtle. In counseling a man to tell his wife, we would go farther, and advise him to keep none of his affairs a secret from her. Many a home has been happily saved, and many a fortune retrieved, by a man's full confidence in his "better-half." Woman is far more a seer and prophet than man, if she be given a fair chance. As a general rule, wives confide the minutest of their plans and thoughts to their husbands, having no involvements to screen from them. Why not reciprocate, if but for the pleasure of meeting confidence with confidence? We are certain that no man succeeds so well in the world as he who, taking a partner for life, makes her the partner of his purposes and hopes. What is wrong of his impulse or judgment, she will check and set right with her almost universally right instincts. "Help-meet" was no insignificant title as applied to man's companion. She is a helpmeet to him in every darkness, difficulty and sorrow of life. And what she most craves and most deserves is confidence—without which love is never free from a shadow.—*Pacific Rural Press.*

HOSPITALITY.

Oliver Goldsmith.

BLEST be that spot where cheerful guests retire
To pause from toil, and trim their evening fire;
Blest that abode, where want and pain repair,
And every stranger finds a ready chair:
Blest be those feasts with simple plenty crown'd,
Where all the ruddy family around
Laugh at the jest or pranks, that never fail,
Or sigh with pity at some mournful tale,
Or press the bashful stranger to his food,
And learn the luxury of doing good.

TRUE HOSPITALITY.

Sir Arthur Helps.

A PERFECT host is as rare a being as a great poet, and for much the same reason, namely, that to be a perfect host requires as rare a combination of qualities as those which are needed to produce a great poet. He should be like that lord in waiting of whom Charles II. said, that he was "never in the way, and never out of the way." He should never degenerate into a showman, for there is nothing of which most people are so soon weary as of being shown things, especially if they are called upon to admire them. He, the perfect host, should always recollect that he is in his own house, and that his guests are not in theirs, consequently those local arrangements which are familiar to him should be rendered familiar to them. His aim should be to make his house a home for his guests, with all the advantage of novelty. If he entertains many guests, he should know enough about them to be sure that he has invited those who will live amicably together, and will enjoy each other's society. He should show no favoritism, if possible, and if he is a man who must indulge in favoritism, it should be to those of his guests who are more obscure than the others. He should be judiciously despotic as regards all proposals for pleasure, for there will be many that are diverse, and much time will be wasted if he does not take upon himself the labor and responsibility of decision. He should have much regard to the comings and goings of his guests, so as to provide for their adit and exit every convenience. Now I am going to insist on what I think to be a very great point. He should aim at causing that his guests should hereafter become friends, if they are not so at present, so that they might, in future days, trace back the beginning of their friendship to their having met together at his house. He, the perfect host, must have the art to lead conversation without absorbing it himself, so that he may develope the best qualities of his guests. His expense in entertainment should not be devoted to what is luxurious, but to what is ennobling and comfortable. The first of all things is that he should be an affectionate, indeed, a loving host, so that every one of his guests should feel that he is really welcome. He should press them to stay, but should be careful that this pressing does not interfere with their convenience, so that they stay merely to oblige him, and not to please themselves. In considering who should be his guests, he should always have a thought as to those to whom he would render most service by having them as his guests, his poorer brethren, his more sickly brethren. Those who he feels would gain most advantage by being his guests, should have the first place in his invitations, and for his considerateness he will be amply rewarded by the benefits he will have conferred.

THE RULE OF HOSPITALITY.

Wm. M. F. Round.

TRUE hospitality is a thing that touches the heart and never goes beyond the circle of generous impulses. Entertainment with the truly hospitable man means more than the mere feeding of the body; it means an interchange of soul gifts. Still it should have its laws as all things good must have laws to govern them.

The obligation to be hospitable is a sacred one, emphasized by every moral code known to the world, and a practical outcome of the second great commandment.

There should never be a guest in the house whose presence requires any considerable change in the domestic economy.

However much the circumstances of business or mutual interests may demand in entertaining a stranger, he should never be taken into the family circle unless he is known to be wholly worthy of a place in that *sanctum sanctorum* of social life; but when once a man is admitted to the home fireside he should be treated as if the place had been his always.

The fact of an invitation gives neither host nor guest the right to be master of the other's time, and does not require even a temporary sacrifice of one's entire individuality or pursuits.

A man should never be so much himself as when he entertains a friend.

THE RULE OF HOSPITALITY.

To stay at a friend's house beyond the time for which one is invited is to perpetrate a social robbery.

To abide uninvited in a friend's home is as much a misdemeanor as borrowing his coat without his permission. It is debasing the coin of friendship to mere dross when a man attempts to make it pay his hotel bills.

The fact of two men having the same occupation and interests in life gives to neither a social right to the other's bed and board. A traveling minister has no more right to go uninvited to a fellow-preacher's house than a traveling shopkeeper or shoemaker has to go uninvited to the house of his fellow-craftsman. Men are ordained to the ministry as preachers, teachers and pastors, and not as private hotel-keepers.

They who go into the country in summer as uninvited guests of their farmer friends should be rated as social brigands and treated accordingly.

These few social maxims are by no means to be taken as a complete code of laws. Others quite as important will spring up out of the personal experience of every reader of this article, and the justice and equity of all may be tested by that infallible standard of society,—the Golden Rule. There can be no true hospitality that in practice is a violation of this rule; and you may safely rest assured that you have given the fullest and most perfect measure of entertainment to your neighbor if you have done exactly as you would be done by.

MAN should never be ashamed to own that he has been in the wrong, which is but saying in other words, that he is wiser to-day than he was yesterday.—*Alexander Pope.*

DON'T BE TOO SENSITIVE.

THERE are people—yes, many people—always looking out for slights. They cannot carry on the daily intercourse of the family without finding that some offense is designed. They are as touchy as hair-triggers. If they meet an acquaintance who happens to be preoccupied with business, they attribute his distraction in some mode personal to themselves, and take umbrage accordingly. They lay on others the fruit of their irritability. Indigestion makes them see impertinence in every one they come in contact with. Innocent persons, who never dreamed of giving offense, are astonished to find some unfortunate word or momentary taciturnity mistaken for an insult. To say the least, the habit is unfortunate. It is far wiser to take the more charitable view of our fellow-beings, and not suppose that a slight is intended unless the neglect is open and direct. After all, too, life takes its hues in a great degree from the color of our own mind. If we are frank and generous, the world will treat us kindly; if, on the contrary, we are suspicious, men learn to be cold and cautious to us. Let a person get the reputation of being "touchy," and everybody is under restraint, and in this way the chances of an imaginary offense are vastly increased.—*Anonymous.*

I THINK the first virtue is to restrain the 'tongue; he approaches nearest to the gods who knows how to be silent, even though he is in the right.—*Cato.*

ADVICE TO A YOUNG MAN.

John Todd, D.D

A MAN who *wills* it can go anywhere and do what he determines to do. We must make ourselves, or come to nothing. We must swim off, and not wait for any one to put cork under us. I congratulate you on being poor, and thus compelled to work; it was all that ever made me what little I am. *Macte virtute.* Don't flinch, flounder, fall, nor fiddle, but grapple like a man, and you will be a man.

ADVICE TO YOUNG MEN.

Noah Porter, D.D.

YOUNG men, you are the architects of your own fortunes. Rely upon your own strength of body and soul. Take for your star self-reliance, faith, honesty, and industry. Inscribe on your banner, "Luck is a fool, pluck is a hero." Don't take too much advice—keep at your helm and steer your own ship, and remember that the great art of commanding is to take a fair share of the work. Don't practice too much humanity. Think well of yourself. Strike out. Assume your own position. Put potatoes in your cart, over a rough road, and small ones go to the bottom. Rise above the envious and jealous. Fire above the mark you intend to hit. Energy, invincible determination, with a right motive, are the levers that move the world. Don't drink. Don't chew. Don't smoke. Don't swear. Don't deceive. Don't read novels. Don't marry until you can support a wife. Be in earnest. Be self-reliant.

Be generous. Be civil. Read the papers. Advertise your business. Make money and do good with it. Love your God and fellow men. Love truth and virtue, Love your country, and obey its laws.

If this advice be implicitly followed by the young men of the country the millennium is near at hand.

EDUCATION.

H. W. Beecher.

EDUCATION is the knowledge of how to use the whole of oneself. Men are often like knives with many blades; they know how to open one, and only one; all the rest are buried in the handle, and they are no better than they would have been if they had been made with but one blade. Many men use but one or two faculties out of the score with which they are endowed. A man is educated who knows how to make a tool of every faculty—how to open it, how to keep it sharp, and how to apply it to all practical purposes.

IDEAS go booming through the world louder than cannon. Thoughts are mightier than armies. Principles have achieved more victories than horsemen or chariots.

W. M. Paxton, D.D.

THE intelligence of the people is the security of the nation.

Daniel Webster.

COUNSELS TO THE YOUNG.

NEVER be cast down by trifles. If a spider breaks his web twenty times, twenty times will he mend it again. Make up your minds to do a thing, and you will do it. Fear not if trouble comes upon you; keep up your spirits, though the day may be a dark one.

"Troubles never last forever;
The darkest day will pass away."

If the sun is going down, look up to the stars; if the earth is dark, keep your eyes on heaven. With God's presence and God's promise, a man or child may be cheerful.

"Never despair when fog's in the air,
A sunshiny morning will come without warning!"

Mind what you run after! Never be content with a bubble that will burst, or a fire-wood that will end in smoke and darkness. But that which you can keep, and which is worth keeping.

"Something sterling, that will stay
When gold and silver fly away!

Fight hard against a hasty temper. Anger will come, but resist it strongly. A spark may set a house on fire. A fit of passion may give you cause to mourn all the days of your life. Never revenge an injury.

"He that revengeth knoweth no rest;
The meek possess a peaceful breast!"

If you have an enemy, act kindly to him, and make him your friend. You may not win him over at once, but try again. Let one kindness be followed by another, till you have compassed your end. By little and by little great things are completed.

> "Water falling day by day,
> Wears the hardest rock away."

And so repeated kindnesses will soften a heart of stone.

Whatever you do, do it willingly. A boy that is whipped at school never learns his lessons well. A man that is compelled to work, cares not how badly it is performed.

Evil thoughts are worse enemies than lions and tigers, for we can get out of the way of wild beasts. Keep your heads and hearts full of good thoughts, that bad thoughts may not find room.—*Anonymous.*

VALUE the ends of life more than its means; watch ever for the soul of good in things evil, and the soul of truth in things false, and beside the richer influence that will flow out from your life on all to whom you minister, you will do something to help the solution of that unsolved problem of the human mind and heart, the reconciliation of hearty tolerance with strong positive belief. *Phillips Brooks.*

No man is so insignificant as to be sure his example can do no hurt. *Lord Clarendon.*

THERE never was a great man, unless through divine inspiration. *Cicero.*

TO YOUNG MEN.

"Sowing Wild Oats," or What shall the Harvest be ?

D. L. Moody.

WHEN a man sows in the natural world he expects to reap. There is not a farmer who goes out to sow, but expects a harvest. Another thing—they all expect to reap more than they sow. And they expect to reap the same as they sow. If they sow wheat, they expect to reap wheat. If they sow oats, they won't expect to gather watermelons. If they plant an apple-tree, they don't look for peaches on it. If they plant a grapevine, they expect to find grapes, not pumpkins. They will look for just the very seed they sow. Let me say right here, that ignorance of what they sowed will make no difference in the reaping. It would not do for a man to say, "I didn't know but what it was wheat I was sowing, when I sowed tares." That makes no difference. If I go out and sow tares, thinking that it is wheat, I've got to gather tares all the same. That is a universal law. If a man learns the carpenter's trade, he don't expect to be a watchmaker, he expects to be a carpenter. The man who goes to college and studies hard, expects to reap for those long years of toil and labor. It is the same in the spiritual world. Whatsoever a man or nation sows, he and they must reap. The reaping time will come. Men may think God is winking at sin now-a-days, and isn't going to punish sin, because he does not execute his judgments speedily, but be not deceived, God is not mocked, and whatsoever a man soweth that shall he reap. I tremble for these young men who laugh in a scoffing way and say, "I am sowing my wild oats." You have got to reap them. There are some before me now reaping them, who only a few years ago were scoffing in the same way. The rich man who fared luxuriously, while the poor man sat at his gate, and the dogs came and licked his sores, the reaping time has come for him now. He would gladly change places with that beggar now.

Yes, there will be a change by and by. Men may go on scoffing and making light of the Bible but they will find it to be true by and by. I think there is one passage that you will admit is true. You very often see it in the daily papers, that "Murder will out" when some terrible crime that has been covered up for years has come to light. And there is one passage I would like to get every one to remember. "Be sure your sin will find you out." There are a great many things in this world we are not sure of, but this we can always be sure of, that our sins will find us out. I don't care how deep you dig the grave in which you try to bury them. Look at those sons of Jacob. They thought they had covered up their sin, and their father never would find out what they had done with Joseph. And the old man mourned him for twenty long years. But at last, after all these years had gone, away down in Egypt, there Joseph stood before them. How they began to tremble. Oh, it had found them out. Their sin had overtaken them. Young men, you may have committed some sin many years ago, and you think nothing is known about it. Don't you flatter yourself. God knows all about it, and be sure your sin will find you out. Your own conscience may turn witness against you by and by. If you sow tares, you will reap disappointment, you will reap despair, you will reap death and hell. If you sow to the Spirit you shall reap peace and joy and happiness and eternal life. The reaping time is coming. What is the harvest going to be? If you confess your sin, God will have mercy; He delights in mercy.

ABILITY AND OPPORTUNITY.

THESE are the conditions of success. Give a man power and a field in which to use it, and he must accomplish something. He may not do and become all that he desires and dreams of, but his life can not be a failure. I never hear men complaining of the want of ability. The most unsuccessful think that they could do great things if they only had the chance. Somehow or other something or somebody has always been in the way. Providence has hedged them in so that they could not carry out their plans. They knew just how to get rich, but they lacked opportunity.

Sit down by one who thus complains and ask him to tell you the story of his life. Before he gets half through he will give you occasion to ask him, "Why didn't you do so at that time? Why didn't you stick to that piece of land and improve it, or to that business and develope it? Is not the present owner of that property rich? Is not the man who took up the business you abandoned successful?" He will probably reply: "Yes, that was an opportunity; but I did not think so then. I saw it when it was too late." In telling his story he will probably say, of his own accord, half a dozen times. "If I had known how things were going to turn I might have done as well as Mr. A. That farm of his was offered to me. I knew that it was a good one, and cheap, but I knew that it would require a great deal of hard work to get it cleared and fenced, to plant trees, vines, etc., and to secure water for irrigation. I did not like to undertake it. I am sorry now that I didn't. It was one of my opportunities."

ABILITY AND OPPORTUNITY.

The truth is, God gives to all of us ability and opportunities enough to enable us to be moderately successful. If we fail, in ninety-five cases out of a hundred it is our own fault. We neglect to improve the talents with which our Creator endowed us, or we failed to enter the door that he opened for us. A man can not expect that his whole life shall be made up of opportunities, that they will meet him at regular intervals as he goes on, like milestones by the roadside. Usually he has one or two, and if he neglects them he is like a man who takes the wrong road where several meet. The further he goes the worse he fares.

A man's opportunity usually has some relation to his ability. It is an opening for a man of his talents and means. It is an opening for him to use what he has, faithfully and to the utmost. It requires toil, self-denial and faith. If he says, "I want a better opportunity than that. I am worthy of a higher position than it offers;" or if he says, "I won't work as hard and economize as closely as that opportunity demands," he may, in after years, see the folly of his pride and indolence.

There are young men all over the land who want to get rich, and yet they scorn such opportunities as A. T. Stewart and Commodore Vanderbilt improved. They want to begin, not as those men did, at the bottom of the ladder, but half way up. They want somebody to give them a lift, or carry them up in a balloon, so that they can avoid the early and arduous struggles of the majority of those who have been successful. No wonder that such men fail, and then complain of Providence. Grumbling is usually a miserable expedient that people resort to to drown the reproaches of conscience. They know that they have been foolish, but they try to persuade themselves that they have been unfortunate.—*Herald and Presbyter.*

HAPPINESS.

Alexander Pope.

ORDER is heaven's first law; and this confessed,
　Some are, and must be, greater than the rest;
　More rich, more wise, but who infers from hence,
That such are happier, shocks all common sense.
Heaven to mankind, impartial, we confess,
If all are equal in their happiness:
But mutual wants this happiness increase,
All nature's difference keeps all nature's peace.
Condition, circumstance, is not the thing;
Bliss is the same in subject or in king,
In who obtains defense, or who defend,
In him who is, or him who finds a friend;
Heaven breathes through every member of the whole,
One common blessing, as one common soul.

DOMESTIC HAPPINESS.

Wm. Cowper.

DOMESTIC happiness! thou only bliss
　Of paradise, that has survived the fall!
　Though few now taste thee, unimpair'd and free,
Or, tasting, long enjoy thee; too infirm,
Or too incautious to preserve thy sweets
Unmixed with drops of bitter.

FAMILY LIFE A TEST OF PIETY.

IT is in the family life that a man's piety gets tested. Let the husband be cross and surly, giving a snap here and a cuff there, and see how out of sorts everything gets! The wife grows cold and unamiable, too. Both are tuned on one key. They vibrate in unison, giving tone for tone, rising in harmony or discord together. The children grow up saucy, and savage as young bears. The father becomes callous, peevish, hard, a kind of two-legged brute with clothes on. The wife bristles in self-defense. They develop an unnatural growth and sharpness of teeth; and the house is haunted by ugliness and domestic brawls.

Is that what God meant the family to be—He who made it a place for love to build her nest in, and where kindness and sweet courtesy might come to their finest manifestations? The divine idea can be realized. There is sunshine enough in the world to warm all. Why will not men come out of their caves to enjoy it? Some men make it a point to treat every other man's wife well but their own,—have smiles for all but their kindred. Strange, pitiable picture of human weakness, when those we love best are treated worst; when courtesy is shown to all save our friends! If one must be rude to any, let it be to some one he does not love—not to wife, sister, brother or parent.

Let one of our loved ones be taken away, and memory recalls a thousand sayings to regret. Death quickens recollection painfully. The grave can not hide the white faces of those who sleep. The coffin and the green mound are cruel magnets. They draw us farther than we would go. They force us to remember. A man never sees so far into human life as when he looks over a wife's or mother's grave. His eyes get wondrous clear then, and he sees as never before what it is to love and be loved; what it is to injure the feelings of the loved.—*Golden Rule.*

AIM AND OBJECT IN LIFE.

Rev. C. H. Spurgeon.

O THAT we could wake men up to exercise the faculty of thinking, and then to direct, to regulate, and to control their thoughts! But thinking is an occupation that a great many persons altogether dislike. They are frivolous. We cannot get them to think about anything. Many minds never get on the wing at all. Not a few men work so hard with their hands, and suffer such fatigue from bodily labor, that they are scarcely able to think much; while there are others who dissipate their time and consume their lives in idleness, till they are utterly disqualified for any vigorous thought. They are lazy and sluggish. They have the dry rot in their very souls. Their brains do not work. They seem to live in one everlasting lethargy and day-dream. O that men were wise, that they were thoughtful! Ask many a man whom you meet with, "Sir, what are you living for?" he would, perhaps, tell you what his trade or what his profession might be; but if you pressed him with the question, "What is the main object of life?" he would not like to say that he was living only to enjoy himself—seeking his own pleasure. He would hardly like to say that he was living to grasp and grab and get a fortune. He would hardly know how to answer you. Many young men are in this condition; they have not a definite object. Now, you will not make a good captain if you do not know the port you are sailing for. You will make a poor life of it, young man, if you go out as an apprentice, and then afterwards out as a master, with no definite aim and end. Say to yourself, "I can only live for two things. I can live for God, or I can live for the devil; which, now, am I going to do?" Get your mind well fixed and firmly resolved as to which it shall be. I will put it to you as boldly and badly as even Elijah did when he said, "If Baal be God, serve Him; and if Jehovah be God, serve Him." If the world, if the flesh, if the devil, be worth serving, go follow out the career of a sensualist, and say so. Let yourself know what you are at; but if God be worth serving, and your soul worth the saving, go in for that; but do not sneak through this world really seeking yourself, and yet not having the courage to say to yourself, "Self, you are living for yourself." Do have a definite and distinct object, or else your vital energies will be wasted, and your most industrious days will be recklessly squandered.

SELFISHNESS.
Wm. Cowper.

OH, if the selfish knew how much they lost,
What would they not endeavor, not endure,
To imitate, as far as in them lay,
Him who his wisdom and his power employs
In making others happy?

WHOEVER thinks of life as something that could be without religion is yet in deadly ignorance of both. Life and religion are one, or neither is anything.
Geo. MacDonald.

MAKE YOUR MARK.

David Barker.

IN the quarries should you toil,
    Make your mark ;
  Do you delve upon the soil,
    Make your mark ;
In whatever path you go,
  In whatever place you stand,
Moving swift or moving slow,
  With a firm and honest hand,
    Make your mark.

Should opponents hedge your way,
    Make your mark ;
Work by night or work by day,
    Make your mark ;
Struggle manfully and well,
  Let no obstacle oppose ;
None, right-shielded, ever fell,
  By the weapons of his foes ;
    Make your mark.

What though born a peasant's son,
    Make your mark ;
Good by poor men can be done,
    Make your mark ;
Peasants' garbs may warm the cold,
  Peasants' words may calm a fear ;

THE USES OF ADVERSITY.

Better far than hoarding gold,
  Is the drying of a tear;
    Make your mark.

Life is fleeting as a shade,
  Make your mark;
Marks of some kind must be made,
  Make your mark;
Make it while the arm is strong,
  In the golden hours of youth;
Never, never make it wrong,
  Make it with the stamp of truth;
    Make your mark.

THE USES OF ADVERSITY.

Joseph Addison.

THE gods in bounty work up storms about us,
  That give mankind occasion to exert
  Their hidden strength, and throw out into practice
Virtues that shun the day, and lie concealed
In the smooth seasons and the calms of life.

THE good are better made by ill:—
  As odors crushed, are sweeter still!

Samuel Rogers.

TROUBLES are hard to take, though they strengthen the soul.
  Tonics are always bitter.   *T. De Witt Talmage.*

FOLLY OF FRETTING.

A. A. Lason.

THE personal sin of fretting is almost as extensive as any other evil. It is not universal, but very general. It is as vain and useless a habit as one can harbor. Nothing so warps man's nature, sours his disposition, breaks up the friendly relationship in the domestic circle. It is a direct violation of the law of God. It is sinful in the beginning, in its progress, and sinful continually. The divine direction is, "Fret not thyself in anywise to do evil." David's knowledge of human nature was as large as it was exact. Scolding is confined to no age or clime. Some bad streak in one's constitution, a little mishap, or a score of causes, may stir and stimulate this irritable disposition. Such a spirit in the family, in the school, or church, may become contagious, and result in great injury. It may be quelled and conquered. When we see its manifestation in time to take a second thought, a determined silence is sure to ward off the most fiery outburst. It is difficult for a quarrel to continue long without opposing agents. Nothing so surprises an angry person as kind words. Let them be few and spoken in a loving manner.

The milk of human kindness, like oil on an axle, lightens the load and eases life's heavy burdens. In the severe school of hardship and adversity—through which all humanity must pass—the law of kindness is the real antidote. Overwork and anxiety produce irritability. Domestic felicity is the oil of consolation. Fault-finding tends to division, rejection, and misery. True perennial happiness is the lot of few mortals in this inconstant world. The effects of scolding are twofold. They give color to one's own character, as truly as they do harm to society. Fretting becomes habitual with some—all is unpleasant.

A fretful habit finds frequent opportunities for indulgence, occasions literally multiplying as the habit increases in strength. Almost everybody displeases the fault-finder. Nothing seems to go right with the constant fretter. Circumstances control and conquer him. There is no self-poise in his soul—no controlling power. Fretting weakens one's self-respect. It breaks asunder the bond of affections. It is impossible to love an habitual fault-finder. If a scolder should be loved through deception for a time, the affections must, sooner or later, be sundered. We might tolerate a person through ignorance, or for some weakness in his constitution, for a time. But a toleration differs materially from genuine friendship. A fretful disposition sours all the relations of life, is a most pernicious acquisition, a dreadful inheritance. Such a habit, too frequently indulged, has driven the best of husbands into dissipation, rendered the most affectionate wives miserable, schools ungovernable, and made congregations noisy and disrespectful. It would fill the state with rebellion, and hell with inmates.

One fretful parent would instill poison into every heart in the domestic circle. In after years the spirit of the early life will reassert its claim, and will insensibly fill other families with discontent. Vice, like virtue, through all the channels of influence, is handed down from sire to son, from mother to daughter. There is no sense, no necessity for fretting. We are to let our moderation be made known. There is no kind of use, no real benefit to come from such a course. It is an injury to man, a curse on society, and a libel on God, who has endowed us with speech. It defeats domestic and school discipline. The great object of genuine government is a willing, ready, hearty obedience from personal choice.

NEVER MIND.

All rightful rulers seek to win the self-respect, the good will of those whom they are to control. Fretting fails to secure these ends. This ill-timed grace is founded in selfishness. Love can not be won by it; respect can not be retained. There remains the love of nobility in every man. To this natural sense of goodness we can not, in kindness, appeal in vain. Fretting resorts to fear, appeals to brute force, and in return awakens only dread and dislike. It is an evil force, that fosters the faults it seeks in vain to correct.

> "Vice is a monster of so frightful mien,
> That to be hated needs but to be seen."

NEVER MIND

"Casting all your care upon him; for he careth for you." I. Peter, v 7.

WHAT'S the use of always fretting
    At the trials we shall find
    Ever strewn along our pathway!
    Travel on, and never mind.

Travel onward, working, hoping,
    Cast no lingering look behind
At the trials once encountered;
    Look ahead, and never mind.

What is past, is past forever;
    Let all the fretting be resigned;
It will never help the matter—
    Do your best, and never mind.

And if those who might befriend you,
  Whom the ties of nature bind,
Should refuse to do their duty,
  Look to heaven, and never mind.

Friendly words are often spoken
  When the feelings are unkind;
Take them for their real value,
  Pass them on, and never mind.

Fate may threaten, clouds may lower,
  Enemies may be combined;
If your trust in God is steadfast,
  He will help you,—never mind.—*Anonymous.*

LITTLE TROUBLES.

Mrs. Amelia E. Barr.

ALTHOUGH general sympathy overlooks small miseries, individuals find it worth their while to take them into account; for the whole history of some people is but a long record of trifling vexations and sufferings: trifling when taken singly, but overwhelming when taken in the mass.

It may not seem a great thing to have a constantly nagging companion, or boots that always hurt your corns, or linen that is never properly starched; or to have to read crossed letters, or go to stupid parties, or consult books without indexes,—but to the sufferer they are very tangible oppressions, and, in our short space of working life, not to be made light of.

Of course, if we were all cast in heroic moulds, we should despise such petty aggravations; but the world does not turn on heroic principles; it is useless to tell a fretful, worried man that his trials are "*absurd;*" and do not think you have effected a cure when you have let that drop of boiling oil fall upon his wounds. "Absurd?" His own common sense has already told him so, and that is the very thing that aggravates his annoyance.

It is equally useless to remind such sufferers "that if they lived with a proper estimate of the present and future before them, they could bear these little trials with a calm and decent philosophy." Perhaps so! but I have seen these same philosophers strongly moved by little disappointments in meals, or weather, that affected themselves; nay, even by such trifling causes as cold shaving-water, or a want of buttons. Most platitudes of this kind are affectations; and the men who pretend to despise little troubles are the very men who exaggerate them.

There are indeed, some characters who have the cheerfulness of fine summer mornings; everything about them laughs and sings, even their tears have the lustre of a fresh shower. But there are other natures equally fine in a contrary direction, whose excessive sensibility makes them the instrument upon which every circumstance plays.

I am going now to make a confession of one of these little troubles—one which will doubtless seem puerile to many, but which I know tens of thousands suffer keenly from—I mean the tyranny of the atmosphere. When a foggy day or a spiteful east wind attacks us, or when there is no blue sky to speak to us of heaven, we are depressed, and full of inexpressible languors. Our work falls from our hands, our inability irritates us, our whole human nature suffers with the physical world.

"What nonsense! Man as an immortal soul ought to float above this terrestrial atmosphere." Ah, yes! but though we envy the strength of such natures as are always equable, we cannot imitate them. And we do not want them to tell us that such depressions are "imaginary," and "ought to be resisted;" we do resist them, and this very struggle assures us of their reality, for in it we feel the difficulty of measuring ourselves against its influence.

Any system of philosophy is too big for the average man—yes, for the Christian man—which overlooks the terrible reality of "little troubles."

It is not the great boulders, but the small pebbles on the road, that bring the traveling horse on his knees; and it is the petty annoyances of life, ever present, to be met and conquered afresh every day, that try most severely the metal of which we are made. And when we are in the very thick of such a fight, how often are we met with that aggravating little bit of sympathy that "it will be all the same a hundred years hence."

There is no comfort in a dictum so mocking and so untrue. It does not touch the question at all; and it is not true. For nothing happens for nothing; and whether we did or did not do a certain thing, or whether we got, or did not get another, may have very important consequences, even a hundred years hence. Besides, this kind of consolation, carried out to its logical conclusion, would take every honest and honorable purpose out of life. A man could easily persuade himself by it, that whether he did his duty or not, whether he earned his bread or stole it, would be "all the same a hundred years hence." We don't live for a hundred years hence, we are here to do *to-day's duty*, and whatever helps us best to-day is the help we need.

What are we then to do with these ever-recurring little trials, from which we see no release this side of the grave? Do not let us blink matters. *Our friends grow weary of them.* Smitten by the same blows, we go on repeating the same cries, and this monotony is hard to bear with. Friendship that can overlook our faults wears out with our complaints. The sympathy that finds us every morning just as it leaves us every night, can no more maintain its life than flame can burn in a vacuum. "To whom then shall we go?" Go to that divine Friend whose pierced hands have so often raised us up. It was not to the unhappy Jesus forbade "repetitions." We may importune him without fear; we may tell him all, and tell it every day.

But will he care for such small troubles as harass our little affairs, and let out our life, as it were, by multitudes of pin-pricks? Yes, for our God is not a God who only occupies himself with weighty matters. He is no overtasked being who sits afar off, and abandons the care of every-day trials and interests to inferior agents. He is a God to whom everything is little, and everything is great, who counts one poor human soul of more value than a world, who numbers the hairs of our heads, and counts our tears. We can never weary God, and nothing that gives us an anxious thought or a weary feeling is beneath his notice.

These little trials are the soul's drill and discipline. We make our lives, as we sew—stitch by stitch; often wearily enough, often faint and discouraged, but perseverance in well doing always touches the heart of God, who seems to say at the last, "*That will do!*"

ANXIETY is the poison of life; the parent of many sins and of more miseries. Why, then, allow it, when we know that all the future is guided by a Father's hand? *Blair.*

MANY dishes bring many diseases. *Pliny.*

TRANSIENT TROUBLES

MOST of us have had troubles all our lives, and each day has brought all the evil that we wished to endure. But if we were asked to recount the sorrows of our lives, how many could we remember? How many that are six months old should we think worthy to be remembered or mentioned? To-day's troubles look large, but a week hence they will be forgotten and buried out of sight.

If you would keep a book, and every day put down the things that worry you, and see what becomes of them, it would be a benefit to you. You allow a thing to annoy you, just as you allow a fly to settle on you and plague you; and you lose your temper (or rather get it; for when men are surcharged with temper they are said to have lost it); and you justify yourselves for being thrown off your balance by causes which you do not trace out. But if you would see what it was that threw you off your balance before breakfast, and put it down in a little book, and follow it out, and ascertain what becomes of it, you would see what a fool you were in the matter.

The art of forgetting is a blessed art, but the art of overlooking is quite as important. And if we should take time to write down the origin, the progress, and outcome of a few of our troubles, it would make us so ashamed of the fuss we make over them, that we should be glad to drop such things and bury them at once in eternal forgetfulness. Life is too short to be worn out in petty worries, frettings, hatreds, and vexations. Let us think only on whatsoever things are pure, and lovely, and gentle, and of good report.
—*Anonymous.*

WORKING AND WAITING.

 HUSBANDMAN who many years
Had ploughed his field and sown in tears
Grew weary with his doubts and fears:
"I toil in vain! these rocks and sands
Will yield no harvest to my hands;
The best seeds rot in barren lands.
My drooping vine is withering;
No promised grapes its blossoms bring;
No birds among the branches sing;
My flock is dying on the plain;
The heavens are brass—they yield no rain;
The earth is iron,—I toil in vain!"

While yet he spake, a breath had stirred
His drooping vine, like wing of bird,
And from its leaves a voice he heard:
"The germs and fruits of life must be
Forever hid in mystery,
Yet none can toil in vain for Me.
A mightier hand, more skilled than thine,
Must hang the clusters on the vine,
And make the fields with harvest shine.
Man can but work; God can create:
But they who work, and watch, and wait,
Have their reward, though it come late.
Look up to heaven! behold, and hear

CONTENT.

...ls and thunderings in thy ear—
...er to thy doubts and fear."

...ed, and lo! a cloud-draped car,
...ailing smoke and flames afar,
...shing from a distant star;
...ery thirsty flock and plain
...sing up to meet the rain,
...ime to clothe the fields with grain;
...n the clouds he saw again,
...ovenant of God with men,
...tten with His rainbow pen:
...d-time and harvest shall not fail,
...though the gates of hell assail,
...truth and promise shall prevail!"—*Anonymous.*

CONTENT.
Mrs. L. H. Sigourney

THINK'ST thou the man whose mansions hold
  The worldling's pomp and miser's gold,
  Obtains a richer prize
Than he, who, in his cot at rest
Finds heavenly peace a willing guest,
And bears the promise in his breast
Of treasure in the skies?

HOW sour sweet music is,
  When time is broke, and no proportion kept!
  So is it in the music of men's lives.
            —*Shakespeare.*

WORKING AND WAITING.

 HUSBANDMAN who many years
Had ploughed his field and sown in
Grew weary with his doubts and fer
"I toil in vain! these rocks and sands
Will yield no harvest to my hands;
The best seeds rot in barren lands.
My drooping vine is withering;
No promised grapes its blossoms bring;
No birds among the branches sing;
My flock is dying on the plain;
The heavens are brass—they yield no rain;
The earth is iron,—I toil in vain!"

While yet he spake, a breath had stirred
His drooping vine, like wing of bird,
And from its leaves a voice he heard:
"The germs and fruits of life must be
Forever hid in mystery,
Yet none can toil in vain for Me.
A mightier hand, more skilled than thine,
Must hang the clusters on the vine,
And make the fields with harvest shine.
Man can but work; God can create:
But they who work, and watch, and wait,
Have their reward, though it come late.
Look up to heaven! behold, and hear

CONTENT.

The clouds and thunderings in thy ear—
An answer to thy doubts and fear."

He looked, and lo! a cloud-draped car,
With trailing smoke and flames afar,
Was rushing from a distant star;
And every thirsty flock and plain
Was rising up to meet the rain,
That came to clothe the fields with grain;
And on the clouds he saw again,
The covenant of God with men,
Rewritten with His rainbow pen:
"Seed-time and harvest shall not fail,
And though the gates of hell assail,
My truth and promise shall prevail!"—*Anonymous.*

CONTENT.
Mrs. L. H. Sigourney

THINK'ST thou the man whose mansions hold
The worldling's pomp and miser's gold,
Obtains a richer prize
Than he, who, in his cot at rest
Finds heavenly peace a willing guest,
And bears the promise in his breast
Of treasure in the skies?

HOW sour sweet music is,
When time is broke, and no proportion kept!
So is it in the music of men's lives.
—*Shakespeare.*

LET BY-GONES BE BY-GONES.

LET by-gones be by-gones. If by-gones were clouded
  By aught that occasioned a pang of regret,
  O, let them in darkest oblivion be shrouded;
    'Tis wise and 'tis kind to forgive and forget.

Let by-gones be by-gones, and good be extracted
  From ill over which it is folly to fret;
The wisest of mortals have foolishly acted—
  The kindest are those who forgive and forget.

Let by-gones be by-gones. O, cherish no longer
  The thought that the sun of affection has set;
Eclipsed for a moment, its rays will be stronger,
  If you, like a Christian, forgive and forget.

Let by-gones be by-gones. Your heart will be lighter
  When kindness of yours with reception has met;
The flame of your love will be purer and brighter,
  If, God-like, you strive to forgive and forget.

Let by-gones be by-gones. O, purge out the leaven
  Of malice, and try an example to set
To others, who, craving the mercy of heaven,
  Are sadly too slow to forgive and forget.

Let by-gones be by-gones. Remember how deeply
  To heaven's forbearance we all are in debt;

They value God's infinite goodness too cheaply
Who heed not the precept, "Forgive and forget.
—*Chambers' Journal.*

THE CHRISTIAN AT HOME.

CHRISTIANITY begins *in the home.* If not there, it is nowhere. We may attend meetings, and sing hymns, and join devoutly in prayer; we may give money to the poor, and send missionaries and Bibles to the heathen; we may organize societies of every description for doing good; we may get up church fairs, and tea-parties and tableaux and picnics; we may, in short, devote all our time and all our means to doing good, and yet not be the true and earnest Christians we ought to be, after all.

If they cannot say of us in the family at home: "He—or she—is a Christian, we know it, we feel it," if home is not a better and happier place for our living in it, if there is not an influence going out from us, day by day, silently drawing those about us in the right direction, then it is time for us to stop where we are, and begin to examine into our title to the name of Christian.

Christianity. *Christ-likeness.* Is that ours? Are we possessed of that? Are we patient, kind, long-suffering, forbearing, seeking with all our hearts to do good, dreading with all our hearts to do evil?

For if we are Christ's we shall be like Him; and the first fruits, and the best fruits, of our daily living, will be in the better and happier lives of those who are about us day by day.—*Anonymous.*

RELIGION IN THE FAMILY.

Bishop F. D. Huntington.

BEGIN, my friends, with your children. Speak cheerfully, but reverently and solemnly, to them of the righteousness of God. Tell them He is their father, and tell them He is their judge. Show them His face of compassion; show them His throne of retribution. Teach them that He loves the good; teach them that He hates lying, and lust, and all iniquity, and that, for His goodness' sake, He will sweep those who do not hate them finally into tribulation. Take care, yourselves, to touch not the unclean thing, so that your counsel to your sons and daughters be not a mockery. Shake off the first dishonest penny from your fingers, as the apostle shook off the venomous viper into the fire. Stand in awe at your conscience; stand in awe of the King of kings. Expect and welcome, from the ministry of Christ, searching message. Pray for prophets who will rebuke you, as their ancient predecessors did Israel, for robbing man by any fraud, for robbing God by keeping back the offerings at His altar which he requires at your hands. And when we, your ministers, are weak, when our lips stammer, or our courage falters, or our poor lives seem to empty our words of power, turn to old Isaiah, and listen to the burden of his advent vision:

"Hear, O, heaven, and give ear, O earth, for the Lord hath spoken. I have nourished and brought up children, and they have rebelled against me. Wash you; make you clean. Cease to do evil; learn to do well. Seek judgment; relieve the oppressed; right the fatherless; plead for the widow. Zion shall be redeemed with judgment, and her converts with righteousness. Say ye to the righteous, it shall be well with them, for the reward of his hand shall be given him. The mouth of the Lord hath spoken it."

CERTAINTIES IN RELIGION.

Rev. Joseph Cook.

A LITTLE while ago we were not in the world—a little while hence we shall be here no longer. This is arithmetic. This is the clock. Demosthenes used to say that every speech should begin with an incontrovertible proposition. Now, it is scientifically incontrovertible that a little while ago, we were not here, and a little while hence we shall be here no more. De Tocqueville said that you will in vain try to make any man religious who has no thought of dying. Now, the first of religious certainties is, that we are going hence soon. As to that proposition there is not a particle of doubt. I defy any man to deny that we are going hence. I defy any man to deny that we want to go hence in peace. I defy any man to show that we can go hence unless we are harmonized with our environment. What is that? Our environment is made up of God, of the plan of our own natures, and of our record in the past; and therefore we must be harmonized with God in conscience, and our record, or, in the very nature of things, there cannot be peace for us. Aristotle built his whole philosophy on the proposition that no thing can exist and not exist at the same time, and in the same sense; that is to say, self-contradiction is the proof of error everywhere. And now, since we have an environment, made up of God, conscience and our record, we must be either in harmony or in dissonance with it; and if we are in dissonance we are not in harmony with it; and if we are in harmony, we are not in dissonance with it. And so it is incontrovertible that with whatever environment we cannot escape from, we must come into harmony, and that environment consists of conscience and of God, and of our record.

Similarity of feeling with God, or a love of what He loves, and a hate of what he hates, is an unalterable natural condition of peace of soul in this life and the next.

WINNING SOULS.

Bishop E. S. Janes.

NOW in some way we can work and live and act for Christ. We can all of us be true soldiers under the great Captain of our salvation, and we may all of us in some way win souls to the Master. I think this one passage of Scripture is enough to prove this: "Let him know, that he which converteth the sinner from the error of his way, shall save a soul from death, and shall hide a multitude of sins." What a work! What a result!

O, what an investment is this rational and immortal nature which God has given us, which qualifies us for divine blessings and for eternal felicity. What majesty, what interest, what value does this give to our souls! O, how much pertinency there was in the question of the Saviour, "What shall it profit a man if he shall gain the whole world and lose his own soul, or what shall a man give in exchange for his soul?" And now if our own salvation be so precious and so important, the salvation of those poor degraded brethren that we see around us, inasmuch as they share this nature, is of equal moment. They are not as cultured, perhaps, as we are; they are not as cleanly in their person, they are not as happy in their condition, their social state as well as their personal character is unlike ours, and yet, this immortality is in them; this capacity for bearing the image of God and enjoying the beatitudes of eternity is in them; consequently their souls are as precious as ours and their salvation as important as ours. And besides this, Jesus died for them as well as he died for us. They are just as much the purchase of his blood and they are as much redeemed of his love as we are. If we should succeed in acquiring the whole world and lose our own souls, then it is a legitimate inference that their salvation is of more importance than all this world. It is a grander enterprise, it is a sublimer result to save a human soul through the mediation of Christ and through the instrumentality of grace than to make a world. No wonder, then, that the inspired writer said he that saves a soul is wise. It is the very highest of human wisdom because we choose the greatest interest, the sublimest and most sacred result, we choose the highest sphere of usefulness to accomplish the greatest and grandest of all results: and if we seek to do this as Christians, by teaching men as God teaches us by his word; by influencing them as God influences us by his truth; by influencing them as God permits us in invoking upon them the divine power and operation of the Holy Spirit—O, if we choose this greatest object of ambition, of effort, of aspiration, and pursue it according to the teachings of the Bible, looking to God to crown our effort with success, I repeat it, we are exercising the very highest of human wisdom. There is nothing to compare with it.

WHEN I think of the agencies which are ceaselessly at work to make this bad world better, I am thankful that I live.

W. Morley Punshon, LL.D.

YOUR MISSION.

Daniel March, D. D.

HARK, the voice of Jesus crying,—
  " Who will go and work to-day?
  Fields are white and harvest waiting!
  Who will bear the sheaves away?"
Loud and strong the Master calleth,
  Rich reward he offers thee;
Who will answer, gladly saying,
  "Here am I; send me, send me!"

If you cannot cross the ocean,
  And the heathen lands explore;
You can find the heathen nearer,
  You can help them at your door.
If you cannot give your thousands,
  You can give the widow's mite;
And the least you do for Jesus,
  Will be precious in his sight.

If you cannot speak like angels;
  If you cannot preach like Paul;
You can tell the love of Jesus,
  You can say He died for all.
If you cannot rouse the wicked
  With the judgment's dread alarms,
You can lead the little children
  To the Saviour's waiting arms.

YOUR MISSION.

If you cannot be the watchman
  Standing high on Zion's wall,
Pointing out the path to heaven,
  Offering life and peace to all;
With your prayers and with your bounties
  You can do what heaven demands;
You can be like faithful Aaron,
  Holding up the prophet's hands.

If among the older people,
  You may not be apt to teach;
"Feed my lambs," said Christ, our **Shepherd**,
  "Place the food within their reach,"
And it may be that the children
  You have led with trembling hand,
Will be found among your jewels
  When you reach the better land.

Let none hear you idly saying,
  "There is nothing I can do,"
While the souls of men are dying,
  And the Master calls for you.
Take the task he gives you gladly;
  Let his work your pleasure be;
Answer quickly when he calleth,
  "Here am I; send me, send me!"

To serve with lofty gifts the lowly needs
  Of the poor race for which the God-man died,
  And do it all for love—oh, this is great!
                                        J. G. Holland.

WHATEVER YOU DO, DO IT WELL.

 A JOB slighted, because it is apparently unimportant, leads to habitual neglect, so that men degenerate, insensibly, into bad workmen.

"That is a good rough job," said a foreman in our hearing, recently, and he meant that it was a piece of work, not elegant in itself, but strongly made and well put together.

Training the hand and eye to do work well, leads individuals to form correct habits in other respects, and a good workman is, in most cases, a good citizen. No one need hope to rise above his present situation who suffers small things to pass by, unimproved, or who neglects, metaphorically speaking, to pick up a cent because it is not a dollar. Some of the wisest law-makers, the best statesmen, the most gifted artists, the most merciful judges, the most ingenious mechanics, rose from the great mass.

A rival of a certain lawyer sought to humiliate him publicly by saying: "You blacked my father's boots once." "Yes," replied the lawyer, unabashed, "and I did it well." And because of his habit of doing even mean things well, he rose to greater.

Take heart, all who toil! all youths in humble situations, all in adverse circumstances. If it be but to drive the plow, strive to do well; if only to cut bolts, make good ones; or to blow the bellows, keep the iron hot. It is attention to business that lifts the feet higher up on the ladder.

Says the good Book: "Seest thou a man diligent in his business, he shall stand before kings; he shall not stand before mean men "— *Anonymous.*

INDUSTRY.

Benjamin Franklin.

THE way to wealth is as plain as the way to market. It depends chiefly on two words, industry and frugality; that is, waste neither time nor money, but make the best use of both. Without industry and frugality, nothing will do, and with them everything.

Sloth makes all things difficult, but industry all easy; and he that riseth late must trot all day, and shall scarce overtake his business at night, while laziness travels so slowly that poverty soon overtakes him.

Industry need not wish, and he that lives upon hopes will die fasting. There are no gains without pains; then help, hands, for I have no lands; or if I have, they are smartly taxed. He that hath a trade hath an estate, and he that hath a calling, hath an office of profit and honor, but then the trade must be worked at, and the calling followed, or neither the estate nor the office will enable us to pay our taxes. If we are industrious, we shall never starve; for, at the working-man's house, hunger looks in, but dares not enter. Nor will the bailiff or the constable enter, for industry pays debts, while despair increaseth them.

Employ thy time well, if thou meanest to gain leisure; and since thou art not sure of a minute, throw not away an hour. Leisure is time for doing something useful; this leisure the diligent man will obtain, but the lazy man never; for a life of leisure and a life of laziness are two things.

ART is the application of knowledge to a practical end.

Sir John Herschel.

KNOW THYSELF.

Mrs. L. H. Sigourney.

WHEN gentle twilight sits
   On Day's forsaken throne,
     'Mid the sweet hush of eventide.
Muse by thyself alone,
And at the time of rest,
   Ere sleep asserts its power,
Hold pleasant converse with thyself
   In Meditation's bower.

Motives and deeds review
   By Memory's truthful glass,
Thy silent self the only judge
   And critic as they pass;
And if thy wayward face
   Should give thy conscience pain,
Resolve with energy divine
   The victory to gain.

When morning's earliest rays
   O'er spire and roof-tree fall,
Gladly invite thy waking heart
   Unto a festival
Of smiles and love to all,
   The lowliest and the least,
And of delighted praise to Him,
   The Giver of the feast.

KNOW THYSELF.

Not on the outer world
  For inward joy depend;
Enjoy the luxury of thought.
  Make thine ownself thy friend;
Not with the restless throng,
  In search of solace roam,
But with an independent zeal
  Be intimate at home.

Good company have they,
  Who by themselves do walk,
If they have learned on blessed themes
  With their own souls to talk;
For they shall never feel
  Of dull ennui the power,
Not penury of loneliness
  Shall haunt their hall or bower.

Drink waters from the fount
  That in thy bosom springs,
And envy not the mingled draught
  Of satraps or of kings;
So shalt thou find at last,
  Far from the giddy brain,
Self-knowledge and self-culture lead
  To uncomputed gain.

They are never alone that are accompanied with noble thoughts
Sir Philip Sidney.

IMPORTANCE OF CHARACTER.

THERE is a difference between character and reputation. Character is what we really are. Reputation is what others suppose we are. A man may have a good character and a bad reputation, or he may have a good reputation and a bad character. The reason of this is, that we form our opinions of men from what they appear to be, and not from what they really are. Some men appear to be much better than they really are, while others are better than they appear to be. Most men are more anxious about their reputation than they are about their character. This is improper. While every man should endeavor to maintain a good reputation, he should especially labor to possess a good character. Our true happiness depends not so much on what is thought of us by others, as on what we really are in ourselves. Men of good character are generally men of good reputation; but this is not always the case, as the motives and actions of the best of men are sometimes misunderstood and misrepresented. But it is important, above everything else, that we be right, and do right, whether our motives and actions are properly understood and appreciated or not. Nothing can be so important to any man as the formation and possession of a good character.

The influences which operate in the formation of character are numerous, and however trivial some of them may appear, they are not to be despised. The most powerful forces in nature are those which operate silently and imperceptibly. This is equally true of those moral forces which exert the greatest influences on our

IMPORTANCE OF CHARACTER.

minds, and give complexion to our characters. Among these, early impressions, example, and habits, are perhaps the most powerful.

Early impressions, although they may appear to be but slight, are the most enduring, and exert the greatest influences on the life. By repetition they acquire strength, become deeply rooted in the mind, and give bent and inclination to its powers. " The tiniest bits of opinion sown in the minds of children in private life, afterwards issue forth to the world, and become its public opinion; for nations are gathered out of nurseries." Examples, it is said, preach to eyes; and there are but few persons, especially among the young, who can avoid imitating those with whom they associate. For the most part, this is so unconscious that its effects are almost unheeded, but its influence is not on that account the less permanent. The models which are daily placed before us, tend to mould our character and shape our course in life. Habit results from the repetition of the same act, until we become so accustomed to it, that its performance requires no mental effort, and scarcely attracts our attention.

By the influence of early impressions, the force of example, and the power of habit, the character becomes slowly and imperceptibly, but at length decidedly formed; the individual acquires those traits and qualities by which he is distinguished, and which bear directly upon his happiness and welfare. It is very important, then, for every one, and especially for the young, to be very careful as to the impressions he cherishes, the example he imitates, and the habits he forms. These are important elements which go to constitute character, and if they are of an improper nature, the result will be ruinous. Character is everything. It matters not what a man's reputation may be, without a good character he cannot be really happy.—*Methodist Recorder.*

INFLUENCE OF CHARACTER.

W. M. Taylor, D. D.

THE influence of character can never be over-estimated. We call it influence, indeed; but we might, perhaps — as Whately somewhere says—with more significance, style it *effluence*, for it is continually radiating from a man, and then most of all when he is least conscious of its emanation. We are moulding others wherever we are; and if we were in every respect to live according to the gospel, we should be the noblest missionaries of the cross that the world has ever seen. Books are only powerful when they are read; sermons are only influential when they are listened to; but character keeps itself at all times before men's attention, and its might is felt by every one who comes within its sphere. Other agencies are intermittent, like the revolving light, which, after a time of brightness, goes out into a period of darkness; but religious principle is continuous in its operation, and shines with the steady radiance of a star. Hence, of all the ways by which Christians may tell on the surrounding world, this is the most potent, and probably there are no means more blessed for the conversion of sinners, and the elevation of spiritual life among believers, than the habitual deportment of the disciples of Jesus. Frequently a servant has been brought to Christ by the sight of the Christian consistency of her mistress; and not seldom all the members of a household have been benefited by the piety of a humble maiden. I have known the young men of an office seriously impressed by the sterling principle of a fellow-clerk; and sometimes the holy walk of a simple-minded artisan has won not only the admiration, but also the imitation of his neighbors. Now, this is a means of usefulness within the reach of every one, and were we thoroughly alive to its importance, we should be more careful than we are of our conduct, for is it not the case that, instead of commending Christ by our lives, we too frequently give occasion to the enemies of the Lord to blaspheme, and mar the force of the truth by our inconsistency? Instead of adding new energy to the gospel by our conduct, we take away from its power by our iniquities; and men say, if the life of a Christian be such as we have manifested, they will be no Christians. Who can tell how many have been thus repelled from the word of truth? And is it not a fact, that one of the strongest evidences of the divinity of our religion may be derived from the consideration that it has survived the injuries inflicted on it by the Christless conduct of its professed adherents? My brethren, is this inconsistency to continue among us? Let us to-day resolve that, God helping us, we shall live more thoroughly in harmony with those noble principles which Christ enforced by his teaching, and adorned by his example. In the family, let us cultivate the graces of patience, forbearance, love, and self-sacrifice; in the social circle, let us seek to manifest meekness and purity; in business pursuits, let us show that we are actuated by justice and integrity; yea, wherever we are, let us endeavor to have our conversation so worthy of the gospel, that men may take knowledge of us that we have been with Jesus.

A GUILTY conscience is like a whirlpool, drawing in all to itself which would otherwise pass by. *Fuller.*

THE character of the soul is determined by the character of its God.

STRENGTH OF CHARACTER.

F. W. Robertson, D.D.

WE mistake strong feeling to be strong character. A man who bears all before him—before whose frown domestics tremble and whose bursts of fury make the children of the house quake—because he has his will obeyed, and his own way in all things, we call him a strong man. The truth is, that he is a weak man; it is his passions that are strong: he, mastered by them, is weak. You must measure the strength of a man by the power of the feelings he subdues, not by the power of those which subdue him. And hence composure is very often the highest result of strength. Did we never see a man receive a flat grand insult, and only grow a little pale and then reply quietly? That was a man spiritually strong. Or did we never see a man in anguish, stand as if carved out of the solid rock, mastering himself? or one bearing a hopeless daily trial, remain silent and never tell the world what it was that cankered his home peace? That is strength. He who, with strong passions, remains chaste—he who, keenly sensitive, with manly power of indignation in him, can be provoked, yet can restrain himself and forgive—these are strong men, spiritual heroes.

ONLY what we have wrought into our characters during life can we take away with us. *Humboldt.*

CHARACTER, good or bad, has a tendency to perpetuate itself.
A. A. Hodge, D. D.

WORTH OF CHARACTER.

Geo. H. Colton.

THE two most precious things this side the grave are our reputation and our life. But it is to be lamented that the most contemptible whisper may deprive us of the one, and the weakest weapon of the other. A wise man, therefore, will be more anxious to deserve a fair name than to possess it, and this will teach him so to live, as not to be afraid to die.

THE purest treasure mortal times afford
Is spotless Reputation; that away,
Men are but gilded loam, or painted clay.

Shakespeare.

EARNESTNESS OF PURPOSE.

Timothy Dwight, D.D.

THE earnest men are so few in the world that their very earnestness becomes at once the badge of their nobility; and as men in a crowd instinctively make room for one who seems eager to force his way through it, so mankind everywhere open their ranks to one who rushes zealously toward some object lying beyond them.

MOUNT upward! Heaven is won by prayer.
Be sober, for you are not there! *John Keble.*

WANT OF DECISION.

Sidney Smith.

A GREAT deal of labor is lost to the world for the want of a little courage. Every day sends to their graves a number of obscure men, who have only remained in obscurity because their timidity has prevented them from making a first effort, and who, if they had only been induced to begin, would in all probability have gone great lengths in the career of fame. The fact is, that in doing anything in the world worth doing, we must not stand shivering on the bank, thinking of the cold and danger, but jump in, and scramble through as well as we can. It will not do to be perpetually calculating risks and adjusting nice chances; it did all very well before the flood, when a man could consult his friends upon an intended publication for a hundred and fifty years, and live to see its success for six or seven centuries afterward; but at present a man waits and doubts, and consults his brother, and uncles, and his particular friends, till one day he finds that he is sixty-five years of age, and that he has lost so much time in consulting first cousins and particular friends, that he has no more time to follow their advice. There is so little time for over-squeamishness at present, that the opportunity slips away. The very period of life at which a man chooses to venture, if ever, is so confined that it is no bad rule to preach up the necessity, in such instances, of a little violence done to the feelings, and efforts made in defiance of strict and sober calculations.

WHAT I admire in Columbus, is not his having discovered a world, but his having gone to search for it on the faith of an opinion. *Turgot.*

DON'T BE DISCOURAGED.

IF a man loses his property at thirty or forty years of age, it is only a sharp discipline generally, by which later he comes to large success. If is all folly for a man or woman to sit down in mid-life discouraged. The marshals of Napoleon came to their commander and said: "We have lost the battle and. we are being cut to pieces." Napoleon took his watch from his pocket, and said: "It is only two o'clock in the afternoon. You have lost the battle, but we have time to win another. Charge upon the foe!" Let our readers who have been unsuccessful thus far in the battle of life not give up in despair. With energy and God's blessing they may yet win a glorious victory.—*Anonymous.*

INFLUENCE.

Charles Dickens.

THERE is nothing—no, nothing—beautiful and good, that dies and is forgotten. An infant, a prattling child, dying in its cradle, will live again in the better thoughts of those who loved it, and play its part, though its body be burned to ashes or drowned in the deepest sea. There is not an angel added to the hosts of heaven, but does its blessed work on earth in those who loved it here. Dead! Oh, if the good deeds of human creatures could be traced to their source, how beautiful would even death appear! for how much charity, mercy and purified affection would be seen to have their growth in dusty graves!

EARTHLY INFLUENCE.

Thomas Carlyle.

IT is a high, solemn, almost awful thought for every individual man, that his earthly influence, which has a commencement, will never, through all ages, have an end! What is done is done, has already blended itself with the boundless, ever-living, ever-working universe, and will work there for good or evil, openly or secretly, throughout all the time. The life of every man is as the well-spring of a stream, whose small beginnings are indeed plain to all, but whose course and destination, as it winds through the expanses of infinite years, only the Omniscient can discern.

Will it mingle with the neighboring rivulets as a tributary, or receive them as their sovereign? We know not: only in either case we know its path is to the great ocean; its waters, were they but a handful, are *here* and cannot be annihilated or permanently held back.

―――――

POWER OF INFLUENCE.

F. W. Faber.

OUR many deeds, the thoughts that we have thought,
  They go out from us thronging every hour;
  And in them all is folded up a power
That on the earth doth move them to and fro;
And mighty are the marvels they have wrought,
In hearts we know not, and may never know.

THE POWER OF INFLUENCE.

INFLUENCE is the power we exert over others by our thoughts, words, and actions—by our lives, in short. It is a silent, a pervading, a magnetic, and a most wonderful thing. It works in inexplicable ways. We neither see nor hear it, yet, consciously or unconsciously, we exert it. No one can think or speak, or act— no one can live—without influencing others. We all sometimes seem unconscious of this very important fact, and appear to have adopted the strange idea that what we do, or think, or say, can affect no one but ourselves. You influence others and mould their characters and destinies for time and for eternity far more extensively than you imagine. The whole truth in this matter might flatter you; it would certainly astonish you if you could once grasp it in its full proportions. It was a remark of Samuel J. Mills that "No young man should live in the nineteenth century without making his influence felt around the globe." At first thought that seems a heavy contract for any young man to take. As we come to apprehend more clearly the immutable laws of God's moral universe we find that this belting of the globe by his influence is just what every responsible being does—too often, alas, unconsciously. You have seen the telephone, that wonderful instrument which so accurately transmits the sound of the human voice so many miles. How true it is that all these wonderful modern inventions are only faint reflections of some grand and eternal law of the moral universe of God! God's great telephone—I say it reverently—is everywhere—filling earth and air and sea, and sending round the world with unerring accuracy, and for a blessing or a curse, every thought of your heart, every word that falls thoughtfully or thoughtlessly from your lips, and every act you do. It is time you awoke to the conviction that, whether you would have it so or not, your influence is world-wide for good or for evil. Which?

There is another immense fact which you or I may as well look squarely in the face. *An influence never dies.* Once born it lives forever. In one of his lyrics, Longfellow beautifully illustrates this great truth:

> " I shot an arrow in the air,
> It fell to earth, I knew not where;
> * * * * *
> I breathed a song into the air,
> It fell on earth, I knew not where;
> * * * * *
> Long, long afterwards, in an oak
> I found the arrow, still unbroke;
> And the song, from beginning to end,
> I found again in the heart of a friend."

No thought, no word, no act of man ever dies. They are as immortal as his own soul. He will be sure to find them written somewhere. Somewhere in this world he will meet their fruits in part; somewhere in the future life he will meet their gathered harvest. It may, and it may not, be a pleasant one to look upon.

An influence not only lives for ever, but it keeps on growing as long as it lives. There never comes a time when it reaches its maturity and when its growth is arrested. The influence which you start into life to-day in the family, the neighborhood, or the social circle, is perhaps very small now, very little cared for now; but it will roll forward through the ages, growing wider and deeper and stronger with every passing hour, and blighting or blessing as it rolls.—*Christian Weekly.*

PERPETUITY OF INFLUENCE.

J. G. Whittier.

NOTHING fails of its end. Out of sight sinks the stone,
In the deep sea of time, but the circles sweep on,
Till the low-rippled murmurs along the shores run,
And the dark and dead waters leap glad in the sun.

DOING GOOD.

Richard Penrose.

LET some noble deed be thine
   Before the day is ended;
   Ere the sun doth cease to shine,
Ere on thy bed thou dost recline,
Go where the fevered brow doth pine,
And see its wants attended,
And learn that in its restless dream
It craves the pure and limpid stream,
And know that in its fitful madness
It drains the cooling draught with gladness;
And the parched lips will bless thee
For the deed of kindness shown,
While some other tongue will tell thee
'Twas not done to one alone;
For an Eye that never sleepeth
Beheld the action from his throne.

Let some tearful eye be dried
Before the day is ended;

DOING GOOD.

Take the wanderer to thy side,
But his sad folly ne'er deride;
A multitude of sins thou'lt hide,
In some poor soul befriended,
And learn that in his reckless race
Ofttimes the pathway he will trace
To some harsh words, unkindly spoken,
And which his sobbing heart hath broken;
Pour the balm of consolation;
While the listening ear is shown,
Wound it not by ostentation;
Do thy Master's work alone,
Remembering He ever keepeth
A faithful record on his throne.

Let some hungry child be fed
Before the day is ended;
Go! the orphan cries for bread,
Where squalor reigns in all its dread,
And where the widow's mournful tread
Should with thy steps be blended,
And see where vile and misery haunt,
Where shriveled babe and woman gaunt
Are stretched on beds where filth is reeking,
And tottering age with ruffians greeting;
Perhaps a word of thine may cheer
Some sad heart whose hope had flown,
And bid it cast aside its fear
For a love before unknown,
Seeking Him who ever meeteth
A suppliant at Mercy's throne.

SYMPATHY NOT LOST.

THE look of sympathy; the gentle word,
　　Spoken so low that only angels heard;
　　The secret art of pure self-sacrifice,
Unseen by men, but marked by angel's eyes;
　　　　These are not lost.

The sacred music of a tender strain,
Wrung from a poet's heart by grief and pain,
And chanted timidly, with doubt and fear,
To busy crowds, who scarcely pause to hear:
　　　　This is not lost.

The silent tears that fall at dead of night
Over soiled robes that once were pure and white;
The prayers that rise like incense from the soul,
Longing for Christ to make it clean and whole:
　　　　These are not lost.

The happy dreams that gladdened all our youth,
When dreams had less of self and more of truth;
The childhood's faith, so tranquil and so sweet,
Which sat like Mary at the Master's feet:
　　　　These are not lost.

The kindly plans devised for others' good,
So seldom guessed, so little understood:

The quiet, steadfast love that strove to win
Some wanderer from the ways of sin;
   These are not lost.

Not lost, O Lord! for in thy city bright
Our eyes shall see the past by clearer light,
And things long hidden from our gaze below
Thou wilt reveal, and we shall surely know
   They were not lost.—*Anonymous.*

TRIALS.

TRIALS come in a thousand different forms, and as many avenues are open to their approach. They come from physical appetites, æsthetic tastes, social habits, bodily ills, the desire for gain, the love of luxury and of ease. They come through every contact with the unrenewed mind of the world, and from the assaults of Satan. They come with the warm throbbings of our youthful lives, keep pace with the measured tread of manhood's noon, and depart not from the descending footsteps of decrepitude and age. "Lead us not into temptation," should ever remind us of our utter weakness and absolute dependence upon Almighty support. But we may not hope to be entirely free from either disciplinary trial or the fiery darts of the enemy, until we reach that land into which shall enter nothing that deceiveth or maketh a lie.

"Courage, my soul; thy bitter cross
 In every trial here,
 Shall bear thee to thy heaven above,
 But shall not enter there."
       —*Anonymous.*

TRIALS, A TEST OF CHARACTER.

Wm. Morley Punshon, LL.D.

VAIN are all the efforts of slander, *permanently* to injure the fame of a good man! There is a cascade in a lovely Swiss valley which the fierce winds catch and scatter so soon as it pours over the summit of the rock, and for a season the continuity of the fall is broken, and you see nothing but a feathery wreath of apparently helpless spray; but if you look further down the consistency is recovered, and the Staubbach pours its rejoicing waters as if no breeze had blown at all. Nay, the blast which interrupts it only fans it into more marvelous loveliness, and makes it a shrine of beauty where all pilgrim footsteps travel. And so the blasts of calumny, howl they ever so fiercely over the good man's head, contribute to his juster appreciation and to his wider fame. What are circumstances,—I wonder, that they should hinder a true man when his heart is set within him to do a right thing! Let a man be firmly principled in his religion, he may travel from the tropics to the poles, it will never catch cold on the journey. Set him down in the desert, and just as the palm tree thrusts its roots beneath the envious sand in search of sustenance, he will manage somehow to find living water there. Banish him to the dreariest Patmos you can find, he will get a grand Apocalypse among its barren crags. Thrust him into an inner prison, and make his feet fast in the stocks, the doxology will reverberate through the dungeon, making such melody within its walls of stone that the jailer shall relapse into a man, and the prisoners hearing it shall dream of freedom and of home.

ELEMENTS OF SUCCESS IN LIFE.

A. D. F.

MANY brilliant students gather into our seminary halls who disappoint the ardent hopes of friends. One of the most prominent sources of failure is a trust in genius, and a forgetting the necessities of labor. In my seminary days I remember few students who gave promise of success, but that prated of genius, and relied upon genius as a power that was to carry them, as poets, as lawyers, as preachers, up to the world's gaze, and no doubt many an old student is plodding in the dust to-day who is just beginning to find out that what we call genius was only an *ignis fatuus*. A *desire* to be somewhat, was mistaken for the *power* to do. They are just beginning to find out that desire; that ardent aspiration is not power, and we are beginning to go to the true sources of strength. Years are wasted, but it may not yet be too late, O ardent-souled alumnus, to rise! "Shut a man alone from the world, bookless and friendless, he will write thoughts of power." That *was* my faith · now I receive as my creed the thought that the truest genius is the genius of hard work. In most cases what is termed bright-eyed genius, is the student's evil genius, the real siren that sings amid the rocks along the student's sail-way to deceive his soul into false hopes! O oblivion! oblivion! how many brilliant students hast thou embosomed in thy waters, who verily thought the lightness of their bodies would carry them gaily on the stream, forgetting that all people must make endeavor to swim, or else consent to sink beneath thy silent waves!

We read the lives of poets, learning how they wrote, but seek no power for ourselves, and write no poetry. We become inspired by the lives of heroes, but perform no heroic acts. We listen to tales of the miners concerning the riches of the inner world, and vainly dream that these are to come at our bidding, but we delve not in the mines. The most common kind of originality and genius is that which makes good use of ideas, let them come from what source they may. Genius is the power which makes good use of knowledge, and presents old truths in a new light. In each new adjustment the kaleidoscope exhibits new beauties; so the true man, with ardent study, adjusts and re-adjusts old thoughts, and what we call genius is, as the country parson has it, the "successful putting of hings." If one would be a true poet, or orator, he must have matter, and to get this he must leave for awhile these poets and these poets' lives, and go down into the under-world, and behold the foundation of things. He must study the first principles of wisdom, strict reasonings on the human mind, the deep and momentous truths of the past world, histories, antiquities, and philosophy. He must leave, for a season, the floating chimeras of the upper world, and search the hidden depths of truth ; must dive deep into his own heart and there trace motives and desires, and when he is an adept there he may come above ground and stalk abroad among the stupendous realities of the world.

The idea of study does not demand that we shall always be poring over books. A man may study as he lolls over a fish-pole, or lies beneath a tree. Under such circumstances, often, a man's best thoughts come to him. Because a man to whom we have accorded genius dashes off at times great things, is no sign there was no forethought. Impromptu thoughts are generally fruits of seeds before sown. The dashing off of a fine poem is often only the outbursting of a volcano that has long been seething, or the overflow of a dam that has long been collecting. The mighty river, which seems to have within itself the elements of an eternal flow, would soon dry up were it not ever fed by the founts and the rains all along its course. It only pours into the ocean waters it has gathered from a thousand sources.

Alas, for the many brilliant young ministers that fade after the first impulses of feeling are calmed! I hardly remember one brilliant young preacher that in the end has amounted to anything. But the plodders, the workers, are the ones that rise and take position. The first blaze out like meteors, and soon are lost in shade; the second by steady step make slow but sure footsteps on to success.

But while matter and power are, in great measure, things of acquirement, it is true that peculiarities of nature or experience give a tinge to all the outgoings of our talents. This peculiar *tone* of the soul is what all the time we have been mistaking for genius. The spirit of earnestness should give tone to every effort, or it will be like a tinking cymbal. Whatever we would do well, we must not only do with our intellect, but with our souls. Our preachings should emanate from the brain, and pass through the warm blood of the heart to the tongue. Some of the sweetest strains of poetry, and the most pathetic peals of oratory have emanated from souls tinged by the mellow hues of sorrow. A man's own life and heart-movings will make an impress on all he does. Can a poet or orator paint remorse who has never been in despair? Can he who has never been bereaved, utter true words of sympathy in a parent's ear as that parent weeps over the tomb? True poetry possesses a kind of divine despair—can a heart pour it forth that has never known the divine frenzy?

> "The grape must be crushed before
> Can be gathered the glorious wine;
> So the poet's heart must be wrung to the core
> Ere his song can be divine."

ELEMENTS OF SUCCESS IN LIFE.

Have you read Poe's Raven—that grandest American poem, which with a weird power deals with the most momentous hopes of a human soul? Poe has printed a statement that the poem was the result of mechanical effort; but to a friend who related to me the fact, Poe communicated what we are ready to receive as a truth, the statement that the poem is a recital of a real experience when within him hope was in terrible conflict with despair, in which conflict, alas! despair comes off victor. Poe's talents, not his genius, wrote the Raven; Poe's heart, with anguish wrung, gave it its peculiar pathos.   .   .   .   .

When Summerfield was on his dying bed, he exclaimed, "Oh, if I might be raised again, how I could preach; I could preach as I never have preached before; I have had a look into eternity."

One more truth let me impress upon you, namely: There is little greatness that is worth the name, that is not founded upon and accompanied by sound, moral, Christian principle. How poor, how vain, how unreliable the acquirements of men, if no religious principle gives tone to the impulses! How many have I known who gave brilliant promise, who have dazzled only to disappoint us because beneath all outside grandeur there was the cankering influence of a corrupt heart. Mankind have two wings—one the love of woman, the other faith in religion; the breaking of either will leave a man an unsymmetrical, lop-sided creature. One of the most common errors we fall into in our ardent vigor and youthful wisdom, is to throw aside religion as a thing beneath us, forgetting it is a thing about and above us.   .   .   .   .

Our free-school system, the maker of innumerable men; our colleges, the conservators of a higher style of thought; our charters of liberty—all that we extol in our land, are outgrowths of Christian principle, or off springs of Christian hearts. Wherever the star-spangled banner with its star-gems, like angel-eyes peering down as watching sentinels, has waved, there, though often invisible, has waved the banner of the Cross, bearing aloft the noble sentence, *Through this conquer!*

All the callings of life have need of men; and men are found in all the callings of life. If you ask what places are vacant in professional life, I answer there are plenty of vacant places on the higher seats. There are plenty of common lawyers; there are a plenty of ordinary physicians; there is an over-stock of mediocre preachers, but those who stand on the higher platforms are few. The hill of fame which, in some sense, is synonymous with the hill of success, is a tall and tapering cone, having, like pictorial representations of the temple of Belus at Babylon, a pathway winding round and round, terrace above terrace, upward. Crowds set out for the top and along the lower terraces multitudes crowd the way; but as you look up the company becomes thinner, till we behold a few daring strugglers going up, up, up! and a still smaller number standing on the apex. Friends, if you are in want of places, go up to the higher terraces of the pyramid of success. Alexander Selkirk, on his lonely isle, could easily sing,

"I am monarch of all I survey,"

For he could also sing,

"My right there is none to dispute."

But an alumnus of to-day goes forth to join in the struggle with one hundred thousand students who are striving to get upon the thrones! Yet, nevertheless, there is always room on the higher seats, and again I say, go up!

PRESS on! for it is God-like to unloose the spirit and forget yourself in thought. *N. P. Willis.*

AMBITION.

AMBITION, the greatest incentive to advancement and civilization; the greatest teacher of morality and wisdom; the foundation of truth and virtue, and at the same time the instrument of crime and iniquity; the instigator of intemperance and rashness; is divided into two classes, godly and ungodly, the latter of which was created in Heaven.

We suppose that Heaven is a place of eternal bliss and happiness, and we have no reason to think otherwise, yet we learn from the Bible that God allowed Satan, who was once an angel in Heaven, to be subjected to temptation. For what reason we know not, and it is not expedient for us to dwell upon the propriety of such an act, unless we may become skeptical. We are not competent to criticise the doings of our Maker. It is simply for us to know that Satan was the sad victim of this ungodly ambition. He was so ambitious that he desired to be upon a level with God, and on account of his sin he was cast out of Heaven into everlasting darkness.

When Adam and Eve were created, Satan, who had become a bitter enemy to God, commenced to go about the earth with the malicious determination of robbing Heaven of the sons of men. He first came to Eve, the weaker of the two in the garden of "Eden," with the same stumbling-block over which he fell. He well knew that if the angels in Heaven were not able to resist such a temptation, Eve would certainly yield to that which would cause her own destruction. And great was the success of his first temptation which he threw upon the path of mankind, for Eve, burning with the eager desire of being a goddess, ate with Adam the forbidden fruit, and fell.

Hence this ambition, which was created in Heaven, and transported to earth, has passed down along the generations until it has attained its height.

Alexander, who sat down and wept because he had no more worlds to conquer, was cursed with this ambition. He fought with no higher principles than the love of glory, and military honors. He fought not so much in the defense of his country, but went into foreign lands and burned cities, made widows and orphans, and robbed proud mothers of their sons, to satisfy the thirst for fame.

Cæsar was upon the same footing with Alexander, in this respect, and thousands of others have lived, and thousands live to-day who are the unfortunate possessors of this ambition.

There is no lack of such examples. We know that the harvest of just ambition is success. She laughs at discouragements. Instead of being weakened by misfortunes, she is strengthened. The way to success may be strewn with impediments, but have ambition as your guide and she will clear the way of all obstacles.

The height of ambition is Heaven. It was the intention of our Maker that this world should be a world of probation. We were not created to live and die as do the inferior animals, but we have been born for a higher and a nobler state. Although we are desirous of leaving a blank at our death, which the world cannot fill; yet to what does all this amount? Life is short at the longest,—a moment compared to eternity. Then when we are ambitious for the things pertaining to this life, let us not forget the great hereafter.

THE drying up a single tear has more
    Of honest fame than shedding seas of gore. *Byron.*

A WORTHY AMBITION.

John B. Gough.

YOUNG man! if God has given you brains, heart and voice, speak out. There are great reforms to be carried on. The whole nation needs awakening. Speak out, sir, and your speech will be welcome, wherever and on whatever particular branch of reforms you choose to make yourself heard. Lift up your voice for that which is "honest, lovely and of good report." Not in mere wordy harangue, not in windy palaver, not in grandiloquent spouting, nor in weary, drawling verbosity—not in the jabbering garrulity which is heard only when the speaker must be delivered of a speech. But in words of true, sanctified earnestness, opening your mouth because you have something useful to say, saying it with the genuine, unstudied eloquence which comes right from the heart, and in all cases closing your mouth the moment you have done.

IT is not what men eat but what they digest, that makes them strong; not what we gain, but what we save that makes us rich; not what men read, but what they remember that makes them learned; and not what we preach but what we practise that makes us Christians. These are great but common truths, often forgotten by the glutton, the spendthrift, the book-worm and the hypocrite. *Lord Bacon.*

WE have not wings—we cannot soar,
    But we have feet to scale and climb,
By slow degrees, by more and more,
    The cloudy summits of our time. *Longfellow.*

MAKE HOME LIFE BEAUTIFUL.

Prof. B. G. Northrop.

LET me say to parents: Make the home-life beautiful, without and within, and they will sow the seeds of gentleness, true kindness, honesty, and fidelity in the hearts of their children, from which the children reap a harvest of happiness and virtue. The memory of the beautiful and happy home of childhood is the richest legacy any man can leave to his children. The heart will never forget its hallowed influences. It will be an evening enjoyment, to which the lapse of years will only add new sweetness. Such a home is a constant inspiration for good and as constant a restraint from evil.

If by taste and culture we adorn our homes and grounds and add to their charms, our children will find the quiet pleasures of rural homes more attractive than the whirl of city life. Such attractions and enjoyments will invest home-life, school-life, the whole future of life with new interests and with new dignity and joyousness, for life is just what we make it. We may by our blindness live in a world of darkness and gloom, or in a world full of sunlight and beauty and joy; for the world without only reflects the world within. Also the tasteful improvement of grounds and home exerts a good influence not only upon the inmates, but upon the community. An elegant dwelling, surrounded by sylvan attractions, is a contribution to the refinement, the good order, the taste, and prosperity of every community, improving the public taste and ministering to every enjoyment. On the other hand, people who are content to dwell in huts and cellars grow barbarous in their ideas. They become dirty and ragged in their dress, uncouth in manner, coarse in habits, brutal in character, without aspiration for a better life. There can be no progress in civilization but improvement in their homes and grounds accompanies, if it does not directly produce the advance in civilization. Improvements, a beautiful village, a fine park, are effective instruments of civilization and education, and there is protection, as well as education, in a fervent love of improvement, with its multitude of associations. Attachment to one's native soil is an antidote to the restless, roaming, and migratory spirit of our youth, as well as safe-guard from temptation. Nobody without local attachment can have genuine patriotism.

WOMAN AT HOME.

T. De Witt Talmage.

THANK God, O woman! for the quietude of your home, and that you are queen in it. Men come at eventide to the home; but all day long you are there, beautifying it, sanctifying it, adorning it, blessing it. Better be there than wear Victoria's coronet. Better be there than carry the purse of a princess. It may be a very humble home. There may be no carpet on the floor. There may be no pictures on the wall. There may be no silks in the wardrobe; but, by your faith in God, and your cheerful demeanor, you may garniture that place with more splendor than the upholsterer's hand ever kindled.

To be womanly is the greatest charm of woman.
Gladstone.

THE HOMESTEAD.

Phœbe Cary.

FROM the old squire's dwelling, gloomy and grand,
Stretching away on either hand,
Lie fields of broad and fertile land.

Acres on acres everywhere
The look of smiling plenty wear,
That tells of the master's thoughtful care.

Here blossoms the clover, white and red,
Here the heavy oats in a tangle spread,
And the millet lifts her golden head;

And, ripening, closely neighbored by
Fields of barley and pale white rye,
The yellow wheat grows strong and high.

And near, untried through the summer days,
Lifting their spears in the sun's fierce blaze,
Stand the bearded ranks of the maize.

Straying over the side of the hill,
Here the sheep run to and fro at will,
Nibbling of short green grass their fill.

Sleek cows down the pasture take their ways,
Or lie in the shade through the sultry days,
Idle, and too full-fed to graze.

THE HOMESTEAD.

Ah! you might wander far and wide,
Nor find a spot in the country's side
So fair to see as our valley's pride!

How, just beyond, if it will not tire
Your feet to climb this green knoll higher,
We can see the pretty village spire;

And, mystic haunt of the whippoorwills,
The wood, that all the background fills,
Crowning the tops to the mill-creek hills.

There, miles away, like a faint blue line,
Whenever the day is clear and fine,
You can see the track of a river shine.

Near it a city hides unseen,
Shut close the verdant hills between,
As an acorn set in its cup of green.

And right beneath, at the foot of the hill,
The little creek flows swift and still,
That turns the wheel of Dovecote mill.

Nearer the grand old house one sees
Fair rows of thrifty apple-trees,
And tall straight pears o'ertopping these.

And down at the foot of the garden, low,
On a rustic bench, a pretty show,
White bee-hives, standing in a row.

Here trimmed in sprigs, with blossoms, each
Of the little bees in easy reach,
Hang the boughs of the plum and peach.

THE HOMESTEAD.

At the garden's head are poplars tall,
And peacocks, making their harsh, loud call,
Sun themselves all day on the wall.

And here you will find on every hand
Walks and fountains and statues grand,
And trees from many a foreign land.

And flowers, that only the learned can name,
Here glow and burn like a gorgeous flame,
Putting the poor man's blooms to shame.

Far away from their native air
The Norway pines their green dress wear;
And larches swing their long, loose hair.

Near the porch grows the broad catalpa tree,
And o'er it the grand wistaria
Born to the purple of royalty.

There looking the same for a weary while—
'Twas built in this heavy, gloomy style—
Stands the mansion, a grand old pile.

Always closed, as it is to-day,
And the proud squire, so the neighbors say,
Frowns each unwelcome guest away.

Though some, who knew him long ago,
If you ask, will shake their heads of snow,
And tell you he was not always so,

Though grave and quiet at any time,
But that now, his head in manhood's prime,
Is growing white as the winter's rime.

HOME.

T. De Witt Talmage.

IF you wanted to gather up all tender memories, all lights and shadows of the heart, all banquetings and reunions, all filial, fraternal, paternal, conjugal affections, and had only just four letters with which to spell out that height and depth and length and breadth and magnitude and eternity of meaning, you would write it all out with these four capital letters: H-O-M-E.

THE POWER OF KINDNESS.

Wm. Morley Punshon, LL.D.

HUNGER and want are conditions surely of extremest need, and a word of kindness in such a strait is welcome as the smile of an angel, for it may redeem from hopelessness and despair, and a helpful hand-grasp, with something in the hand the while, is worth a hundredfold its cost, for it may have ransomed for all future time the most kingly thing on earth, *the manhood of a man*, for industry, and society and God.

RULE OF CONDUCT.

Seneca.

I WILL govern my life and my thoughts, as if the whole world were to see the one and read the other; for what does it signify, to make anything a secret to my neighbor, when to God (who is the searcher of our hearts) all our privacies are open!

FIRESIDE MUSINGS.

Ada A. Chaffee.

SITTING where the fitful firelight
    Shines and glimmers on the wall,
    Listening to the ceaseless patter
  Of the raindrops as they fall,
Musing like an idle dreamer
    While the moments come and go,
Weaving fancies sad and tender
    Into *now* and long ago.

Fire! oh tell me, am I sitting
    Lowly at the Master's feet,
With a filial heart accepting
    Joy and sorrow, bitter, sweet!
Sitting where, perchance, a mission
    Is to shed one little ray
For a beacon to some pilgrim
    Groping for the heavenly way!

Falling raindrops! tell me, tell me,
    Do I heed the still, small voice?
Listening to the call of duty?
    In the Saviour's love rejoice?
Listening to another's sorrow,
    With a hope to soothe the pain!
Do I scatter love and sunshine
    As the clouds the falling rain!

FIRESIDE MUSINGS.

Roving thought! oh, whither, whither,
    In thy musings dost thou speed?
To some brother weary, toiling,
    That perhaps of aid has need?
Seeking out the spirit wand'ring?
    Culling tares from golden grain?
Pondering on Christ's example,
    That this life be not in vain?

Child of earth! say, art thou weaving
    In the tangled web of life
Something *more* than tender fancies—
    Strength to brave the coming strife?
Weaving in each little duty,
    Better far than wordly fame,
Weaving patience, love, forbearance,
    Humbly in the Saviour's name?

Would that we were ever sitting
    Where we'd shed a steady light,
Listening to the voice of conscience,
    Constant, always to the right;
Musing on that better country,
    Free from sorrow, care, or blight,
Where we'll weave our heav'nly fancies
    If while *here* we weave aright.

THE voices that spoke to me when a child, are now speaking through me to the world.   *Bishop Simpson.*

I WOULD rather be right than be President.   *Henry Clay.*

A PLEA FOR HOME.

Theodore L. Cuyler, D.D.

NOW that the long winter evenings have come again it is a good time to put it in a plea for *home*. This is the seeding season for the mind. We have sometimes thought that one reason why the Scottish people are such readers and so many of their humblest cottagers have taken high rank intellectually is that their winter evenings are so prodigiously long and afford such opportunities for study.

There is no country in the globe—not even excepting Britain—which contains more happy and cultured homes than our own. The Germans make much of their domestic life, observing birthdays, weddings, anniversaries, etc., with abundant merry-makings. The French love cafés and crowds. They have not the word "home" in their language and not enough of the thing itself in their social existence. After peeping into some of the smoky, ill-furnished chalets of Switzerland this year, I could not but feel a new pride and satisfaction in the homes of the American laborers and small farmers. Some of the brightest and richest homes in our land are found under the low, broad roof of the Yankee farm-house. Look in a moment at the group which glows in the blaze of the hickory fire. The old father is running the sharp coulter of his mind through a tough volume of science or theology or politics as steadily as he put his plow through a stiff sod last summer. Mother lays down her knitting to read a letter from the tall son at Yale or Williams or Dartmouth; perhaps a letter from a missionary daughter in the Orient or another who is settled in a Colorado parsonage. A stack of books loads the center-table. There is an antique "sampler" on the walls, which dear old grandma worked when she was sweet sixteen. One of the younger girls touches a lively tune from the piano before the winter evening is over. One of the older lads gets back from the singing-school or an apple-bee in time for family prayers. The old family Bible—with its chronicle of wedlock and births and burials—is read devoutly; and prayer puts its strong *hem* around the finished day's work.

This is no mere fancy picture. The real wealth and stability and virtue and future hope of our republic lie in just such homes of industry and honest thrift. The best society roots there. The church of God has its roots there too. If thousands of our young men in the rural regions truly appreciated the quiet joys and blessings of having such a home for themselves and their children, they would not be in such hot haste to rush off to the large towns to "seek their fortunes" and find only a precarious clerkship and a cold fourth-story room in a boarding-house. If our humble voice would be heard and heeded, we would take up Horace Greeley's old refrain and cry aloud: "Stay out of the cities! They are too full already." And of nothing are they more full than of evil haunts, broken expectations, lost characters, and ruined lives. But young men of ambition will pour into the cities in spite of all our notes of warning. Employers have a duty to them also which is too seldom discharged. It is the duty of thinking about the young clerk, or salesman, or book-keeper, when the store, the office, or the counting-room is locked up. Those young men must either have a home or a—haunt. Their evenings must be spent somewhere. The devil will light up his decoy-lamps all over town. Now cannot our rich employers occasionally invite the young men in their employ to their own residences, and thus strengthen their own influence and put in a new tether to hold their young "wards" to personal and

A PLEA FOR HOME.

social purity! There are no more thoroughly homeless class than the thousands of youths from the country; none appreciate more a friendly invitation to the table or the fireside of a pleasant home. Church sociables, prayer meetings, Young Men's Christian Associations, lectures, libraries, etc., are all excellent in their way. But no one of them exactly fills the aching void and satisfies the hunger for a glimpse of *home*.

Business men themselves need to be nudged, too, in regard to the claims of home and household. Many of them live in an atmosphere of excitement and bake their daily bread in a very hot oven. Many of you need the soothing sedative and cooling of the mind which only a quiet home can give. When affairs go prosperously with you, here is an outlet for a portion of your gains. Make your own homes attractive. Indulge yourself in the luxury of cheerful, open fires, instead of black flues in the floor. A glowing open fire is a "means of grace" to the children. It makes a bright rallying-point for the whole family. Tom will not be so anxious to run off to the theater, and Mary will not be so hungry for an invitation to the ball or the opera, and all the children will feel the visible influence of one warm, cheerful heart-shrine. Before that fire spend as many evenings as you can. If a bad day's business has made you sore and unhappy, let your daughter's piano be to your ruffled spirit what David's harp was to the distempered mind of Saul. Watch your boy as he piles his blocks on the carpet, and see how easy it is to topple over the most ambitious structures when they get out of the *perpendicular*. Learn the lesson of some of your own failures from it, and how to begin again and pile better. A good romp with your children or a half-hour with them over their lessons will make them love you the more, and will expel many a "blue devil" that found entrance into you during the day.

To have such a home you must make it. The husband who forsakes his household for his evening haunts elsewhere does not deserve to have a home in this world; he materially lessens his hope for a good home in eternity. Beshrew all clubs! Every true wife hates the very name of them. She is jealous of such rivals with a "godly jealousy." If there was a righteous uprising of indignant wives to make a clean conflagration of every club-house and drinking-haunt in our cities, I should esteem it a noble exercise of "women's rights" that ought not to provoke the interference of the fire department.

God meant, when he made us, that we should live in families. It is the only way that the two sexes can come together without impairing virtue and purity. There is no such school of true religion on the globe as a happy, God-fearing home. No church is so effective for restraint from evil and for growth in all graces as "the church in the *house*." There stands the domestic altar. There speaks the word of truth and authority on every day in the whole seven. There is felt a religion which acts and molds from the cradle clear on to the judgment-seat. It is a nursery for the noblest life. It is the earliest, the best, the surest preparation for the Home not made with hands, eternal in the heavens.

MAKE SOME ONE HAPPY.

T. DeWitt Talmage.

THAT is a good day in which you make some one happy. It is astonishing how little it takes to make one happy. Feel that the day is wasted in which you have not succeeded in this.

MAN's best powers point him Godward.

Spurgeon.

THE TRIALS OF HOME.

W. K. Tweedie, D.D.

"Sorrowing yet always rejoicing."

WHEN the first death happens in a home it speaks with a voice which scarcely any other form of tribulation can equal. We read of wars, and battles, and thousands slain, but even these are far-off echoes to most, compared with our own first death. That blow falls upon the very heart, and though faith may enable even a mother to close the dying eye of her little one, and smile through her tears, exclaiming—

"My Saviour, I do this for thee;"

yet nature may be wrung with anguish, even while grace enables the tried one to triumph.

And the pang is often rendered more acute, or the stroke more severe, by the inscrutable mystery of a little infant's death. Why the terrible convulsions? Why that low wail—that smothered cry far worse for the parent to bear than a blow? Why that little frame pining slowly away, while skill is baffled in its attempts to discover the cause? Why is every breath a sigh or a moan, till even a mother sometimes flees from the sight and the sound, and feels that it would be a relief could her little sufferer die? And when all is over—when the little one is coffined, and the marble dust is about to be borne to the tomb, why that death at all? That little hand never did sin; that little heart never thought sin; and why, then, this living only to die—this infant shroud, that infant coffin and grave? Have my sins, a parent may ask, brought down this woe? Is this the inquity of the fathers visited on the children?

Of this, at least, we are sure, "death passes upon all, for that all have sinned." "In Adam all die." Thus God shows the mystery, and bids us, when we cannot understand, be silent and adore. What we know not now, we shall know hereafter; and though our rifled homes may cause the heart to ache, yet if such bereavements urge the parents more sedulously to prepare for glory, the present tribulation will deepen and prolong the future hosannas of the tried. And nature may symbolically teach us the same lesson. When we enter a mist cloud as it drifts or hovers along the mountain-side which we are climbing, it sometimes dissolves around us so that the sunshine becomes undimmed. In like manner, if not here, at least hereafter, all the mist clouds will clear away from before the parent who believes. Concerning his children torn from his embrace to the tomb, he may learn to say,—

"For us they sicken and for us they die."

Meanwhile, could parents remember that they are encountering their cares, and weeping their tears, and bearing their cross, and seeing their hopes deferred to-day, or blighted to-morrow, while attempting to train their children for God, they would be stimulated to persevere, and not "faint in their minds."

But there is one form of grief more intense than even this. The trials which crowd our homes are numerous, and no doubt, one of the reasons may be that some would make their home their heaven. Their affections center there; and their family is the Alpha and Omega of their exertions, their joys, and their hopes. Now to prevent such idolatry, a thorn is often placed in the nest, and men find labor and sorrow where they expected only sunshine and smiles. There may be poverty, and that is bitter, or some dis-after may threaten to strip our homes bare, but it is when trials assume the character of retributions that they convulse a household the most. It was hard for David to know that Absalom was no more; and that he perished a rebel against his king and father, made the pang more poignant still. But if that father associated that death with his own home misdeeds, his sorrow would be the most acute that man is doomed to feel. His touching wail, his characteristic Oriental outcry over his lost son, thus acquires a deeper meaning than before. "Would God I had died for thee," becomes not merely pathetic but profound. And that is the climax of all anguish—to see an object of affection go down, we fear, to a darker home than the grave. It is sad for a widowed one to see the delight of her eyes, the husband of her youth, snatched away by death. It is agony to an affectionate family to see the mother who bore them, and bore with them, carried to the narrow house. But a moral death causes a deeper wound—a more remediless sorrow, and nothing but omnipotent grace can carry a sufferer through such a grief. While he drinks "the wine of astonishment" his solace may be—"It is the Lord," and "the Judge of all the earth will do right." But if the mourner find cause for self-accusation in connection with his grief, his sorrow culminates there, and amid such sadness the nightfall of life may often find us weeping over the errors of its morning. If, on the other hand, our sorrows come directly from another, our solace is more easily found. It will then be the believer's endeavor to be silent where he cannot understand; and while he prays for repentance to the wanderer, he himself will forgive, remembering that he is what he is only by the grace of God.

For all this innumerable company of sorrowers, Christ pronounced the benediction we are speaking of. But we must not limit it to them. "Blessed are they that mourn, *over sin*." Not over its final penalty of perdition, but over the hateful and Christ-wounding thing itself. Genuine sorrow over sin is probably the one heart-grief which commands the tenderest symyathy of Jesus. How tenderly He always treated the penitent—from that weeping woman who bathed His feet, clear on to that dying ruffian who prayed to him from the adjoining cross! There is no heart in the universe that so sympathizes with us when we cry out in contrition as the heart of Calvary's Redeemer. No pain does Jesus look upon so kindly as the pain felt by the conscience over sin committed and the spirit grieved.

Selfishness says: "*Cover* sin," and the sin thus covered up kills like a cancer. Jesus says: "*Confess* sin and I will have mercy. Abandon sin and flee unto me!" And never do we draw so closely to Jesus as when our inmost soul has been wounded by the arrows of conviction, and we have felt what an abominable thing it is to wound our Master in the house of His friends. The only way to obtain peace of mind is to fling ourselves into the arms of Jesus. He never loves us so tenderly as when we lie thus on his bosom—as a child hushes its last sobs on the bosom of its mother. And when we look up into Christ's countenance, and say: "Dear Master, forgive me!" His answer is: "Blessed are they that mourn for sin; they shall be comforted." He is faithful and just to forgive us our sins, and to cleanse us from all unrighteousness.

Blessed are they that mourn; for he who never mourns *never mends.* Compunction, if it is of the godly sort, tends to growth in grace. There are too many dry-eyed Christians in this world. There ought to be more tears of penitence over our neglects of Christ, more tears of sympathy with the afflicted, and more tears of joy over the infinite good things which Jesus brings to us. They that sow in the tears of contrition shall reap in the joys of pardon, and the Saviour's smile. Such tears water the roots of our piety.

Blessed are they that mourn—and *mend!* The ladder to the higher Christian life starts from the dust of self-abasement, but every round in it is a new grasp on Christ.

> " Pining soul ! draw nearer Jesus,
> Come—but come not doubting thus;
> Come, with faith that trusts more freely
> His great tenderness for us.
>
> " If our love were but more simple,
> We should take him at his word;
> And our lives would be all sunshine,
> In the sweetness of our Lord."

SANCTIFIED AFFLICTION

AFFLICTIONS, if sanctified, are good. They ungrasp our hold upon the world, and lift the eye to God. Temptations are good; they make us flee to Christ and cling closer to his hands. Like spies from the enemy of souls they serve to keep us on the alert. Good are our inward conflicts with sin, they make us yearn for heaven. God plucks from us our earthly friends that we may look upon Him as He is—our very best friend. He foils our earthly hopes that we may not fail of the hope of heaven. He plunges us into sorrow here that we may escape the sorrow that is to come. He plants around the tree of pleasure angry briers, that we may be induced to pluck the fruit of the tree of life. He, at times, gives this life a bitter taste only to give a keener relish for the life to come. If sanctified, every trial is a treasure; each wound a scar of glory; each drop of grief will glitter a diamond in the Christian's crown of bliss.

Are our trials sometimes great? Great is our reward. Sometimes the victims of disappointment here are tantalized by the hope of often offered but seldom tasted good. The branches of the tree of life do not withdraw themselves from the hand, and the water of the river of life never retires from the lip.

The mariner in the midst of a storm longs for the break of day. The storm-tossed Christian, too, sometimes feels that his night is long and dark and wearisome. Let him be of good cheer; behind it all is coming up a brighter day. By the eye of faith and the aid of revelation we can already see its streaks. At times we can almost feel the winds of that fresh morning breaking in upon us! Christians, never despond in temptation, nor repine under losses, nor murmur in afflictions. Bear them with a smile, for the eternal joys of heaven far exceed the brief sufferings of earth.

He who was in afflictions, distresses, tumults, labors, who was beaten, stoned, shipwrecked, imprisoned; was in journeyings often, in perils of robbers, in perils in the city, in the wilderness, in the sea; who was in stripes, in prisons, and in deaths often, could say, I take pleasure in infirmities, necessities, reproaches, distresses, and persecutions. Why? For I reckon that the sufferings of this present time are of no account in comparison with the glory hereafter to be revealed in us.

Now could that white-robed company be permitted to speak to us, we should hear them from the heights of bliss exclaim, in triumph, "Weeping may endure for the night, but joy cometh in the morning. The night is already past, the day is at hand. Then lift up your heads, for the time of your redemption draweth nigh."

And from the Captain of our salvation—made perfect through sufferings—there comes the exhortation, "Forasmuch as Christ hath suffered in the flesh, arm yourselves likewise with the same mind; for if you suffer with him, you shall also reign with him. These light afflictions which are but for a moment, work out a far more exceeding and eternal weight of glory!" The cup which my Father giveth me, shall I not drink? "Why should I murmur?" said Henry Martyn, in his last sickness; "weakness, peril, and pain are but the ministering angels whose office it is to conduct me to glory." "Oh, what owe I," says Rutherford, "to the file, to the hammer, to the furnace of my Lord Jesus!"— *Watchman and Reflector.*

I HOLD it true, whate'er befall,
I feel it when I sorrow most—
'Tis better to have loved and lost
Than never to have loved at all.
Alfred Tennyson.

THE stars shall fade away; the sun himself
Grow dim with age, and nature sink in years,
But thou shalt flourish in immortal youth,
Unhurt amidst the war of elements,
The wreck of matter and the crush of worlds.
Robert Pollock.

DEATH'S but a path that must be trod
If man would ever pass to God.
Thomas Parnell.

CONSOLATION.

Mary H. Houghton.

NOT always can we tell when the most vivid lightning and startling thunder are to come. Light clouds gather here and there, the sun is temporarily obscured, nothing ominous appears in air or sky, when, quick as thought, the atmosphere seems bursting with crash and peal and roar and flashings of fire, that leave a wonder that everything is not shivered and aflame.

Again the sun shines, and a light shower falls. Soon a rainbow's broad and brilliant arch repeats itself on the inky clouds that bank the east. A little later sunset tints of surpassing beauty, pale-blue and amber, brown and gold, sea-green and rose, purple and gray, paint floating argosies of cloud that rise from the bosom of the west, linger at the north, like ships at anchor, then slowly pass from sight where the fading arches had been. Long rifts of clearer sky, like far-off, soft-tinted seas, exquisite and of varying color, stretch beyond and between the shifting fleet.

Some of the saddest experiences of life come without premonition. Yesterday life went well, hope was in the ascendant; it was easy to be content. To-day all is reversed; the crushed heart can scarcely lift itself to pray; speech seems paralyzed. It appears cruel that such calamity should be permitted when we might have been so happy. Was there not some way by which it could have been foreseen and avoided? Where are life's compensations now? What are its ambitions worth in the face of this?

In other homes and in the busy streets move on, in close procession, life's hurrying cares. There is no pause with the world at large because grief and desolation sit at our hearthstone.

The clanging bells, from their high towers, call to worship and to prayer. Their voices are unutterably sad. They did not sound like this a week ago. A ripple of childish laughter floats into the lonely house. Across the street a proud father leads his innocent, sunny-haired boy. Further on a cheerful mother walks with her trio of little ones. They are not tearful, or anxious, or bereaved; and their happiness, which yesterday would have made us glad, to-day smites us with a keen sense of contrast. Night comes on, with its gathering silence and shadow, and is even more dreadful than the day. Thinking of the loved dead at night, our thoughts, per force, take the gloom of the grave where their bodies lie; but Nature is tender and God is merciful, and there is sure to come with the triumphant dawn some bright and comforting thought of that morning-land where their souls are dwelling.

For the saddest day some duty waits; and when one would with folded hands keep idle company with grief, temporary consolation comes unbidden. A little child, with its unceasing activity, its numberless wants, its quick recovery from tears, its wonder that we can not be entirely consoled by its caresses and comforted with its toys,—even this shallow comprehension of the storm that is beating at one's heart, is better than to be left in uninterrupted communion with sadness.

Whatever the loss, ours is not long a solitary case. To the one who has it to bear, every trial is a peculiar trial. When God's hand hath touched us we shrink and cry, "What have I done that this calamity should fall on me?" We question if there "*is* any sorrow like unto our sorrow." If we take thought only of our own cross, it appears the heaviest of any. But when we begin to recognize the losses and trials of others, and extend a helpful sympathy even beyond our family and household, we experience the blessedness of giving in a way to react upon and comfort our own hearts.

Our burdens, whether of bereavement or disappointment, or

wrong or regret, weigh heavier or lighter at different times, according to our moods and occupations, or the want of them. We find some way to bear the grief we cannot escape and which in prospect we could not endure. Bitter, indeed, would be all chastening, if no good came of it. Who shall say that this rending of the soul, this breaking up of all the depths of our nature, this strain upon our capacities for suffering, is but the inevitable chance-work of existence!

What does it mean? "That the trial of your faith being much more precious than of gold that perisheth, though it be tried with fire, might be found unto praise, and honor, and glory, at the appearing of Jesus Christ." Were we perfect in sympathy? Was our charity unfailing? Lacked we not in all directions that symmetry of faith and purity of practice needed to effect a resemblance to the divine model? Would we be strong? We must often be put to the trial of our strength. Covet we the best gifts? They are not granted to the undisciplined.

We "rise on stepping-stones of our dead selves to higher things." No one soul is so obscure that God does not take thought for its schooling. The sun is the central light of the universe, but it has a mission to the ripening corn and the purpling clusters of the vine. The sunshine that comes filtering through the morning mists, with healing in its wings, and charms all the birds to singing, should have, also, a message from God to sad hearts. No soul is so grief-laden that it may not be lifted to sources of heavenly comfort by recognizing the Divine love in the perpetual recurrence of earthly blessings:

> "The night is mother of the day,
>   The winter of the spring ;
> And even upon old decay
>   The greenest mosses cling.
> Behind the cloud the star-light lurks ;
>   Through showers the sunbeams fall ;
> For God, who loveth all his works,
>   Hath left his hope with all."

OUR LAMBS.

I LOVED them so,
    That when the Elder Shepherd of the fold
    Came, covered with the storm, and pale and cold,
And begged for one of my sweet lambs to hold,
        I bade Him go.

        He claimed the pet—
A little fondling thing, that to my breast
Clung always, either in quiet or unrest—
I thought of all my lambs I loved him best,
        And yet—and yet—

        I laid him down
In those white, shrouded arms, with bitter tears;
For some voice told me that, in after-years,
He should know naught of passion, grief or fears,
        As I had known.

        And yet again
That Elder Shepherd came. My heart grew faint.
He claimed another lamb, with sadder plaint.
Another! She who, gentle as a saint,
        Ne'er gave me pain.

        Aghast I turned away.
There sat she, lovely as an angel's dream,
Her golden locks with sunlight all agleam,

Her holy eyes with heaven in their beam.
    I knelt to pray.

    "Is it Thy will?
My Father, say, must this pet lamb be given?
Oh! Thou hast many such in heaven."
And a soft voice said: "Nobly hast thou striven,
    But—peace, be still."

    Oh! how I wept,
And clasped her to my bosom, with a wild
And yearning love—my lamb, my pleasant child.
Her, too, I gave. The little angel smiled,
    And slept.

    "Go! go!" I cried:
For once again that Shepherd laid His hand
Upon the noblest of our household band.
Like a pale spectre, there He took His stand,
    Close to his side.

    And yet how wondrous sweet
The look with which he heard my passionate cry:
"Touch not my lamb; for him, oh! let me die!"
"A little while," He said, with smile and sigh,
    "Again to meet."

    Hopeless I fell;
And when I rose, the light had burned so low,
So faint, I could not see my darling go:
He had not bidden me farewell, but, oh!
    I felt farewell.

OUR LAMBS.

      More deeply far
Than if my arms had compassed that slight frame,
Though could I but have heard him call my name—
"Dear Mother!"—but in heaven 'twill be the same.
      There burns my star!

      He will not take
Another lamb, I thought, for only one
Of the dear fold is spared, to be my sun,
My guide, my mourner when this life is done.
      My heart would break.

      Oh! with what thrill
I heard Him enter; but I did not know
(For it was dark) that He had robbed me so,
The idol of my soul—he could not go—
      O heart! be still!

      Came morning, can I tell
How this poor frame its sorrowful tenant kept?
For waking, tears were mine; I, sleeping, wept,
And days, months, years, that weary vigil kept.
      Alas! "Farewell."

      How often it is said!
I sit and think, and wonder too, sometime,
How it will seem, when, in that happier clime
It never will ring out like funeral chime
      Over the dead.

      No tears! no tears!
Will there a day come that I shall not weep?
For I bedew my pillow in my sleep,

Yes, yes; thank God! no grief that clime shall keep,
   No weary years.

    Ay! it is well;
Well with my lambs, and with their earthly guide,
There, pleasant rivers wander they beside,
Or strike sweet harps upon its silver tide—
    Ay! it is well.

    Through the dreary day,
They often come from glorious light to me;
I cannot feel their touch, their faces see,
Yet my soul whispers, they do come to me.
    Heaven is not far away.—*Anonymous.*

MY BABY.

SUCH a little break in the sod!
 So tiny to be a grave!
Oh! how can I render so soon to God
 The beautiful gift he gave!

Must I put you away, my pet—
 My tender bud unblown—
With the dew of the morning upon you, yet,
 And your blossom all unshown?

My heart is near to break,
 For the voice I shall not hear,
For the clinging arms around my neck,
 And the footsteps drawing near.

MY BABY.

The tiny, tottering feet,
   Striving for mother's knee,
For the lisping tones so sweet,
   And the baby's kiss to me.

For the precious mother-name,
   And the touch of the little hand,
O! am I so very much to blame
   If I shrink from the sore demand?

How shall I know her voice,
   Or the greeting of her eyes,
'Mid the countless cherubs that rejoice,
   In the gardens of Paradise?

How shall I know my own,
   Where the air is white with wings—
My babe, so soon from my bosom flown,
   To the angels' ministerings?

And this is the end of it all!
   Of my waiting and my pain—
Only a little funeral pall,
   And empty arms again.

O, baby! my heart is sore
   For the love that was to be,
For the untried dream of love, now o'er,
   'Twixt thee, my child, and me.

Yet over this little head,
   Lying so still on my knee,
I thank my God for the bliss of the dead,
   For the joy of the soul set free.

THANKSGIVING—THE FAMILY GATHERING.

CHILDHOOD.

'Tis a weary world, at best,
  This world that she will not know.
Would I waken her out of such perfect rest,
  For its sorrow and strife? Ah, no!

Escaped are its thorns and harms;
  The only path she has trod
Is that which leads from the mother's arms
  Into the arms of God.—*The Evangelist.*

CHILDHOOD.
John G. Whittier.

BEFORE life's sweetest mystery still
  The heart in reverence kneels;
The wonder of the primal birth
  The latest mother feels.

We need love's tender lessons taught
  As only weakness can;
God hath his small interpreters;
  The child must teach the man.

We wander wide through evil years,
  Our eyes of faith grow dim;
But he is freshest from His hands
  And nearest unto Him!

And haply, pleading long with Him
  For sin-sick hearts and cold,

OUR DEAR ONES.

The angels of our childhood still
　　The Father's face behold.

Of such the kingdom ! Teach thus us,
　　O Master most divine,
To feel the deep significance
　　Of these wise words of thine !

The haughty feet of power shall fail
　　Where meekness surely goes ;
No cunning find the key of heaven,
　　No strength its gates unclose.

Alone to guilelessness and love
　　Those gates shall open fall ;
The mind of pride is nothingness,
　　The child-like heart is all.

OUR DEAR ONES.

James Aldrich.

GOD gives us ministers of love,
　　Which we regard not, being near ;
　Death takes them from us, then we feel
　　That angels have been with us here !

TIS a blessing to live, but a greater to die ;
　And the best of the world, is its path to the sky.

John K. Mitchell.

THE LITTLE CHILDREN.

Henry W. Longfellow.

 LITTLE feet; that such long years
Must wander on through hopes and fears;
   Must ache and bleed beneath your load;
I, nearer to the wayside inn,
Where toil shall cease and rest begin,
   Am weary thinking of your road.

O, little hands; that weak or strong,
Have still to serve or rule so long,
   Have still so long to give or ask;
I, who so much with book and pen
Have toiled among my fellow-men,
   Am weary, thinking of your task.

O, little hearts; that throb and beat
With much impatient, feverish heat,
   Such limitless and strong desires;
Mine, that so long has glowed and burned,
With passions into ashes turned,
   Now covers and conceals its fires.

O, little souls; as pure and white,
As crystalline, as rays of light
   Direct from Heaven, their source divine;
Refracted through the mist of years,
How red my setting sun appears;
   How lurid looks this sun of mine!

ARE ALL THE CHILDREN IN?

Mrs. S. T. Perry.

THE darkness falls, the wind is high,
   Dense black clouds fill the western sky;
     The storm will soon begin.
The thunders roar, the lightnings flash,
I hear the great round rain-drops dash—
   Are all the children in?

They're coming softly to my side;
Their forms within my arms I hide—
   No other arms as sure.
The storm may rage with fury wild,
With trusting faith each little child
   With mother feels secure.

But future days are drawing near—
They'll go from this warm shelter here,
   Out in the world's wild din.
The rain will fall, the cold winds blow;
I'll sit alone and long to know,
   Are all the children in.

Will they have shelters then secure,
Where hearts are waiting strong and sure,
   And love is true when tried?
Or will they find a broken reed,
When strength of heart they so much need
   To help them brave the tide?

God knows it all; His will is best;
I'll shield them now, and leave the rest
  In His most righteous hand.
Sometimes souls He loves are riven
By tempests wild, and thus are driven
  Nearer the better land.

If He should call me home before
The children go, on that blest shore,
  Afar from care and sin,
I know that I shall watch and wait
Till He, the Keeper of the gate,
  Lets all the children in.

ARE THE CHILDREN AT HOME?

Mrs. M. E. Sangster.

EACH day when the glow of sunset
  Fades in the western sky,
And the wee ones, tired of playing,
  Go tripping lightly by,
I steal away from my husband,
  Asleep in his easy-chair,
And watch from the open doorway
  Their faces fresh and fair.

Alone in the dear old homestead
  That once was full of life,
Ringing with girlish laughter,
  Echoing boyish strife,

ARE THE CHILDREN AT HOME?

We two are waiting together;
    And oft, as the shadows come,
With tremulous voice he calls me,
    "It is night! are the children home?"

"Yes, love!" I answer him gently,
    "They're all home long ago;"
And I sing, in my quivering treble,
    A song so soft and low,
Till the old man drops to slumber,
    With his head upon his hand,
And I tell to myself the number
    Home in a better land.

Home, where never a sorrow
    Shall dim their eyes with tears!
Where the smile of God is on them
    Through all the summer years!
I know!—Yet my arms are empty
    That fondly folded seven,
And the mother heart within me
    Is almost starved for heaven.

Sometimes in the dusk of evening,
    I only shut my eyes,
And the children are all about me,
    A vision from the skies;
The babes whose dimpled fingers
    Lost the way to my breast,
And the beautiful ones, the angels,
    Passed to the world of the blessed.

ARE THE CHILDREN AT HOME?

With never a cloud upon them,
   I see their radiant brows;
My boys that I gave to freedom—
   The red sword sealed their vows!
In a tangled Southern forest,
   Twin brothers, bold and brave,
They fell; and the flag they died for,
   Thank God! floats over their grave.

A breath, and the vision is lifted
   Away on wings of light,
And again we two are together,
   All alone in the night.
They tell me his mind is failing,
   But I smile at idle fears;
He is only back with the children,
   In the dear and peaceful years.

And still as the summer sunset
   Fades away in the west,
And the wee ones, tired of playing,
   Go trooping home to rest,
My husband calls from his corner,
   "Say, love! have the children come?"
And I answer, with eyes uplifted,
   "Yes, dear! they are all at home!"

A BABE in a house is a well-spring of pleasure,
   A messenger of peace and love,
A resting-place for innocence on earth; a link between angels
   and men.   *M. F. Tupper.*

THE DEATH OF CHILDREN.

Chas. Wadsworth, D.D.

IN His moral tillage, God cultivates many flowers seemingly only for their exquisite beauty and fragrance. For when bathed in soft sunshine they have burst into blossom, then the Divine hand gathers them from the earthly fields to be kept in crystal vases in the deathless mansions above. Thus little children die—some in the sweet bud, some in the fuller blossom; but never too early to make heaven fairer and sweeter with their immortal bloom.

Verily, to the eye of Faith, nothing is fairer than the death of young children. Sight and sense, indeed, recoil from it. The flower that, like a breathing rose, filled heart and home with an exquisite delight, alas! we are stricken with sore anguish to find its stem broken and the blossom gone. But unto Faith, eagle-eyed beyond mental vision, and winged to mount like a singing lark over the fading rainbow unto the blue heaven, even this is touchingly lovely.

The child's earthly ministry was well done, for the rose does its work as grandly in blossom as the vine with its fruit. And having helped to sanctify and lift heavenward the very hearts that broke at its farewell, it has gone from this troublesome sphere,—ere the winds chilled or the rains stained it, leaving the world it blessed and the skies through which it passed still sweet with its lingering fragrance,—to its glory as an ever-unfolding flower in the blessed garden of God. Surely, prolonged life on earth hath no boon like this! For such mortal loveliness to put on immortality—to rise from the carnal with so little memory of earth that the mother's cradle seemed to have been rocked in the house of many mansions—to have no experience of a wearied mind and chilled affections, but from a child's joyous heart growing up in the power of an archangelic intellect—to be raptured as a blessed babe through the gates of Paradise—ah! this is better than to watch as an old prophet for the car of fire in the Valley of Jordan.

MY BOY.

John Moultrie.

I HAVE a son, a third, sweet son; his age I cannot tell,
For they reckon not by years and months where he is gone to dwell.
I cannot tell what form is his, what looks he weareth now,
Nor guess how bright a glory crowns his shining seraph brow;
But I know (for God hath told me this) that he is now at rest,
Where other blessed infants be, on their Saviour's loving breast.
I know the angels fold him close beneath their glittering wings,
And soothe him with a song that breathes of heaven's divinest things.
I know that we shall meet our babe (his mother dear and I),
Where God for aye shall wipe away all tears from every eye.

THE maelstrom attracts more notice than the quiet fountain; a comet draws more attention than the steady star; but it is better to be the fountain than the maelstrom, and star than comet, following out the sphere and orbit of quiet usefulness in which God places us. *John Hall, D.D.*

HOME BEREAVEMENTS.*

Henry Ward Beecher.

WE are joined together, many of us, by a common experience. Many of us have met in each others' houses and in each others' company on just such errands of grief and sympathy and Christian triumph as this. How many of us have sent children forward; and how many of us feel to-day that all things are for our sakes; and that those things which for the present are not joyous but grievous, nevertheless work in us the peaceable fruit of righteousness! So we stand in what may be called a relationship of grief. We are knit together and brought into each other's company by the ministration of grief, made Christian and blessed.

To be sure, if we were to ask this life what would be best, there is no father, there is no mother, who would not plead with all the strength which lies in natural affection, "Spare me, and spare mine." For the outward man this is reasonable and unrebukable; and yet, if it be overruled by Him who loves us even better than He loves His own life, then there comes the revelation of another truth: namely, that the things which are seen are the unreal things, and that the real things are the things which are invisible.

When our children that are so dear to us are plucked out of our arms, and carried away, we feel, for the time being, that we have lost them, because our body does not triumph; but are they taken from our inward man? Are they taken from that which is to be saved—the spiritual man? Are they taken from memory? Are they taken from love? Are they taken from the scope and

* Remarks made at the funeral of a child in Plymouth Church, Brooklyn.

reach of the imagination, which, in its sanctified form, is only another name for faith? Do we not sometimes dwell with them more intimately than we did when they were with us on earth? The care of them is no longer ours, that love-burden we bear no longer, since they are with the angels of God and with God; and we shed tears over what seems to be our loss; but do they not hover in the air over our heads? And to-day could the room hold them all?

As you recollect, the background of the Sistine Madonna, at Dresden (in some respects the most wonderful picture of maternal love which exists in the world), for a long time was merely dark; and an artist, in making some repairs, discovered a cherub's face in the grime of that dark background; and being led to suspect that the picture had been overlaid by time and neglect, commenced cleansing it; and as he went on, cherub after cherub appeared, until it was found that the Madonna was on a background made up wholly of little heavenly cherubs.

Now, by nature motherhood stands against a dark background; but that background being cleaned by the touch of God, and by the cleansing hand of faith, we see that the whole heaven is full of little cherub faces. And to-day it is not this little child alone that we look at, which we see only in the outward guise; we look upon a background of children innumerable, each one as sweet to its mother's heart as this child has been to its mother's heart, each one as dear to the clasping arms of its father as this child has been to the clasping arms of its father; and it is in good company. It is in a spring-land. It is in a summer-world. It is with God. You have given it back to Him who lent it to you.

Now, the giving back is very hard, but you cannot give back to God all that you received with your child. You cannot give back to God those springs of new and deeper affection which were awakened by the coming of this little one. You cannot give back to God the experiences which you have had in dwelling with your darling. You cannot give back to God the hours which, when you look upon them now, seem like one golden chain of linked happiness.

You are better, you are riper, you are richer, even in this hour of bereavement, than you were. God gave; and he has not taken away except in outward form. He holds, he keeps, he reserves, he watches, he loves. You shall have again that which you have given back to him only outwardly.

Meanwhile, the key is in your hand; and it is not a black iron key; it is a golden key of faith and of love. This little child has taught you to follow it. There will not be a sunrise or a sunset when you will not in imagination go through the gate of heaven after it. There is no door so fast that a mother's love and a father's love will not open it and follow a beloved child. And so, by its ministration, this child will guide you a thousand times into a realization of the great spirit-land, and into a faith of the invisible, which will make you as much larger as it makes you less dependent on the body, and more rich in the fruitage of the spirit.

To-day, then, we have an errand of thanksgiving. We thank God for sending this little gift into this household. We thank God for the light which he kindled here, and which burned with so pure a flame, and taught so sweet a lesson. And we thank God, that, when this child was to go to a better place, it walked so few steps, for so few hours, through pain. Men who look on the dark side shake the head, and say, "Oh, how sudden!" but I say, Since it was to go, God be thanked that it was permitted to pass through so brief a period of suffering; that there were no long weeks or months of gradual decay and then a final extinction; that out of the fullness of health it dropped into the fullness of heaven, leaving its body as it lies before you to-day a thing of beauty. Blessed be God for such mercy in the ministration of sickness and of departure.

I appreciate your sorrow, having myself often gone through this experience; and I can say that there is no other experience which throws such a light upon the storm-cloud. We are never ripe till we have been made so by suffering. We belong to those fruits which must be touched by frost before they lose their sourness and come to their sweetness. I see the goodness of God in this dispensation as pointing us toward heaven and immortality. In this bereavement there is cause for rejoicing; for sure it is that you and your child shall meet again never to be separated.

THE ANGEL-CHILD.

Mrs. C. L. Rice.

SHE may not return, but to her thou shalt go,
   When thy days are numbered and finished below;
   And it may to thy angel child be given
First to meet and to welcome her mother to heaven;
And there, reunited to part never more
One song shall ye sing and one Saviour adore.

AN angel stood and met my gaze
   Through the low door-way of my tent;
   The tent is struck, the vision stays:
I only know she came and went.

J. Russell Lowell.

EMPTY CRADLES.

Mrs. Georgie A. H. McLeod.

OH, the empty, empty cradles,
   That must now be put away,
   For the little ones will need them
     Never more by night or day,
For the pure and dreamless sleepers,
   Never more they'll rock to rest,
Their bright heads upon the pillows,
   Shall no more be softly prest!

In the still and solemn nightfall,
   Death's pale angel noiseless sped,
"I have gathered only Lilies,
   For my Lord, to-day," he said;
Oh, the Lilies, the White Lilies,
   That made earthly homes so bright,
How many, many buds are missing,
   Since the happy morning light!

Waxen hands, with blossoms in them,
   Faces very white and fair,
Curtained eyes, like hidden star-light,
   Silken rings of sunny hair.
Hushed and still, we gaze upon them
   And we scarcely know our loss;
But to-morrow we shall feel it,
   Almost crushed beneath the cross.

EMPTY CRADLES.

Little robes, so richly broidered,
    Wrought with so much love and pride,
Dainty laces, pale, pure ribbons,
    They must all be laid aside;
For in glorious robes of brightness
    Are the little ones arrayed,
All unstained by earth the whiteness,
    Such a little while they stayed.

Ah, the busy, busy mornings,
    And the nights of anxious care;
Now, there is no need of watching,
    There'll be time enough to spare.
There's no baby's voice, we'll listen,
    Thinking that we hear it oft;
On our face no baby fingers,
    Touches like the rose leaves soft.

Never mind the noisy household,
    Nor loud foot-falls on the stair,
'Twill not wake the peaceful sleeper,
    There's no baby anywhere.
In a casket, white as snow-flakes,
    Nestling all among the flowers,
Are the pure and stainless Lilies,
    That a little while were ours.

In our dreams, 'midst dazzling brightness,
    And a rapturous burst of song,
Through our tears, we saw above us,
    Oh! the radiant spirit throng!
In their arms so softly cradled
    Our own little ones we know,

And we hear them whisper gently,
"The White Lilies from below."

Wide the shining gates are opened,
For the children are at home,
Back to us, come the sweet echoes,
"Oh, suffer them to come!"
Put away the empty cradles,
Keep we only in our sight
That bright glimpse of the fair dwelling
Which the children have to-night!

MY CHILD.

John Pierpont.

CANNOT make him dead!
His fair sunshiny head
Is ever bounding round my study-chair;
Yet when my eyes, now dim
With tears, I turn to him,
The vision vanishes—he is not there!

I walk my parlor floor,
And, through the open door,
I hear a footfall on the chamber stair;
I'm stepping toward the hall,
To give the boy a call,
And then bethink me that—he is not there!

I thread the crowded street,
A satcheled lad I meet,

MY CHILD.

With the same beaming eyes and colored hair;
And, as he's running by,
Follow him with my eye,
Scarcely believing that—he is not there!

I cannot make him dead!
When passing by the bed,
So long watched over with parental care;
My spirit and my eye
Seek him inquiringly,
Before the thought comes that—he is not there!

Not there? Where, then, is he?
The form I used to see
Was but the raiment that he used to wear.
The grave, that now doth press
Upon that cast-off dress,
Is but his wardrobe locked—he is not there!

He lives! In all the past
He lives; nor, to the last,
Of seeing him again will I despair;
In dreams I see him now;
And on his angel brow,
I see it written, "Thou shalt see me *there!*"

Yes, we all live to God!
FATHER, thy chastening rod
So help us, thine afflicted ones, to bear,
That in the spirit land,
Meeting at thy right hand,
'Twill be our heaven to find that—he is there!"

SUNSHINE FOR THE SORROWING.

Rev. Theo. L. Cuyler.

AMONG the readers of this paper there must be many who "wear mourning." Every minister, as he runs his eye over his congregation, sees the black badge of sorrow in every part of the house. Yet many of the deepest and sorest griefs of the heart do not hoist any outward signal of distress. For who ever puts on crape for a family disgrace, or a secret heartache, or loss of character, or an acute contrition for sin, or a backsliding from Christ? Set it down as a fact that God sees ten-fold more sorrow than the human eye ever detects.

What a clear streak of sunshine our Lord let into this legion of sorrowing hearts when he pronounced that wonderful benediction: "Blessed are they that mourn!" Perhaps some poor Galilean mother who came up that day to hear Jesus of Nazareth, with her eyes red from weeping over a lost child, whispered to herself: "That is for me; I am a mourner." "Ah!" thought some penitent sinner who felt the plague of his guilty heart, "that means me; I am in trouble to-day." It did mean them. Christ's religion is the first and only religion ever known in this world which recognizes human sorrow, and has any sunshine of consolation for broken hearts. Do cold-blooded infidels realize that fact when they attempt to destroy men's faith in the Gospel of Calvary?

We are apt to limit this benediction of Jesus to one class of sufferers. We take this sweet little text into sick rooms, or to funerals, or into the lonely group which gather around a mother's deserted chair or a little empty crib. It was meant for them. It has fallen upon such stricken hearts like the gentle rain upon the new-mown grass. Many of us know full well how good the balm felt when it touched our bruised and bleeding hearts. I remember how, when one of my own "bairns" was lying in his fresh-made grave, and another one was so low that his crib seemed to touch against a tomb, I used to keep murmuring over to myself Wesley's matchless lines:

> "Leave, oh leave me not alone,
> Still support and comfort me!"

In those days I was learning (what we pastors have to learn) just how the arrow feels when it enters, and just how to sympathize with our people in their bereavements. Somehow a minister is never fully ready to emit the fragrance of sympathy for others until he has been bruised himself. There is a great lack about all Christians who have never suffered. Paul abounded in consolation because he had known sharp tribulations in his own experience. What a precious spilling of his great sympathetic heart that was when he overflowed into that sublime passage which ends the fourth and begins the fifth chapter of his Epistle to the Corinthians. The outward man perishing—the inward man renewed day by day. The affliction growing "light" in proportion to the transcendent weight of the eternal glory! The old tent dropping to pieces and the heavenly mansion looming up so gloriously that his homesick soul longed to quit the fluttering tent, and to "be present with the Lord." These are indeed mighty consolations to bear with us into our houses of mourning. They are the foretastes which make us long for the full feast and the seraphic joys of the marriage-supper of the Lamb. We experience what the old godly negro, "Uncle Johnson," did when he said: "Oh, yes, massa, I feel bery lonesome since my Ellen died, but den de Lord comes round ebery day and gibs me a *taste ob de kingdom*, jus' as a nus would wid de spoon; but oh, how I wants to get holds *ob de whole dish!*"

WE KNOW NOT WHAT IS BEFORE US.

Mary G. Brainard.

I KNOW not what shall befall me,
   God hangs a mist o'er my eyes,
   And each step in my onward path
   He makes new scenes to rise,
And every joy He sends to me
   Comes as a sweet surprise.

I see not a step before me
   As I tread on another year,
But the past is still in God's keeping,
   The future His mercy shall clear,
And what looks dark in the distance
   May brighten as I draw near.

For perhaps the dreaded future
   Has less bitter than I think;
The Lord may sweeten the waters
   Before I stoop to drink;
Or, if Marah must be Marah,
   He will stand beside its brink.

It may be He has, waiting
   For the coming of my feet,
Some gift of such rare value,
   Some joy so strangely sweet,
That my lips shall only tremble
   With the thanks they cannot speak.

O, restful blissful ignorance!
  'Tis blessed not to know:
It keeps me still in those arms
  Which will not let me go,
And hushes my soul to rest
  In the bosom that loved me so!

So I go on—not knowing;
  I would not if I might,
Rather walking with God in the dark
  Than going alone in the light;
Rather walking with Him by faith
  Than walking alone by sight.

My heart shrinks back from trials
  Which the future may disclose,
Yet I never had a sorrow
  But what the dear Lord chose;
So I send the coming tears back
  With the whispered word, "He knows!"

PASSING AWAY.
Mrs. F. D. Hemans.

IT is written on the rose
  In its glory's full array;
Read what those buds disclose—
  "Passing away."

It is written on the skies
  Of the soft blue summer day;

PASSING AWAY.

It is traced in sunset's dyes—
    "Passing away."

It is written on the trees,
    As their young leaves glistening play,
And on brighter things than these—
    "Passing away."

It is written on the brow
    Where the spirit's ardent ray
Lives and burns, and triumphs now —
    "Passing away."

It is written on the heart,
    Alas! that there decay
Should claim from love a part—
    "Passing away."

Friends, friends! O shall we meet
    In a land of purer day?
There lovely things and sweet
    Pass not away.

Shall we know each others' eyes
    And the thoughts that in them lay,
When we mingled sympathies?—
    Passing away.

O, if this may be so,
    Speed, speed, thou closing day.
How blest, from earth's vain show
    To pass away!

BY-AND-BYE.

Mrs. Preston.

WHAT will it matter by-and-bye,
    Whether my path below was bright,
    Whether it wound, through dark or light,
Under a gray or golden sky,
When I look on it by-and-bye?

What will it matter by-and-bye,
    Whether unhelped I toiled alone,
    Dashing my foot against a stone,
Missing the charge of the angel high,
Bidding me think of the by-and-bye?

What will it matter by-and-bye,
    Whether with dancing joy I went
    Down through the years with a gay content,
Never believing—nay, not I,
Tears would be sweeter by-and-bye?

What will it matter by-and-bye,
    Whether with cheek to cheek I've lain,
    Close to the pallid angel, Pain,
Soothing myself with sob and sigh—
"All will be elsewise by-and-bye?"

What will it matter? Naught if I
    Only am sure the way I've trod,
    Gloomy or gladdened, leads to God,

Questioning not of the how, the why,
If I but reach Him by-and-bye.

What will I care for the unshared sigh,
   If, in my fear of lapse or fall,
   Close I have clung to Christ through all,
Mindless how rough the road might lie,
Sure He will smoothen it by-and-bye?

What will it matter by-and-bye?
   Nothing but this—That joy or pain
   Lifted me skyward—helped to gain,
Whether through rack, or smile, or sigh,
Heaven—home—all in all—by-and-bye!

BROKEN TIES.

HOW many there are in every human experience! How many even apart from those that death occasions! Your memory goes back to the home of your childhood. All its belongings became, as it were, a part of your nature. You recall the familiar surroundings. Your interests were bound up with them. And then the time came when those ties must be sundered. You went forth from the old home into new scenes. You found new ties binding themselves about you, but the old ones were broken.

And so it has been all the way along. You became attached to persons and the shifting scenes of life have carried them away from you, and though you hear now and then of their well-being, the old intimacy is perforce gone, the old ties are sundered. The ties that

SORROWS OF CHILDHOOD—Burial of the Pet Bird.

hold us to our surroundings are continually breaking. No year is like that which preceded it, no month, no day even.

Let us guard against those things that may give offense or that may through any fault of ours break the tie that binds us to an old friend. There is the bitterness of parting and the added bitterness of self-reproach, the sad recollection of what might have been.

And, since all things and relations change, since ties must be broken, it is well for us to learn to enjoy to the utmost our present. The time is coming when your home ties perhaps must be sundered. Enjoy, then, the present relations. It may be a humble home, and you are planning for one larger, and, to your imagination, more enjoyable. Very well; only do not fail to take all the enjoyment you can from your present surroundings. Your friend will go to some distant place by and by. Enjoy his society while you have it. Your children, while they will always be your children, will nevertheless grow up and go out from the home-nest. The ties that bind you to their youth will be severed. Enjoy them while you have them with you. It is well for us to plan as wisely as may be for the future; but it is folly for us to seek our enjoyment in the future. Let us enjoy what we have now, for "change" is written on all our transitory and mutable life. It will be only when we have sundered the last bonds that bind us to this life that we shall be where there is no more breaking of ties, no more regrets over pleasures that are gone, but sweet enjoyment of an eternal present.—*Christian Weekly.*

LIVE WELL.

John Milton.

NOR love thy life, nor hate; but whilst thou livest,
Live well, how long or short, permit to heaven.

LIFE.—A PLAY.

Shakespeare.

ALL the world's a stage,
    And all the men and women merely players.
    They have their exits and their entrances,
And one man, in his time, plays many parts;
His acts being seven ages. At first the infant,
Mewling and puking in the nurse's arms;
And then the whining school-boy, with his satchel
And shining morning face, creeping like a snail
Unwillingly to school. And then the lover,
Sighing like furnace, with a woful ballad
Made to his mistress' eye-brow. Then a soldier,
Full of strange oaths and bearded like the pard;
Jealous in honor, sudden and quick in quarrel;
Seeking the bubble reputation
Even in the cannon's mouth. And then the justice,
In fair, round belly, with good capon lined,
With eyes severe, and beard of formal cut,
Full of wise saws and modern instances,
And so he plays his part. The sixth age shifts
Into the lean and slipper'd pantaloon,
With spectacles on nose, and pouch on side;
His youthful hose well saved, a world too wide
For his shrunk shank; and his big manly voice,
Turning again toward childish treble, pipes

And whistles in his sound. Last scene of all
That ends this strange eventful history,
Is second childishness, and mere oblivion,
Sans teeth, *sans* eyes, *sans* taste, *sans* everything.

COMPUTATION OF LIFE.

J. R. Planché.

THREESCORE and ten, by common calculation,
The years of man amount to—but we'll say
He turns fourscore; yet, in my estimation,
In all those years he has not lived a day.
Out of the eighty, you must first remember
The hours of night you pass asleep in bed;
And counting from December to December,
Just half your life you'll find you have been dead.

To forty years at once by this reduction
We come; and sure the first five of your birth,
While cutting teeth and living upon suction,
You are not alive to what this life is worth!
From thirty-five next take for education,
Fifteen, at least, at college and at school,
When, notwithstanding all your application,
The chances are, you may turn out a fool.

Still twenty we have left us to dispose of,
But during them your fortune you've to make;
And granting, with the luck of some one knows of,
'Tis made in ten, that's ten from life to take.

LIFE'S EPITAPH.

Out of the ten you must allow for yet left
The time for shaving, tooth and other aches—
Say four, and that leaves six—too short, I vow, for
Regretting past and making fresh mistakes!
Meanwhile each hour dispels some fond illusion,
Until at length, *sans* eyes, *sans* teeth, you may
Have scarcely sense to come to this conclusion,
You've reach'd fourscore, but haven't lived a day.

LIFE'S EPITAPH.

WE are all very busy—busy writing epitaphs. We do not let a day pass without doing something in this line, and we are all busy, not in writing epitaphs for others, but in writing our own. And we are making it very sure that people will read what we have written when we are gone. Shall we not be remembered? If not by many, we certainly shall by a few, and that remembrance we are making sure of by the tenor of our lives. Our characters are the inscriptions we are making on the hearts of those who know, and who will survive us. We do not leave this office to others. We are doing it ourselves. Others might falsify and deceive by what they might say of us, but we are telling the truth. The actions of our passing life are facts visible, plain, undeniable. We engrave them on the mind of all observers. How interesting the question, What kind of epitaphs are we writing! Will they be read with joy or sorrow? Remember the epitaphs we write are not for the marble that tells where we lie, but for the memory of every one that knew us.—*Congregationalist.*

THE LIFE CLOCK.

THERE is a little mystic clock,
   No human eye hath seen;
That beateth on and beateth on,
   From morning until e'en.

And when the soul is wrapped in sleep,
   And heareth not a sound,
It ticks and ticks the live-long night,
   And never runneth down.

Oh, wondrous is that work of art,
   Which knells the passing hour;
But art ne'er formed or mind conceived,
   This life clock's magic power.

Nor set in gold, nor decked with gems,
   By wealth and pride possessed;
By rich or poor, or high or low,
   Each bears it in his breast.

When life's deep stream, 'mid beds of flowers,
   All still and softly glides,
Like the wavelet's step, with a gentle beat,
   It warns of passing tides.

When threatening darkness gathers o'er,
   And hope's bright visions flee,

LIFE'S BOUNDARY LINE.

Like the sullen stroke of the muffled oar,
  It beateth heavily.

When passion nerves the warrior's arm
  For deeds of hate and wrong,
Though heeded not the fearful sound,
  Its knell is deep and strong.

When eyes to eyes are gazing soft,
  And tender words are spoken,
Then fast and wild it rattles on,
  As if with love 'twere broken.

Such is the clock that measures life,
  Of flesh and spirit blended,
And thus 'twill run within the heart
  Till that strange tie is ended.—*Anonymous.*

LIFE'S BOUNDARY LINE.
(THE DOOMED MAN.)
J. Addison Alexander, D.D.

THERE is a time, we know not when,
  A place, we know not where,
That marks the destiny of men,
  To glory or despair.

There is a line by us unseen,
  That crosses every path,
The hidden boundary between
  God's patience and His wrath.

LIFE'S BOUNDARY LINE.

To pass that limit is to die,
   To die as if by stealth;
It does not quench the beaming eye,
   Or pale the glow of health.

The conscience may be still at ease,
   The spirits light and gay;
That which is pleasing still may please,
   And care be thrust away.

But on that forehead God has set
   Indelibly a mark—
Unseen by man, for man as yet
   Is blind and in the dark.

And still the doomed man's path below
   May bloom as Eden bloomed—
He did not, does not, will not know,
   Or feel, that he is doomed.

He knows, he feels that all is well,
   And every fear is calmed;
He lives, he dies, he wakes in hell,
   Not only doomed but damned!

O! where is this mysterious bourne,
   By which our path is crossed;
Beyond which, God Himself hath sworn
   That he who goes is lost?

How far may men go on in sin?
   How long will God forbear?
Where does hope end, and where begin
   The confines of despair?

An answer from the skies is sent,—
"Ye that from God depart,
While it is called to-day repent,
And harden not your heart!"

BREVITY OF LIFE.

Henry King.

LIKE to the falling of a star,
   Or as the flights of eagles are,
   Or like the fresh spring's gaudy hue,
Or silver drops of morning dew,
Or like a wind that chafes the flood,
Or bubbles which on water stood—
E'en such is man, whose borrowed light
Is straight called in, and paid to-night.
The wind blows out, the bubble dies,
The spring entombed in autumn lies,
The dew dries up, the star is shot,
The flight is past—and man forgot!

THE RESPONSIBILITIES OF LIFE.

Alexander Reed, D.D.

THIS world is a solemn fact; we are in it; let us try to understand it, let us grapple with its mysteries, let us think much of its responsibilities, let us ponder the thoughts of the inquiring minds of past ages, let us prize all the light we have from man—from God, so that we may be guided aright amid its perils and changing experiences.

LIFE.

Lord Byron.

BETWEEN two worlds life hovers, like a star
   'Twixt night and morn upon the horizon's verge,
   How little do we know that which we are!
How less what we may be! The eternal surge
Of time and tide rolls on, and bears afar
Our bubbles; as the old burst, new emerge,
Lashed from the foam of ages, while the graves
Of empires heave but like some passing waves.

MYSTERY OF LIFE.

Anna Letitia Barbauld.

LIFE! I know not what thou art,
   But know that thou and I must part;
   And when, or how, or where we met,
I own to me's a secret yet.

Life, we've been long together,
Through pleasant and through cloudy weather;
'Tis hard to part when friends are dear;
Perhaps 'twill cost a sigh, a tear;

Then steal away, give little warning,
Choose thine own time;
Say not Good-night, but in some brighter clime
Bid me Good-morning.

BOUNDARIES OF LIFE.

Oliver Wendell Holmes.

BETWEEN two breaths what crowded mysteries lie—
    The first short gasp, the last and long-drawn sigh!
    Like phantoms painted on the magic slide,
Forth from the darkness of the past we glide,
As living shadows for a moment seen
In airy pageant on the eternal screen,
Traced by a ray from one unchanging flame,
Then seek the dust and stillness whence we came.

THE VANITY OF LIFE.

Edw. Young

WHY all this toil for triumphs of an hour!
    What though we wade in wealth or soar in fame!
    Earth's highest station ends in "Here he lies:"
And "Dust to dust" concludes her noblest song.

LIFE, A BOOK.

John Mason.

MAN'S life's a book of history;
    The leaves thereof are days;
    The letters, mercies closely joined;
    The title is God's praise.

OUR LIFE A SERMON.

T. De Witt Talmage.

OUR birth is the text from which we start. Youth is the introduction to the discourse. During our manhood we lay down a few propositions and prove them. Some of the passages are dull, and some sprightly. Then come inferences and applications. At seventy years we say "Fifthly and Lastly." The doxology is sung. The benediction is pronounced. The book closed. It is getting cold. Frost on the window pane. Audience gone. Shut up the church. Sexton goes home with the key on his shoulder.

HOW TO LIVE.

Wm. C. Bryant.

SO live that when thy summons comes to join
    The innumerable caravan that moves
    To the pale realms of shade, where each shall take
His chamber in the silent halls of death,
Thou go not like the quarry-slave at night,
Scourged to his dungeon; but, sustain'd and soothed
By an unfaltering trust, approach thy grave
Like one who wraps the drapery of his couch
About him, and lies down to pleasant dreams.

GOD demands an account of the past; that we must render hereafter. He demands an improvement of the present, and this we must render now.   *W. Jay.*

THE VOYAGE OF LIFE.*

'TWAS my purpose, on a day,
To embark and sail away,
As I climbed the vessel's side,
Love was sporting in the tide;
"Come," he said, "ascend—make haste,
Launch into the boundless waste."

Many mariners were there,
Having each his separate care;
They that rowed us held their eyes
Fixed upon the starry skies;
Others steered or turned the sails
To receive the shifting gales.

Love, with power divine supplied,
Suddenly my courage tried;
In a moment it was night,
Ships and skies were out of sight;

---

* This poem is from the pen of Madame Guyon—a woman of great wealth, high intellectual culture, and intense suffering for the cause of Christ. She lived two hundred years ago, and was a zealous member of the Roman Catholic Church. Through a long train of complicated providences, involving the keenest trials, she was at length led to an experience of peculiar richness and depth. Self was crucified, and she sank into the perfect will of God. Surrounded by the darkness and superstition of papacy, and tempted by all the blandishments which wealth and social position could offer, she reached a plane of Christian experience which comparatively few attain among the Protestant Churches. "God is no respecter of persons."

THE VOYAGE OF LIFE.

On the briny wave I lay,
Floating rushes all my stay.

Did I with resentment burn
At this unexpected turn?
Did I wish myself on shore,
Never to forsake it more?
No! "*My soul,*" I cried, "*be still;
If I must be lost, I will.*"

Next he hastened to convey
Both my frail supports away;
Seized my rushes; bade the waves
Yearn into a thousand graves.
Down I went, and sunk as lead,
Ocean closing o'er my head.

Still, however, life was safe;
And I saw him turn and laugh;
"Friend," he cried, "adieu! lie low,
While the wintry storms shall blow;
When the Spring has calmed the main,
You shall rise, and float again."

Soon I saw him, with dismay,
Spread his plumes and soar away;
Now I mark his rapid flight;
Now he leaves my aching sight;
He is gone whom I adore,
'Tis in vain to seek him more.

How I trembled then, and feared,
When my Love had disappeared!

THE VOYAGE OF LIFE.

"Wilt thou leave me thus," I cried,
"Whelmed beneath the rolling tide ?"
Vain attempt to reach his ear!
Love was gone, and would not hear.

Ah! return and love me still;
See me subject to thy will;
Frown with wrath, or smile with grace,
Only let me see thy face!
Evil I have none to fear;
All is good, if thou art near.

Yet he leaves me—cruel fate!
Leaves me in my lost estate;
Have I sinned? Oh, say wherein?
Tell me, and forgive my sin!
King and Lord, whom I adore,
Shall I see thy face no more!

Be not angry—I resign
Henceforth all my will to thine.
I consent that thou depart,
Though thine absence break my heart;
Go, then, and forever too;
All is right that thou will do.

This was just what love intended;
He was now no more offended.
Soon as I became a child,
Love returned to me and smiled.
Never strife shall more betide
'Twixt the Bridegroom and his bride.

CHRISTIAN LIVING.

TRUE Christian living in the world is like a ship sailing on the ocean. It is not the ship being in the water which will sink it, but the water getting into the ship. So, in like manner, the Christian is not ruined by living in the world, which he must needs do whilst he remains in the body, but by the world living in him. The world in the heart has ruined millions of immortal souls. How careful is the mariner to guard against leakage, lest the water entering into the vessel should, by imperceptible degrees, cause the vessel to sink; and ought not the Christian to watch and pray, lest Satan and the world should find some unguarded inlet to his heart?—*New York Observer.*

FALSE PRIDE IN LIFE.

John G. Saxe.

BECAUSE you flourish in worldly affairs,
   Don't be haughty and put on airs,
      With insolent pride of station;
Don't be proud and turn up your nose
At poorer people in plainer clothes,
But learn, for the sake of your mind's repose,
That wealth's a bubble that comes and goes;
And that all Proud Flesh, wherever it grows,
      Is subject to irritation.

LIFE RE-ACTING UPON LIFE.

Mrs. Elizabeth B. Browning.

NO stream from its source
    Flows seaward, how lonely soever its source,
    But what some land is gladdened.
        No star ever rose
And set without influence somewhere. Who knows
What earth needs from earth's lowest creature? No life
Can be pure in its purpose and strong in its strife,
And all life not be purer and stronger thereby.

OUR lives are albums, written through
    With good or ill, with false or true;
    And as the blessed angels turn
        The pages of our years,
God grant they read the good with smiles,
    And blot the bad with tears.

John Milton.

THERE is none made so great, but he may both need the help and service, and stand in fear of the power and unkindness, even of the meanest of mortals.   *Seneca.*

Do to-day thy nearest duty.   *Goethe.*

YOUNG MEN LEAVING HOME.

THE critical period in a young man's life is when he leaves home, the presence and influence of his parents, his instructors and early associates, to start in life for himself, and to make new companions and acquaintances. A large majority leave the country and settle in our large towns and cities. They are drawn to these centers supposing the chances of success are more favorable, and the sphere of operation much larger. They come with their ambition on fire, and with visions of wealth before them. They come with a mother's prayers, youthful purity and vigor, inexperienced in crime, ignorant of the devices of wicked men, unsuspicious, and consequently easily entrapped. Soon they find themselves among strangers, and with entirely new surroundings. The quiet of their country home is exchanged for the din and bustle of business. Instead of spending their evenings around the bright and pleasant hearthstone of the old homestead, they find themselves in the crowded street, amid the glare of temptations. It is a great disadvantage,—in fact, a misfortune,—for a young man to be a stranger. The devil is sure to tempt him when lonely.

How weak we all are when alone. How little we seem when among absolute strangers. How much of life is wrapped up in our hearts. How love strengthens character and surrounds it with bulwarks. All this the young man forfeits when he leaves home and takes the risk of unfavorable surroundings in a strange city.

A young man without a home, or some special friends whom he can visit in their own private homes, in a large city, is to be pitied.

YOUNG MEN LEAVING HOME.

For a whole year young men in our cities never sit down in quiet conversation with a family group. They know no families. They are only acquainted with those like themselves, whose chief attraction is the street or the theater. Society, in the higher sense of the term, they know nothing about. They are not at ease in the company of the refined and religious. Their taste is gross and sensual; their conversation has the ring of coarseness; their manners are rough; their ease and grace in virtuous company are gone. Such society becomes distasteful. They prefer the club-room to the parlor, the ball to the private circle at home, the boisterous crowd of the street to the intelligent society of ladies or the elevating influence of music.

Thus we see hundreds and thousands of young men slowly going down to ruin. One restraint after another is broken; old friendships lose their power; early recollections fade slowly away; home is forgotten, or seldom visited; church is neglected; the old Bible, the mother's gift, is unread and unstudied; and deeper and deeper they plunge for gratification. To silence conscience they benumb their feelings with strong drink. To bury thoughts of former innocence and of home, they rush into all kinds of amusements and excitements. Reflection, self-examination, thoughts of accountability to God,—these become purgatory to the soul,—hence, they must be thoughtless, indifferent, and even scoffers at religion. They soon destroy health, blast character, and come down to a sick and dying bed. They break a mother's heart, fill an untimely grave, and lose their souls.

How sad and heartrending this scene. O, God! pity and save these straying lambs, lost in our city vices, and on the road to hell! Christian young men, unite, combine, organize, pray, work, and turn their feet into the royal highway of God's redeemed people. Church-members, welcome them to your churches, your pews.

YOUNG MEN LEAVING HOME.

hem; invite them to come again. Be kind to them, and pluck a jewel from the mire to shine in Christ's coronet. in saving one soul, set in motion a wave of influence and good that shall roll on through the ages, and never cease.
an Voices.

---

mix with the world for the pleasure it affords, we shall be ly to be among the first to be reconciled to the freedom nd laxity it allows. The world is not brought up to us, nk down to the world; the drop becomes of the consistence of the ocean into which it falls; the ocean itself remains d.
Dr. James Walker.

---

are judged not by their intentions, but by the result of ir actions. *Lord Chesterfield.*

---

generous heart should scorn a pleasure which gives others n. *James Thomson.*

R is the true alchemist which beats out in patient transmution the baser metals into gold.
W. Morley Punshon, LL.D.

---

only strike while the iron is hot, but make it hot by striking.
Oliver Cromwell.

For a whole year young men in our cities never sit down i
conversation with a family group. They know no families.
are only acquainted with those like themselves, whose chief
tion is the street or the theater. Society, in the higher sense
term, they know nothing about. They are not at ease in th
pany of the refined and religious. Their taste is gross and s
their conversation has the ring of coarseness; their mann
rough; their ease and grace in virtuous company are gone.
society becomes distasteful. They prefer the club-room
parlor, the ball to the private circle at home, the boisterous cr
the street to the intelligent society of ladies or the elevating in
of music.

Thus we see hundreds and thousands of young men slowly
down to ruin. One restraint after another is broken; old
ships lose their power; early recollections fade slowly away
is forgotten, or seldom visited; church is neglected; the old
the mother's gift, is unread and unstudied; and deeper and
they plunge for gratification. To silence conscience they b
their feelings with strong drink. To bury thoughts of forme
cence and of home, they rush into all kinds of amusemer
excitements. Reflection, self-examination, thoughts of ac
bility to God,—these become purgatory to the soul,—henc
must be thoughtless, indifferent, and even scoffers at religion.
soon destroy health, blast character, and come down to a si
dying bed. They break a mother's heart, fill an untimely
and lose their souls.

How sad and heartrending this scene. O, God! pity an
these straying lambs, lost in our city vices, and on the road t
Christian young men, unite, combine, organize, pray, work, a
their feet into the royal highway of God's redeemed
Church-members, welcome them to your churches, your

YOUNG MEN LEAVING HOME.

Speak to them; invite them to come again. Be kind to them, and you may pluck a jewel from the mire to shine in Christ's coronet. You may, in saving one soul, set in motion a wave of influence and power for good that shall roll on through the ages, and never cease. —*Christian Voices.*

IF we mix with the world for the pleasure it affords, we shall be likely to be among the first to be reconciled to the freedom and laxity it allows. The world is not brought up to us, but we sink down to the world; the drop becomes of the consistence and color of the ocean into which it falls; the ocean itself remains unchanged. *Dr. James Walker.*

MEN are judged not by their intentions, but by the result of their actions. *Lord Chesterfield.*

THE generous heart should scorn a pleasure which gives others pain. *James Thomson.*

LABOR is the true alchemist which beats out in patient transmutation the baser metals into gold.
W. Morley Punshon, LL.D.

Not only strike while the iron is hot, but make it hot by striking.
Oliver Cromwell.

RETURNING HOME.

Miss Mulock.

WE sometimes meet with men who seem to think that any indulgence in an affectionate feeling is weakness. They return from a journey, greet their families with a distant dignity, and move among their children with the cold and lofty splendor of an iceberg surrounded by its broken fragments.

There is hardly a more unnatural sight than one of those families without a heart. A father had better extinguish a boy's eyes than take away his heart. Who that has experienced the joys of friendship, and values sympathy and affection, would not rather lose all that is beautiful in Nature's scenery than be robbed of the hidden treasure of his heart? Cherish, then, your heart's best affection. Indulge in the warm and gushing emotions of filial and fraternal love.

TRAVELING HOME.

Byran W. Proctor.

TOUCH us gently, Time,
   Let us glide adown thy stream
   Gently—as we sometimes glide
Through a quiet dream.
Humble voyagers are we,
Husband, wife, and children three;
One is lost—an angel, fled
To the azure overhead!

HOME, SWEET HOME!
John Howard Payne.

'MID pleasures and palaces though we may roam,
    Be it ever so humble, there's no place like home!
    A charm from the skies seems to follow us there,
Which, seek through the world, is ne'er met with elsewhere.
        Home, home! Sweet home!
        There's no place like home!

An exile from home, splendor dazzles in vain;
O, give me my lowly thatched cottage again!
The birds singing gaily, that came at my call:
Give me these, and the peace of mind dearer than all.
        Home, home! Sweet home!
        There's no place like home!

MEMORY OF HOME.
T. Buchanan Read.

BETWEEN broad fields of wheat and corn
    Is the lowly home where I was born.
    The peach-tree leans against the wall,
And the woodbine wanders over all.
There is the barn, and as of yore
I can smell the hay from the open door,
And see the busy swallows throng,
And hear the peewee's mournful song.
Oh, ye who daily cross the sill,
Step lightly, for I love it still.

JOYS OF HOME.

John Bowring.

Sweet are the joys of home,
    And pure as sweet; for they
Like dews of morn and evening come,
    To make and close the day.

The world hath its delights,
    And its delusions, too;
But home to calmer bliss invites,
    More tranquil and more true.

The mountain flood is strong,
    But fearful in its pride;
While gently rolls the stream along
    The peaceful valley's side.

Life's charities, like light,
    Spread smilingly afar;
But stars approached, become more bright,
    And home is life's own star.

The pilgrim's step in vain
    Seeks Eden's sacred ground!
But in home's holy joys again
    An Eden may be found.

A glance of heaven to see,
    To none on earth is given;
And yet a happy family
    Is but an earlier heaven.

HARVEST HOME.

Jas. Montgomery.

SOW in the morn thy seed,
  At eve hold not thy hand;
To doubt and fear give thou no heed;
  Broadcast it o'er the land.

Beside all waters sow,
  The highway furrows stock;
Drop it where thorns and thistles grow,
  Scatter it on the rock.

The good, the fruitful ground,
  Expect not everywhere;
O'er hill and dale, by plots, 'tis found;
  Go forth, then, everywhere.

Thou knowest not which may thrive,
  The late, or early sown;
Grace keeps the precious germ alive,
  When, and wherever strown.

And duly shall appear,
  In verdure, beauty, strength,
The tender blade, the stalk, the ear,
  And the full corn at length.

Thou canst not toil in vain;
    Cold, heat and moist and dry,
Shall foster and mature the grain
    For garners in the sky.

Hence, when the glorious end,
    The day of God is come,
The angel reapers shall descend
    And heaven cry " Harvest Home."

OUR LAST FAREWELLS.
Carlos Wilcox.

OUR life is like the hurrying on the eve
    Before we start on some long journey,
    When our preparing to the last we leave,
Then run to every room the dwelling round,
And sigh that nothing needed can be found;
    Yet go we must, and soon as day shall break;
    We snatch an hour's repose, when loud the sound
For our departure calls; we rise and take
    A quick and sad farewell, and go ere well awake.

FAREWELL TO HOME.
Robert Southey.

FAREWELL, my home, my home no longer now,
    Witness of many a calm and happy day;
    And thou, fair eminence, upon whose brow
Dwells the last sunshine of the evening ray.

WELCOME HOME.

Farewell! Mine eyes no longer shall pursue
The westering sky beyond the utmost height,
When slowly he forsakes the fields of light.
No more the freshness of the falling dew,
Cool and delightful here shall bathe my head,
As from this western window dear, I lean
Listening the while I watch the placid scene—
The martins twittering underneath the shed.
Farewell, my home, where many a day has passed
In joys, whose loved remembrance long shall last.

THE FAMILY MEETING.

Charles Sprague.

WE are all here!
    Father, mother, sister, brother,
      All who hold each other dear.
Each chair is fill'd; we're all at *home:*
To-night, let no cold stranger come:
It is not often thus around
Our old familiar hearth we're found:
Bless then the meeting and the spot;
For once, be every care forgot;
Let gentle Peace assert her power,
And kind Affection rule the hour;
    We're *all—all* here.

    We're *not* all here!
Some are away, the *dead* ones dear,
Who thronged with us this ancient hearth,
And gave the hour to guiltless mirth.

THE FAMILY MEETING.

Fate, with a stern, relentless hand,
Look'd in and thinn'd our little band;
Some, like a night-flash, pass'd away,
And some sank lingering day by day;
The quiet grave-yard—some lie there—
And cruel ocean has *his* share :
      We're *not* all here.

      We *are* all here!
Even *they*, the *dead*—though dead, so dear,
Fond Memory, to her duty true,
Brings back *their* faded forms to view.
How life-like through the mist of years,
Each well-remember'd face appears!
We see them as in times long past;
From each to each kind looks are cast;
We hear their *words*, their *smiles* behold,
They're round us, as they were of old—
      We *are* all here!

      We are all here!
Father, mother, sister, brother,
    You that I love with love so dear.
This may not long of us be said;
Soon must we join the gather'd dead,
And by the hearth we now sit round,
Some *other* circle will be found.
Oh! then, that wisdom may we know,
Which yields a life of peace below;
So, in the world to follow this,
May each repeat, in words of bliss,
      We're *all—all—here!*

HEAVEN.

The way to heaven.—*You have only to turn to the right and go straight forward.* BISHOP OF LONSDALE.

He who seldom thinks of heaven is not likely to get there. The way to hit the mark is to keep the eye fixed upon it.
BISHOP HORNE

THE ANGEL OF PEACE.

HEAVEN.

[WRITTEN EXPRESSLY FOR THIS WORK.]

By *Fanny J. Crosby.*

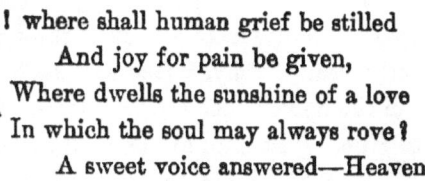

! where shall human grief be stilled
   And joy for pain be given,
Where dwells the sunshine of a love
In which the soul may always rove ?
   A sweet voice answered—Heaven.

O, heart, I said, when death shall come
   And all thy cords be riven,
What lies beyond the swelling tide ?
The same sweet voice to mine replied
   In loving accents—Heaven.

Where, where shall friendship never die ?
   Nor parting hand be given ?
My heart was filled with strange delight,
For in that silent hush of night,
   I heard the answer—Heaven.

O, voyager on life's fitful sea ;
   By stormy billows driven ;
Say, what can soothe thy aching breast,
Or, give thee comfort, joy and rest,
   Like Mother, Home and Heaven ?

THE APOSTLE JOHN'S IDEA OF HEAVEN.
James W. Alexander, D.D.

"We know not what we shall be; but we know that when He shall appear we shall be like Him, for we shall see Him as he is."

THIS is the apostle John's idea of heaven. "We shall see Him as He is." This will be enough. Here we have seen by glimpses, cloudily, in an enigma, "through a glass darkly;" but then clearly, nearly, fully, "face to face." And the object so seen is of all in the universe the most worthy of being contemplated. God shines in Him. "In Him dwelleth all the fullness of the Godhead bodily." To see Him, in the fullness of his unvailed excellence, will be a celestial pleasure, well worth dying for.

PAUL'S ESTIMATE OF HEAVEN.
Hannah More.

"I RECKON," he says, like a man skilled in spiritual arithmetic. "I reckon," after a due estimate of their comparative value, "that the sufferings of this present time are not worthy to be compared with the glory that shall be revealed."

No man was ever so well qualified to make this estimate. Of the sufferings of the present world, he had shared more largely than any other man. Of the glory that shall be revealed, he had a glimpse granted to no other man. He had heard the words of God, and seen the vision of the Almighty, and the result of this privileged experience was, he "desired to depart and be with Christ;" he desired to escape from this valley of tears; he was impatient to recover the celestial vision, eager to perpetuate the momentary foretaste of the glories of immortality.

HEAVEN A HOME.

Thomas Guthrie.

HOME! oh, how sweet is that word! what beautiful and tender associations cluster thick around it; compared with it, house, mansion, palace, are cold, heartless terms. But home! that word quickens the pulse, warms the heart, stirs the soul to its depths, makes age feel young again, rouses apathy into energy, sustains the sailor in his midnight watch, inspires the soldier with courage on the field of battle, and imparts patient endurance to the worn-down sons of toil. The thought of it has proved a seven-fold shield to virtue; the very name of it has a spell to call back the wanderer from the paths of vice; and far away, where myrtles bloom, and palm-trees wave, and the ocean sleeps upon coral strands, to the exile's fond fancy it clothes the naked rock, or stormy shore, or barren moor, or wild Highland mountain with charms he weeps to think of, and longs once more to see. Grace sanctifies these lovely affections, and imparts a sacredness to the homes of earth by making them types of Heaven. As a home, the believer delights to think of it. Thus, while lately bending over a dying saint, and expressing our sorrow to see him lay so low, with the radiant countenance rather of one who had just left Heaven, than of one about to enter it, he raised and clasped his hands, and exclaimed in ecstasy, "I am going home."

IN Heaven hands clasp forever.
Greek Proverb.

HEAVEN.

Daniel March, D.D.

WE are warranted in ascribing to that blessed state all that is most genial and ennobling in occupation; all that is most enduring and satisfying in possession; all that is most pure and excellent in character. The occupations of heaven are endless praise, triumph, joy. The possessions of heaven are infinite glory, riches, knowledge. The character of heaven is perfect love, holiness, peace. These things we can at present know only in part, and the word of divine revelation itself must of necessity tell us much of what heaven is by telling us what it is not. With all our studies and all deepest experience we shall never fathom the full meaning of the one word—Heaven.

HEAVEN A CITY.

Thomas Guthrie.

A CITY never built with hands, nor hoary with the years of time; a city whose inhabitants no census has numbered; a city through whose streets rush no tide of business, nor nodding hearse creeps slowly with its burden to the tomb; a city without griefs or graves, without sins or sorrows, without births or burials, without marriages or mournings; a city which glories in having Jesus for its king, angels for its guards, saints for citizens; whose walls are salvation, and whose gates are praise.

HEAVEN A RESTING-PLACE.

Chas. Mackay.

TELL me, ye winged winds,
   That round my pathway roar,
   Do ye not know some spot,
Where mortals weep no more?
Some lone and pleasant dell,
Some valley in the west,
Where, free from toil and pain,
The weary soul may rest?
The loud wind dwindled to a whisper low
And sighed for pity as it answered, no!

Tell me, thou mighty deep,
Whose billows round me play,
Know'st thou some favored spot,
Some island far away,
Where weary man may find
The bliss for which he sighs,
Where sorrow never lives
And friendship never dies?
The loud waves rolling in perpetual flow,
Stopped for a while, and sighed to answer, no!

And thou, serenest moon,
That with such holy face
Dost look upon the earth
Asleep in night's embrace,

MY FATHER'S HOUSE.

Tell me, in all thy round,
Hast thou not seen some spot
Where miserable man
Might find a happier lot?
Behind a cloud the moon withdrew in woe,
And a voice sweet but sad responded, no!

Tell me, my secret soul,
Oh, tell me, hope and faith,
Is there no resting-place,
From sorrow, sin, and death,
Is there no happy spot,
Where mortals may be blest,
Where grief may find a balm,
And weariness a rest?
Faith, hope and love, best boons to mortal given,
Waved their bright wings and whispered, yes, yes, in Heaven.

MY FATHER'S HOUSE.

Mrs. H. B. Stowe.

"LET not your heart be troubled," then He said,
    "My Father's house has mansions large and fair;
    I go before you to prepare your place;
I will return to take you with Me there."
And since that hour, the awful foe is charmed,
And life and death are glorified and fair;
  Whither He went, we know—the way we know,
And with firm step press on to meet him there.

THE HEAVENLY PLACE.

Howard Crosby, D.D.

WE are accustomed to say that space and time are only conditions of our finite and composite natures, and that to unfettered spirits there would be recognition of neither space nor time. Whether this be so or not, no man can tell. It is a transcendentalism that it is folly to talk about. Time and space are absolute necessities to our thinking. Every conception of our mind is formed on them as a foundation; and we can have no idea of God himself except as in time and space. Hence we must (whether we will or no), take the word "place" of our text literally. Even if it be not literally a place, we *think of it* as a place, for we cannot think of it in any other way. We are not up to this. And, moreover, from the words being used when our Saviour might have said simply, "I go to *prepare* for you," we may infer that it is actually a place (as we understand the word) that is meant here. Farther than that perhaps would be only fancy, and in that region of fancy we cannot find it profitable to wander. But that on which we may dwell with profit is, first, that the place is prepared *by our Lord;* and, secondly, that it is prepared *for us.* What a place that must be which Christ prepares, which His almighty power and infinite love combined make ready for our abode! It must be a place where every purified desire of the heart shall have perpetual satisfaction, and where Christ's own happiness shall be shared by those for whom he died. If these are to be the characteristics of that future home, it makes very little difference what the special forms of occupation, or the objective elements beheld by the soul in that better world may be. The inner soul longs for happiness—it is only the outward and changeable sense that would dictate its form. That it is pure and holy and that it has Christ, our Lord and Saviour in it—this is enough. We know the delicious contents of the vessel, if we do not know the shape and color of the vessel containing.

Imagery may be valuable as a help, provided we do not rest our hope and affections and desires upon the images, but upon the ineffable and indescribable beyond. The Christians of the earliest age were always looking forward. Christ's coming was the controlling and encouraging thought of their daily life. The patriarchs and holy saints of the other dispensation were always looking forward—toward the heavenly country. In different ways the Spirit of God led them to anticipate the developments of God's saving grace in the enjoyment of glory. This lifted them above earthly despondences and saved them from a thousand snares. As God's people, that should be *our* position, and looking unto Jesus, unto him *preparing our place,* our eternal place. Our conversation or citizenship is in heaven. Our treasures are there. Our hearts should be there. God's consolations are not like men's, mere soothers of the troubled mind, but seeds of positive and independent joy. God's grace comes with a set-off that belittles the earthly care and sorrow. If a soldier in the ranks is wounded, it is one thing to apply soothing cataplasms to stay the pain, but it is a grander thing and a better thing for his general to come to him and bestow upon him the title, rank and insignia of a high officer. And so our God gives us in the heavenly title and its pledges, the possession of a divine and eternal joy as against all the aches and pains of this little day of earth. Yea, he makes the aches subserve the glory and work directly into it. "This light affliction, which is but for a moment, *worketh for us* a far more exceeding and eternal weight of glory." We have had those who are very dear to us pass beyond this narrow world, out of our sight. How the Lord stays our tears by these words of our text!

They are in the place prepared for them and for us by Jesus. "To depart" is "to be with Christ." This is the "*far better*" of the apostles which those dear ones now know all about. And still the place with its many abodes, is being prepared by the same Jesus; and you and I, conducted by Him, will one after another enter into the joy of our Lord.

THOUGHTS OF HEAVEN.
Wm. Pearce.

I LOVE to think of heaven, it seems not far away,
Its crystal streams refresh me as I near the closing day;
Its balmy winds are wafted from the heavenly hills above,
And they fold me in an atmosphere of purity and love.

I love to think of heaven, I long to join the choir,
To sing the song of Jesus my soul would never tire;
The loved ones gone before me, are joining in the song,
They cast their crowns before the Lamb who sits upon the throne.

I love to think of heaven, where the weary are at rest,
No sorrow there can enter the mansions of the blest;
All tears are wiped away by the Saviour's loving hand,
And sin and death are banished from that glorious happy land.

I love to think of heaven, and the greetings I shall meet,
From the loving band of loved ones, who walk the golden street;
And the patriarchs and prophets I shall know them every one:
It is written in the Word, "We shall know as we are known."

RECOGNITION IN HEAVEN.

The gospel seer Isaiah, and the plaintive Jeremiah,
And Elijah, who ascended in the chariot of fire;
And Daniel, the beloved, and the Hebrew children three,
The robed in white, and crowned, will be known by you and me.

But oh, the rapturous vision when our eyes behold the King,
And hear the thrilling welcome, "Ye blessed, enter in!"
Ten thousand suns encircle Him, ten thousand crowns adorn
The sacred head that bow'd in death—the head once crowned with
  thorns.

Assemble, all ye hosts, ye thrones, dominions, powers!
There is no king like Jesus! there is no heaven like ours!
All glory hallelujah! let heaven and earth unite
To celebrate His praises with infinite delight.

RECOGNITION IN HEAVEN.
Robert Southey

OWHEN a Mother meets on high
  The babe she lost in infancy,
  Hath she not then for pains and fears,
The day of woe, the watchful night—
For all her sorrows, all her tears,
An over-payment of delight?

FRIENDS, even in heaven, one happiness would miss
  Should they not know each other when in bliss.
                              Bishop Thomas Ken.

ATTRACTIONS OF HEAVEN.

Bernard Barton.

THOUGH earth has fully many a beautiful spot,
As a poet or painter might show,
Yet more lovely and beautiful, holy and bright,
To the hopes of the heart and the spirit's glad sight,
Is the land that no mortal may know.
O! who but must pine in this dark vale of tears,
From its clouds and its shadows to go,
To walk in the light of the glory above,
And to share in the peace, and the joy, and the love,
Of the land that no mortal may know!
There the crystalline stream, bursting forth from the throne,
Flows on, and forever will flow;
Its waves as they roll are with melody rife,
And its waters are sparkling with beauty and life,
In the land which no mortal may know.
And there on its margin, with leaves ever green,
With its fruits healing sickness and woe,
The fair tree of life, in its glory and pride,
Is fed by that deep, inexhaustible tide
Of the land which no mortal may know.

THE truest end of life is to know the life that never ends.
William Penn.

ENTERING HEAVEN.

Rev. J. L. Harris.

DID you ever try to imagine the soul's impressions when it first enters heaven? I remember distinctly my impressions when entering for the first time the city of New York. It was on the evening of a beautiful May-day. The soft strains of music from the band which had accompanied us on our journey were wafted out on the evening air, and fell sweetly on many a listening ear. The sun was just setting. His departing rays hung lingeringly upon the distant hill-tops, as if loath to bid the city adieu.

The noble steamer which had borne us down the Hudson was rounding to at the pier. I had heard and thought much about this great city, of its bustling throng, its crowded Broadway, its shaded avenues, its enchanting parks, its stately mansions, and magnificent churches; and now it lies just before me in all its reality. There were its forests of ship-masts, its domes and lofty spires glittering in the evening sunlight. I could hear the hum of voices, the roll of wheels, and the tramp of hurrying footsteps, while from a passing band there came notes of sweetest music. In a few moments I was to mingle with that human throng, and look with my own eyes upon the wonders of the great metropolis. I shall never forget the impressions of that hour.

If earthly scenes so impress us, how then must it be with the saint when first entering the great metropolis of heaven? The old ship upon which he has crossed the swelling sea is just gliding into the quiet harbor, and rounding to at the heavenly pier. The eternal city is just before him; the sunlight of glory floods all its streets, and bathes its "many mansions" and beautiful landscapes in mellow splendor. The God-built stories of the New Jerusalem rise before him in all their matchless grandeur. He sees the golden streets, the gates of pearl, the sea of glass, the river of life, and the throne of God.

The song of angels mingling with the harps of heaven now fall upon his ear. Never has he heard such music. He may have heard the loud swell of the rich-toned organ, and the majestic burst of praise which has gone up from a thousand well-trained voices. But now, when he hears even the *first* notes of the ransomed throng, the thoughts of all earthly music are forgotten. John says, "I heard a great voice of much people in heaven saying, Alleluia! Salvation, and glory, and honor, and power, unto the Lord our God. And I heard as it were the voice of a great multitude, and as the voice of many waters, and as the voice of mighty thunderings, saying Alleluia, for the Lord God omnipotent reigneth." As this mighty chorus comes swelling up the vales, trembling along the hills, and echoing over the plains, his rapt spirit is filled with an intensity of bliss known only to heavenly hearts.

Friends who had preceded him to glory now meet him. Angels come and bid him welcome to the skies, while those who had borne him from earth to his home in heaven lead him to the Lamb. He sees now, not "through a glass darkly," but face to face. He sees the Saviour "as He is." The vail has been removed, and he looks with undimmed vision upon the "King in his beauty."

He stands transfixed, and gazes with mute and inexpressible wonder. Gushing streams of bliss come pouring in upon him, flooding every avenue of his wonder-stricken soul. The Saviour, rising, addresses him, saying, "Well, done, good and faithful servant," and then places a crown upon his head.

O, bliss of bliss! O, joys of joys! Heaven itself has no language to express the rapture which a blood-washed soul will experience when Jesus shall place the crown of life upon its brow and a harp within its hand.

See him now as the Lamb leads him out "into green pastures, and beside the still waters." He stands upon the banks of the crystal stream which flows from the throne of God; as he gazes upon its placid surface, the voicings and harpings of saints and angels come trembling along the shore. Their sweet vibrations strike every chord of his immortal heart, tuning it to sing in unison with the heavenly choir, when, for the *first* time, he joins with the blood-washed throng in singing, "Worthy is the Lamb that was slain to receive power, and riches, and wisdom, and strength, and honor, and glory and blessing. Glory and honor, and power be unto Him that sitteth upon the throne, and unto the Lamb for ever and ever."

Surely one such moment of bliss would more than balance all the woes and sorrows of earth. It is more than language can express or imagination conceive. "Eye hath not seen, nor ear heard, neither have entered into the heart of man the things which God hath prepared for them that love Him." I wait in joyous hope to see the day that "crowns me at His side." I long to feel the unutterable bliss; to experience the consciousness of the first full draught from the fountain of immortality.

WHEN I get to Heaven, I shall see three wonders there. The first wonder will be to see people there that I did not expect; the second wonder will be to miss many persons whom I did expect to see; and the third and greatest wonder of all will be to find myself there. *John Newton.*

DELIGHTS OF HEAVEN.

Isaac Watts.

THERE is a land of pure delight,
   Where saints immortal reign;
Infinite day excludes the night,
   And pleasures banish pain.

There everlasting spring abides,
   And never-with'ring flowers;
Death, like a narrow sea, divides
   This heavenly land from ours.

Sweet fields beyond the swelling flood
   Stand dress'd in living green;
So to the Jews old Canaan stood,
   While Jordan roll'd between.

Could we but climb where Moses stood,
   And view the landscape o'er,
Not Jordan's stream, nor death's cold flood,
   Should fright us from the shore.

MY knowledge of that life is small,
   The eye of faith is dim,
But 'tis enough that Christ knows all,
And I shall be with him.   *Baxter.*

BEAUTIFUL HEAVEN.

Delia E. Walker.

BEAUTIFUL Heaven, blissful abode,
   Evergreen fields in the city of God;
   The gate ajar by faith I see,
      And the blessed Saviour that died for me.

Beautiful fields, ever green,
With nothing but the vail between.
When life is spent and the vail is rent,
Our vision bright shall behold the sight.

The jasper walls, the streets of gold,
The Lamb of God, the Shepherd's fold,
The saint's sweet rest,
 In the land of the blest.

My soul in its vision would fain take its flight,
And soar to that beautiful land of light,
Away to that blissful home on high,
Where we shall live to love and never die.

And there, where the white-robed angels are,
Within the gate that's left ajar,
Would seek to dwell in the land of the blest,
Forever with God's saints at rest.

Oh! beautiful home, sweet Eden land,
No storms ever beat on thy glittering strand;
O! my dear Saviour, fain would I flee,
And be forever at rest with thee.

SONGS IN HEAVEN.

M. T. B.

IF music be so very sweet,
   While here we plod along,
What must it be when our tired feet
   Shall tread the Shore of Song!

If Christian fellowship can bind
   Our hearts in bonds of love,
What may it not be when we find
   Ourselves at Home, above?

If here we take delight in prayer,
   And love God's throne of grace,
Then may we long, without a fear,
   To meet Him face to face.

'Tis said, perhaps it may be true,
   " Prayer ends with earthly days;
Or, rather, that it flows into
   One ceaseless song of praise."

When we shall tread the shore of song,
   Where music ever rings;
When we shall join the radiant throng
   And see the King of kings;

Then shall the worth of prayer be shown,
   The soul of song be given,
And sweetest fellowship be known
   To all who're safe in Heaven.

HYMNS OF HEAVEN.

Theo. L. Cuyler, D.D.

I HAD rather be the author of "Rock of Ages"—that crown-jewel of sacred minstrelsy—than of either of President Edwards' masterly treatises. Charles Wesley did more for Christ when he sang

"Jesus, lover of my soul!"

than if he had written fifty volumes of sound theology. The hymn itself would be enough to make Wesley's and Calvin's spirits embrace each other before the throne of their Redeemer, and weep that they ever had a controversy while in the flesh.

Among the ancient hymns of heaven we must not overlook that noble lyric composed by old Bernard of Cluny. Its opening verse is,

"Jerusalem, the golden!
With milk and honey blest,
Beneath thy contemplation
Sink heart and voice oppressed!"

The whole hymn reads like one of holy Rutherford's "Letters," turned into rhyme. It is rich in scriptural imagery, without degenerating into the coarser sensuous language which disfigures some of the pious doggerel in our Sabbath-school music books. In fact, some of these descriptions of heaven would answer about as well for Mohammed's Paradise. They give children the idea that the glorified spirits on high are enjoying a sort of celestial *picnic*, with no end of good things to eat, and of angels to sing to them under the green bowers.

In my own childhood I got a very different conception of the holy habitation of the redeemed, when I heard that glorious hymn of Isaac Watts:

> "There is a land of pure delight
> Where saints immortal reign,
> Infinite day excludes the night,
> And pleasures banish pain."

As the inspired singer of this lay looked across Southampton water to the verdant banks of the Isle of Wight, he caught a beautiful image of death as a "narrow sea" dividing the heavenly land from ours. He imagines the lovely island across the water to be a type of that land, and writes—

> "Sweet fields beyond the swelling flood
> Stand dressed in living green;
> So to the Jews old Canaan stood
> While Jordan rolled between."

Of many another hymn of heaven I wish I had time and space to write. In our days several fine additions have been made to this celestial hymnology. Among them are "Rest for the Weary," and Dr. Muhlenberg's "I would not Live alway."

ECHOES FROM HEAVEN.

John Cumming, D.D.

ON the shores of the Adriatic, the wives of fishermen whose husbands have gone far out upon the deep, are in the habit, at eventide, of going down to the seashore and singing, as female voices only can, the first stanza of a beautiful hymn. After they have sung it, they listen till they hear, borne by the winds across the desert sea, the second stanza, sung by their gallant husbands as they are tossed by the gale upon the waves. Perhaps, if we could listen, we too might hear on this desert world of ours, some sound, some whisper, borne from afar, to remind us that there is a heaven and a home.

HEAVENLY REALITIES.

Miss Marsh.

WE are invited to enjoy a perfect sympathy with the Bridegroom of our souls, to have a complete oneness of interest with Him in all that concerns His kingdom and glory; as well as to live constantly upon His grace, holiness, wisdom, power, and love.

Just as we live our natural lives by breathing in the air that surrounds us, unconsciously, more often than consciously, we may still live and move, and have our being in Christ, even when we are necessarily occupied with other thoughts and duties; and be ready, the instant we are "let go" from outward objects and claims, to return joyfully "to our own company," our Blessed Lord himself.

Into this purer, higher atmosphere, all who have accepted Jesus as their Saviour might be lifted up—simply by looking unto Him with the same look of hope and trust with which they passed from death unto life.

"Looking unto Jesus—to be made patient with His patience, active with His activity, loving with His love; asking, not 'What can I?' but, 'What cannot He!' and waiting upon His strength, which is made perfect in weakness. Looking unto Jesus, in order that the brightness of His face may be the light of our darkness, that our joys may be holy, and our sorrows calm."

> " Higher, higher, every thought
> More into His presence brought,
> Every passion, every feeling,
> More His hidden life revealing.
> Less of self, from hour to hour,
> More of Christ's transforming power,

Yearnings heavenward to aspire
Unto Jesus, higher, higher.

"Higher, higher, till at length,
Going on from strength to strength,
Passing up, from grace to grace.
I behold that longed-for face,
Which is ever o'er me leaning
With its deep and tender meaning,
And doth into light retire
But to lead me higher, higher."

THE CHRISTIAN IN HEAVEN.

John S. C. Abbott, D.D.

THE question often is asked, "If Christians in heaven know all that is transpiring upon earth, suppose a sainted mother sees a son or a daughter here going in the ways of ruin, how can she be happy?"

This is a mystery which God has not yet explained to us. It seems, now, impossible that a mother can be happy in heaven with her child forever banished from her. But let us remember that God is more truly the parent of every being on earth than its earthly father or mother can possibly be.

We are God's sons and daughters in a far higher sense than we are the sons or daughters of our earthly parents. God made our bodies and our spirits. God became man, and, by his own humiliation and sufferings upon the cross, made atonement for our sins. Year after year, with yearning utterance, God has cried out to us, "My son, my daughter, give me thine heart." Yes, God is our father in a far more exalted sense than any earthly parent can be. Earthly love is frail and variable. God's love is unchanging.

In the heavenly world we shall be like God. "Beloved, now are we the sons of God, and it doth not yet appear what we shall be; but we know that when He shall appear we shall be like Him." 1 John, iii. 2. God will open to us there views of which here we can form no conception. And if God, our living, heavenly Father, can be happy on His eternal throne while some of His children are in persistent rebellion against Him and are suffering the rebels' dreadful doom, earthly parents, translated to heaven, sharing God's nature, with souls ennobled, expanded, illumined with celestial light, will certainly witness nothing in the administration of God's government which will thrill their souls with anguish.

The intelligence of every hearer will assent to the remark that it cannot be that our happiness in heaven will be based upon our *ignorance*. It cannot be that God, in order to save us from sorrow, will, when we are in heaven, find it necessary for our happiness to conceal from us what is transpiring under His government. There we shall be like God, and shall know even as we are known.

The question may arise, "What bearing has this subject upon the doctrine of modern Spiritualism?" It is sufficient to remark that in all the descriptions which the Bible gives us of the visits of angels to this world, they came in dignity worthy of their exalted character. They were ever intrusted with the fulfillment of some sublime mission—as in all the instances recorded in the Old Testament; as in the annunciation to the Virgin; as when the celestial retinue accompanied the Son of God to his birth in the manger; as when Moses and Elias, in anticipation of the dreadful scenes of the cross, met Jesus upon the Mount of Transfiguration.

It will require stronger evidence than has ever yet been presented to my mind to lead me to believe that the spirits of the just made perfect in heaven can ever come to earth in degrading guise, performing ignoble functions and bearing but idle tales.

THE CHRISTIAN IN HEAVEN.

It must be to all minds a cheering thought that our loved ones in heaven are still with us in spirit on earth. It is a cheering thought that when we die we shall still be interested in all that is transpiring on this globe; that we shall know, far more intimately than we can now know, every event which is taking place here. Our vision is now limited. Then we shall embrace in one view all the nations, tribes, and families, from the equator to the poles.

Such is the prospect which is presented to the Christian in the future world. Such is the home, and such the enjoyments we may have forever. To extricate man from the ruin in which he is involved by the fall, Jesus, the Son of God, has died, in atoning sacrifice, upon the cross. To influence the sinner to abandon rebellion, and return to his allegiance to the heavenly King, the Holy Spirit pleads in all the earnest voices of nature and of providence. And our heavenly Father bends over us with parental love, his earnest entreaty being, "My son, my daughter, give me thine heart."

Reader, can you renounce such offers, and live in rejection of the Saviour, when such love invites, and when such dignity and glory are offered to you? Become a Christian, and your life upon earth will be far more happy than it can otherwise be; your nature will be ennobled as your name is enrolled in the sacramental hosts of God's elect; you may then lead others to the Saviour, and thus be a co-worker with God in redeeming a lost world.

Become a Christian, and death shall then be to you but translation to a higher and nobler sphere of action; then, through all the ages of immortality, you shall soar in perfect holiness and ever-increasing bliss. Every possible consideration urges you to become a Christian. To accept Jesus as your Saviour brings upon you, eventually, every conceivable blessing. To reject him dooms you to woe. Delay not this decision. Every hour of delay is full of peril. Now is the accepted time. To-morrow, to you may never come.

THE LAND OF BEULAH.

O. Huntington.

 GLORIOUS land of heavenly light,
Where walk the ransomed, clothed in white,
On hills of myrrh, through pastures green,
No curse, no cloud upon the scene!

Land where the crystal river glides,
And fruits immortal deck its sides;
O land of rest in Eden's bowers.
No dreary days, no weary hours!

No nights of unavailing grief,
Nor crying which brings no relief;
For God shall wipe away all tears,
And into the past are passed our fears.

Beulah, if e'er my weary feet
Shall press thy blissful shore,
And tread each shining, golden street,
To go out thence no more,

What shall I care for all the way
That led to thee at last—
For every dark, despairing day,
For ever, ever past?

If e'er the loved of earthly years
Shall welcome me to thee,
What shall I care for all these tears
Oft flowing bitterly?

THE SILENT SHORE.

If I may stand before His throne,
And look upon His face,
What shall I care that oft, alone,
Like Him, I ran my race?

Safe on thy ever blissful plains,
My heart's own treasure gathered there;
Farewell for ever, sins and pains,
Farewell, bereavement, sorrow, care!

THE SILENT SHORE.
Charles Lamb.

MY sprightly neighbor, gone before
To that unknown and silent shore,
Shall we not meet as heretofore
Some summer morning,
When from thy cheerful eyes a ray
Hath struck a bliss upon the day,
A bliss that would not go away,
A sweet forewarning!

IT is little matter at what hour of the day
The righteous fall asleep. Death cannot come
To him untimely who has learned to die.
The less of this brief life, the more of heaven;
The shorter time, the longer immortality.
Dean Millman.

HEAVEN—NOT FAR AWAY.

OH, heaven is nearer than mortals think,
    When they look with trembling dread,
At the misty future that stretches on,
    From the silent home of the dead.

'Tis no lonely isle on a boundless main,
    No brilliant, but distant shore,
Where the lovely ones who are called away,
    Must go to return no more.

No, heaven is near us; the mighty vail
    Of mortality blinds the eye,
That we can not see the angel bands
    On the shores of eternity.

The eye that shuts in a dying hour,
    Will open the next in bliss;
The welcome will sound in the heavenly world
    Ere the farewell is hushed in this.

We pass from the clasp of mourning friends,
    To the arms of the loved and lost;
And those smiling faces will greet us there,
    Which on earth we have valued most.

Yet oft in the hours of holy thought,
    To the thirsting soul is given,
That power to pierce through the mist of sense,
    To the beauteous scenes of heaven.

FALLING LEAVES—Typical of the Autumn of Life.

Then very near seem its pearly gates,
    And sweetly its harpings fall;
Till the soul is restless to soar away,
    And longs for the angel's call.

I know when the silver cord is loosed,
    When the vail is rent away,
Not long and dark shall the passage be,
    To the realm of endless day.—*Anonymous.*

THERE IS NO DEATH.
Bulwer Lytton.

THERE is no death! The stars go down
    To rise upon some fairer shore;
And bright in Heaven's jeweled crown
    They shine forevermore.

There is no death! The dust we tread
    Shall change beneath the summer showers
To golden grain or mellow fruit,
    Or rainbow-tinted flowers.

The granite rocks disorganize
    To feed the hungry moss they bear,
The forest leaves drink daily life
    From out the viewless air.

There is no death! The leaves may fall,
    The flowers may fade and pass away;
They only wait through wintry hours
    The coming of the May.

THERE IS NO DEATH.

There is no death! An angel form
   Walks o'er the earth with silent tread;
He bears our best-loved things away,
   And then we call them "dead."

He leaves our hearts all desolate,
   He plucks our fairest, sweetest, flowers,
Transplanted into bliss, they now
   Adorn immortal bowers.

The bird-like voice, with joyous tones
   Made glad these scenes of sin and strife,
Sings now an everlasting song
   Amid the tree of life.

And where he sees a smile too bright,
   Or hearts too pure for taint and vice,
He bears it to that world of light,
   To dwell in Paradise.

Born unto that undying life,
   They leave us but to come again;
With joy we welcome them—the same,
   Except in sin and pain.

And ever near us, though unseen,
   The dear, immortal spirits tread;
For all the boundless universe
   Is life—there is no dead.

OUR FRIENDS IN HEAVEN.

HOW beautiful is the belief of man's immortality! The dead alive again, and forever. "Earth to earth, ashes to ashes, dust to dust," is only spoken over the body, when consigned to "the house appointed for all the living." Not such the requiem of the soul. A refrain of immortality concludes earth's history and announces eternity's beginnings. "Not lost, but gone before." Such is the cherished and beautiful faith of man in all ages and lands; a mere glimmering indeed in minds unirradiated with divine truth; and only a power and a joy when God's voice audibly falls upon the ear in words of counsel and prophecy.

The sainted dead dwell in life; beholding "the king in his beauty;" shining "as the brightness of the firmament, and as the stars for ever and ever." They fade no more, nor realize pain; a wealth of love is theirs, a heritage of goodness, a celestial habitation; and in them thoughts, hopes, feelings expand and move forward in ceaseless progressions. We may feel sad because they are lost to us; but while we weep and wonder, they are wrapped in garments of light and warble songs of celestial joy. They will return to us no more; but we shall go to them; share their pleasures; emulate their sympathies; and compete with them in the path of endless development. We would not call them back. In the homes above they are great, and well-employed and blest. Shadows fall upon them no more; nor is life ruffled with anxious cares; love rules their life and thoughts; and eternal hopes beckon them forever to the pursuit of infinite good.

To whom are these thoughts strange and dull? Who has no

treasure in Heaven—well-remembered forms hallowed by separation and distance—stars of hope illumining with ever increasing beauty life's utmost horizon? What family circle has remained unbroken —no empty chair—no cherished mementoes—voices and footsteps returning no more—no members transferred to the illimitable beyond? Where is he who has stood unhurt amid the chill blasts, that have blighted mortal hopes, and withered mortal loves? Alas! the steps of death are everywhere; his voice murmuring in every sweep of the wind; his ruins visible on towering hill and in sequestered vale. We all have *felt* or *seen* his power. Beneath the cypress we rest and weep; our hearts riven with memories of the loved and lost; and yet hope springing eternal from earth's mausoleums to penetrate and possess the future.

Heaven is ours; for is it not occupied by our dead? Heaven and earth lay near together in the myths of the ancients; and shall it be otherwise in the institutions of Christianity? We need faith. Our paths are surrounded by the departed; our assemblies multiplied by their presence; our lives bettered by their ministries. From beneath night shadows we look forward into the approaching day; and while we gaze the beams of the morning spread light and loveliness over the earth. It is not otherwise, as from beneath the night of time we peer anxiously after the pure day of Heaven.

Faith penetrates the vail, and bids the invisible stand disclosed; while its magic wand wakens into life forms well-known, but holier and lovelier far than we knew them here. Such thoughts make us better, purer, gentler. We cannot keep society with the sainted dead, and with the great God in whose presence they dwell, without feeling a nobler life throbbing through us. They draw us upward. We grow less earthly, more heavenly; and God-like aspirations come to us, as we wander along the border land where dwell the sainted dead. Too little do we seek such communings. Our time is so absorbed with perishable and unsatisfying forms of good; and so we lose the image of the heavenly, and grow carnal. The beauty of our life fades; and we are left to hanker after passing shadows and unsubstantial dreams. Let us tear away oftener from these earthly moorings; let us walk more steadily in the light of celestial companionship; and so attain to the true and the good, as they have attained who roam the hills of immortality.

> "They dwell with thee—the dead;
> Pavilioned in auroral tents of light;
> Their spheres of heavenly influence round thee spread,
> Their pure transparence vailing them from sight,
> Angelic ministers of love and peace,
> Whose sweet solicitudes will never cease."

Communion by faith with the immortals can not fail to strengthen us for the stern conflicts of life. At once this earthly existence is seen in its true light; the opening of a day that shall never close; the spring-time of a year that will know no end, the initial chapter in a volume whose records shall find no final page nor incident. When life is thus truly gauged, we learn to place a proper estimate upon its passing pomps and pleasures; and we grow less sensitive to the world's smiles and frowns; more careful to seek after the eternal good. The example of the sainted dead, who toiled and endured till they now reign, affects us; and we feel strong for like conflicts, and ready for equal labors, till in us too the mortal shall put on the immortal. Divine ties spring up, and last forever, binding the heart to the good, the beautiful, the true, and making it strong for the work and trials of life.

And communion with the dead, whom we have known and loved on earth, will make Heaven more real and attractive to us; dissipating the vagueness of the notion with which it is too often regarded; begetting within us abiding attachments for celestial seats. God, who created the world, and whose providence is everywhere visible in promoting our welfare, is there; and Jesus, who died for us, and with whom we have grown familiar in his earthly history; and the Holy Spirit, the sanctifier of the church, and whose gentle influences we have felt within us. And our friends are there, —changeless, loving spirits now,—yet with lineaments familiar and forms well remembered. The homes of the blest are no longer vague, indistinct, poorly defined. We see them—the beautiful city, the outlined hills of immortality—the on-flowing river making glad the palaces of God. And we can have an idea of what they must be —how substantial in their foundations—how vast in their proportions—how rich in their furnishings—to be fitting habitations for the immortals. Heaven comes nearer to us, and grows more attractive, as we think of the loved ones who dwell there.—*Anonymous.*

MINISTERING ANGELS.

THE beautiful have gone with their bloom from the gaze of human eyes. Soft eyes that made it springtime to our hearts are seen no more. We have loved the light of many a smile that has faded from us now; and in our hearts have lingered sweet voices that now are hushed in the silence of death. Seats are left vacant in our earthly homes, which none again can fill. Kindred and friends, loved ones, have passed away one by one; our hearts are left desolate; we are lonely without them. They have passed with their love to "that land, from whose bourne no traveler returns." Shall we never see them again? Memory turns with lingering regret to recall those smiles and the loved tones of those

MINISTERING ANGELS.

dear familiar voices. In fancy they are often by our side, but their home is on a brighter shore. They visit us in our dreams, floating over our memory like shadows over moonlit waters. When the heart is weary with anguish, and the soul is bowed with grief, do they not come and whisper thoughts of comfort and hope? Yes, sweet memory brings them to us, and the love we bore them lifts the heart from earthly aspirations and we long to join them in that better land. They hover round us, the ethereal, dear, departed ones —the loving and the loved, they watch with eyes that slumber not. When gentle dreams are wandering to the angel land, in whispers wake the hymning strains of that bright and happy choir, revealing many a tale of hope, and bliss, and tenderness, and love. They tell of sunny realms, ne'er viewed by mortal eye—of forms arrayed in fadeless beauty—and lofty anthems to their great Creator's praise are sounded forth in sweet, seraphic numbers. And this bright vision of the blest dissolves the tumult of life's jarring scenes; they fade in air, and then we glory in the thought that we are heirs of immortality. And why is it that we regard with such deep reverence and love, those bright, celestial beings of another sphere? Ah, it is because they take an interest in our welfare, and joy over our success in the great battle of life. They are not selfish in their happiness, but fain would have us share it with them.—*Kingswood Chronicle.*

WE have, amid all changes, three unchangeables—an unchangeable covenant, an unchangeable God, and an unchangeable heaven; and while these three remain " the same yesterday, to-day, and forever," welcome the will of our Heavenly Father in all events that may happen to us. Come what will, nothing can come amiss. *Rev. Matthew Henry.*

THE STARLESS CROWN.

J. L. H.

WEARIED and worn with earthly care, I yielded to repose,
And soon before my raptured sight a glorious vision rose.
I thought, while slumbering on my couch in midnight's solemn gloom,
I heard an angel's silvery voice, and radiance filled my room.
A gentle touch awakened me; a gentle whisper said,
"Arise, O sleeper, follow me!" and through the air we fled:
We left the earth so far away that like a speck it seemed,
And heavenly glory, calm and pure, across our pathway streamed.

Still on he went; my soul was wrapped in silent ecstasy;
I wondered what the end would be, what next would meet my eye.
I knew not how we journeyed through the pathless fields of light,
When suddenly a change was wrought, and I was clothed in white.
We stood before a city's walls, most glorious to behold;
We passed through streets of glittering pearl, o'er streets of purest gold.
It needed not the sun by day, nor silver moon by night;
The glory of the Lord was there, the Lamb himself its light.

Bright angels paced the shining streets, sweet music filled the air,
And white-robed saints, with glittering crowns, from every clime were there;
And some that I had loved on earth stood with them round the throne.
"All worthy is the Lamb," they sang, "the glory His alone."

THE STARLESS CROWN.

But, fairer far than all beside, I saw my Saviour's face,
And as I gazed, He smiled on me, with wondrous love and grace,
Slowly I bowed before His throne, o'erjoyed that I at last
Had gained the object of my hopes, that earth at length was past.

And then in solemn tones He said, "Where is the diadem
That ought to sparkle on thy brow, adorned with many a gem?
I know thou hast believed on Me, and life, through Me, is thine,
But where are all those radiant stars that in thy crown should shine!
Yonder thou seest a glorious throng, and stars on every brow;
For every soul they led to me, they wear a jewel now;
And such thy bright reward had been, if such had been thy deed,
If thou hadst sought some wandering feet in paths of peace to lead.

"I did not mean that thou should'st tread the way of life alone,
But that the clear and shining light which round thy footsteps shone
Should guide some other weary feet to my bright home of rest,
And thus in blessing those around, thou had'st thyself been blest."
The vision faded from my sight; the voice no longer spake;
A spell seemed brooding o'er my soul, which long I feared to break,
And when at last I gazed around, in morning's glimmering light,
My spirit fell, o'erwhelmed amid that vision's awful night.

I rose and wept with chastened joy that yet I dwelt below—
That yet another hour was mine, my faith by works to show,
That yet some sinner I might tell of Jesus' dying love,
And help to lead some weary soul to seek a home above.
And now while on the earth I stay, my motto this shall be,.
"To live no longer to myself, but Him who died for me."
And graven on my inmost soul this word of true divine,
"They that turn many to the Lord bright as the stars shall shine."

"BRINGING OUR SHEAVES WITH US."

Elizabeth Akers.

THE time for toil is past, and night has come,
The last and saddest of the harvest eves;
Worn out with labor long and wearisome,
Drooping and faint, the reapers hasten home,
    Each laden with his sheaves.

Last of the laborers, Thy feet I gain,
Lord of the harvest! and my spirit grieves
That I am burdened, not so much with grain
As with a heaviness of heart and brain;—
    Master, behold my sheaves!

Few, light, and worthless—yet their trifling weight
Through all my frame a weary aching leaves;
For long I struggled with my hapless fate,
And staid and toiled till it was dark and late,
    Yet these are all my sheaves!

Full well I know I have more tares than wheat,
Brambles and flowers, dry stalks and withered leaves;
Wherefore I blush and weep, as at Thy feet
I kneel down reverently, and repeat,
    Master, behold my sheaves!

I know these blossoms, clustering heavily
With evening dew upon their folded leaves,
Can claim no value nor utility;
Therefore shall fragrancy and beauty be
    The glory of my sheaves.

So do I gather strength and hope anew;
For well I know Thy patient love perceives
Not what I did, but what I strove to do—
And though the full, ripe ears be sadly few,
      Thou wilt accept my sheaves.

THE SHORE OF ETERNITY.
F. W. Faber, D.D.

ALONE! to land alone upon that shore,
  With no one sight that we have ever seen before;
    Things of a different hue.
    And the sounds all new,
  And fragrances so sweet the soul may faint.
  Alone! Oh, that first hour of being a saint.

Alone! to land upon that shore,
On which no wavelets lisp, no billows roar,
  Perhaps no shape of ground,
  Perhaps no sight or sound,
No forms of earth our fancies to arrange—
But to begin, alone, that mighty change!

Alone! to land alone upon that shore,
Knowing so well we can return no more;
  No voice or face of friend,
  None with us to attend
Our disembarking on that awful strand,
But to arrive alone in such a land!

THE SHORE OF ETERNITY.

Alone! to land alone upon that shore!
To begin alone to live forevermore,
   To have no one to teach
   The manners or the speech
Of that new life, or put us at our ease;
Oh! that we might die in pairs or companies!

Alone? The God we know is on that shore,
The God of whose attractions we know more
   Than of those who may appear
   Nearest and dearest here;
Oh, is He not the life-long friend we know
More privately than any friend below?

Alone? The God we trust is on that shore,
The Faithful One whom we have trusted more
   In trials and in woes
   Than we have trusted those
On whom we leaned most in our earthly strife;
Oh, we shall trust Him more in that new life!

Alone? The God we love is on that shore—
Love not enough, yet whom we love far more,
   And whom we loved all through
   And with a love more true
Than other loves—yet now shall love Him more;
True love of Him begins upon that shore!

So not alone we land upon that shore;
'Twill be as though we had been there before;
   We shall meet more we know
   Than we can meet below,
And find our rest like some returning dove,
And be at home at once with our Eternal love.

HYMNS OF LONGING FOR REST.

Theodore L. Cuyler, D.D.

"OTHAT I had wings like a dove, for then would I fly away, and be at rest!" The reference in this beautiful verse is to the turtle-dove of Palestine, a bird of such free spirit that if confined in a cage, it soon droops and dies. How often the child of God breathes this yearning aspiration for a higher and a holier atmosphere. How often, in seasons of grief and disappointment, and utter disgust with the inconsistency of our fellow-creatures, the homesick heart pines for escape into the very bosom of Jesus. For there only is rest, full, sweet, and all-satisfying.

This aspiration is not only breathed in prayer. It is uttered in song. Many of our richest hymns are prayers in metre. And few yearnings break forth oftener in the psalmodics of God's people than the yearning for soul-rest. Of the hymns that are pitched to this key we might mention many. Of the hymnists who have composed them, none is more celebrated than James Montgomery.

He is the Cowper of the nineteenth century—not in the poetry of nature, but in sacred song. Scotland gave him birth, as she did to Henry Lyte and Horatius Bonar. He was born in Ayrshire, the land of Robert Burns, in 1771. His father was a Moravian missionary, who labored and died in the West Indies. James united with the Moravian Church at the age of forty-three, and his memory is held in high veneration among that small, but true-hearted band of Christians. The Moravian body is like a tuberose, small in bulk, but sends its sweet odors afar off. With this communion Montgomery worshiped until in his later years, and then he attended an Evangelical Episcopal church (St. George's) in Sheffield, England.

HYMNS OF LONGING FOR REST.

During my student days I spent some time at Sheffield, and often met the venerable poet. He was small of stature, with hair as white as snow. Although he had long been an editor (and once been imprisoned for his bold utterances in his newspaper, the *Iris*), he would be easily mistaken for a clergyman. He wore an exceedingly conspicuous white cravat, which reached close to his chin, and gave you the impression that he was suffering from a chronic sore throat. When I first called on him at his residence, "The Mount," several of his most familiar lines began to repeat themselves to me, such as:

> "Friend after friend departs,
> Who hath not lost a friend ?"

And that other exquisite verse which often weaves itself into our secret devotions:

> "Here in the body pent,
> Absent from Him I roam,
> Yet nightly pitch my moving tent,
> One day's march nearer home."

There are few finer verses in the whole range of devotional poetry. It is a pilgrim's wayfaring song, as he pulls up the tent-pins every morning, and moves onward towards his everlasting rest.

Montgomery never visited this country, but he was full of warm enthusiasm toward America, in whose churches his hymns are sung every Sabbath. He was also full of honest indignation that so many people would persist in confounding him with the spasmodic Robert Montgomery, whose poem on "Satan" has been impaled, like a buzzing beetle on a pin, by the sharp pen of Macaulay. "Only think," said the dear old poet to me, "that I should have just got a letter, telling me that my poem on Satan is the best I ever wrote." I do not wonder that his wrath waxed warm under such an imputation. The last time I ever saw the veteran, he was sitting in his

HYMNS OF LONGING FOR REST.

pew at St. George's, the "good gray head" bending reverently over his prayer-book, as he joined in the responses. He "flew away and was at rest" in 1854, at the ripe old age of eighty-three.

Montgomery's most popular hymn is that one which breathes out the longing of a weary heart:

> "O where shall rest be found,
>   Rest for the weary soul?
> 'Twere vain the ocean depths to sound
>   Or pierce to either pole."

Ten thousand times have God's best beloved children, when made sick at the worthlessness and emptiness of worldly treasures, broke out in the fervid protestation:

> "This world can never give
>   The bliss for which I sigh;
> 'Tis not the whole of life to live,
>   Nor all of death to die."

Of Montgomery's other favorite hymns, "Prayer is the Soul's Sincere Desire," and "What are these in Bright Array?" I wish I had space to speak. But we must confine ourselves in this brief article to those songs of Zion which are full of longings for the better life and the better land.

Of this class of hymns there is one which everybody knows, and everybody sings, and yet almost nobody knows its authorship, for *Robert Seagrave* is one of God's "hidden ones" from all celebrity in the world of letters. He was a minister of the English Established Church, but being a caged dove there, he broke loose into dissent. This unfettered spirit of his gave birth to that vigorous hymn whose uplift has carried us often into the higher climes:

> "Rise, my soul, and stretch thy wings,
>   Thy better portion trace;
> Rise from transitory things,
>   Towards heaven, thy native place."

Seagrave sang this one bird-song about the year 1748, but I never heard that he sang again; but his inspiring lyric is ringing yet, like the notes of a lark at the gates of heaven. Probably all the sermons preached that year throughout Christendom have not lifted so many souls towards the gates of pearl as that single melody of Robert Seagrave. We must all seek to become acquainted with him in our Father's house.

Yes, and we shall all love to know Horatius Bonar there, and thank him for his many hymns so full of heavenward aspiration. Another songstress from our own land, too, who has lately flown above the clouds—sweet, sorrowful Phebe Cary. For she taught us all to sing, amid our care-burdens and our crosses:

> "One sweetly solemn thought,
>   Comes to me o'er and o'er;
> I am *nearer home* to-day,
>   Than I ever have been before."

AT EVENTIDE IT SHALL BE LIGHT.

"OLD age," says one whose words have survived his name, "is a blessed time, when looking back over the follies, sins, and mistakes of past life—too late, indeed, to remedy, but not too late to repent—we may put off earthly garments one by one, and dress ourselves for heaven. Griefs that are heavy to the young are to the old calm and almost joyful, as tokens of the near and ever-nearing time when there shall be no more death, neither sorrow, nor crying, neither any more pain." Even though walking in darkness for awhile, the aged have the sure promise, "**At eventide it shall be light.**"—*Anonymous.*

REUNION IN HEAVEN.

Wm. Morley Punshon.

HEAVEN is not a solitude; it is a peopled city, a city in which there are no strangers, no homeless, no poor, where one does not pass another in the street without greeting, where no one is envious of another's minstrelsy or of another's more brilliant crown. When God said in the ancient Eden, "It is not good for man to be alone," there was a deeper signification in the words than could be exhausted or explained by the family tie. It was the declaration of an essential want which the Creator in His highest wisdom has impressed upon the noblest of His works. That is not life—you don't call that life—where the hermit in some moorland glade drags out a solitary existence, or where the captive in some cell of bondage frets and pines unseen? That man does not understand solitude.

Life, all kinds of life, tends to companionship, and rejoices in it, from the larvæ and buzzing insect cloud up to the kingly lion and the kinglier man. It is a social state into which we are to be introduced, as well as a state of consciousness. Not only, therefore, does the Saviour pray for His disciples, "Father, I will that those whom thou hast given me be with me where I am, that they may behold my glory," but those who are in that heavenly recompense are said to have come "to the general assembly and church of the first-born written in heaven." Aye, and better than that, and dearer to some of us, "to the spirits of just men made perfect."

The question of the recognition of departed friends in heaven, and special and intimate reunion with them, Scripture and reason enable us to infer with almost absolute certainty. It is implied in the fact that the resurrection is a resurrection of individuals, that it is this mortal that shall put on immortality. It is implied in the fact that heaven is a vast and happy society; and it is implied in the fact that there is no unclothing of nature that we possess, only the clothing upon it of the garments of a brighter and more glorious immortality.

Take comfort, then, those of you in whose history the dearest charities of life have been severed by the rude hand of death, those whom you have thought about as lost are not lost, except to present sight. Perhaps even now they are angel watchers, screened by a kindly Providence from everything about, that would give you pain; but if you and they are alike, in Jesus, and remain faithful to the end, doubt not that you shall know them again. It were strange, don't you think, if amid the multitude of earth's ransomed ones that we are to see in heaven, we should see all but those we most fondly and fervently long to see? Strange, if in some of our walks along the golden streets, we never happen to light upon them! Strange, if we did not hear some heaven song, learned on earth, trilled by some clear ringing voice that we have often heard before!

WHAT MUST IT BE TO BE THERE!

Mrs. Elisabeth Mills.

WE speak of the realms of the blessed,
    Of that country so bright and so fair;
And oft are its beauties confessed—
    But what must it be to be there!

JOY IN THE MORNING.

We speak of its pathways of gold,
   Of its walls decked with jewels so rare,
Of its wonders and pleasure untold—
   But what must it be to be there!

We speak of its service of love,
   The robes which the glorified wear,
The Church of the First-born above—
   But what must it be to be there!

We speak of its freedom from sin,
   From sorrow, temptation, and care,
From trials without and within—
   But what must it be to be there!

Do thou, Lord, midst pleasure or woe,
   For heaven our spirits prepare;
Then soon shall we joyfully know
   And feel what it is to be there.

JOY IN THE MORNING—Ps. xxx. 5.

Rev. Dwight Williams.

THOUGH dark the night and dreary,
   And eyes that watch are weary,
The daylight cometh after
   With song and love and laughter,
And down the mountains cold
The sunlight pours its gold.

JOY IN THE MORNING.

If while the world is sleeping,
Lone vigils thou art keeping,
And midnight skies are stooping,
O'er thee in sadness drooping,
  This know, the King of light
  Is speeding in his flight.

He cometh from his chamber,
O'er paths of gold and amber;
The gates are backward swinging,
The morning chime is ringing;
  He comes with wheels of fire,
  And steeds that never tire.

Poor soul, in storm o'ertaken,
With cold and hunger shaken!
The conqueror is riding,
The night itself is hiding,
  And flies in swift dismay,
  O'er the mountains far away.

Christian, a royal weeper
Is evermore thy keeper;
The night he passed in waiting,
From dark to light translating,
  Hath brought the matin song
  And thou shall listen long.

THE most important thought I ever had was that of *my personal responsibility* to God.   *Daniel Webster.*

THE SUNSET HOUR OF LIFE.

THE stream is calmest when it nears the tide,
And flowers are sweetest at the eventide,
And birds most musical at close of day,
And saints divinest when they pass away.

Morning is holy, but a holier charm
Lies folded close in evening's robes of balm,
And weary man must ever love her best,
For morning calls to toil, but night to rest.

She comes from Heaven, and on her wings doth bear
A holy fragrance, like the breath of prayer;
Footsteps of angels follow in her trace,
To shut the weary eyes of day in peace.

All things are hushed before her as she throws
O'er earth and sky her mantle of repose;
There is a calmer beauty and a power
That morning knows not, in the evening hour.

Until the evening we must weep and toil—
Plow life's stern furrow, dig the weedy soil—
Tread with sad feet our rough and thorny way,
And bear the heat and burden of the day.

Oh! when our sun is setting may we glide,
Like summer evening down the golden tide;
And leave behind us, as we pass away,
Sweet, starry twilight round our sleeping clay.

—*Anonymous.*

THE JOY OF INCOMPLETENESS.

IF all our lives were one broad glare
   Of sunlight, clear, unclouded;
  If all our path were smooth and fair,
   By no soft gloom enshrouded;
If all life's flowers were fully blown
  Without the sweet unfolding,
And happiness were rudely thrown
  On hands too weak for holding,
Should we not miss the twilight hours,
  The gentle haze and sadness?
Should we not long for storms and showers,
  To break the constant gladness?

If none were sick and none were sad,
  What service could we render?
I think if we were always glad,
  We scarcely could be tender.
Did our beloved never need
  Our patient ministration,
Earth would grow cold, and miss indeed
  Its sweetest consolation;
If sorrow never claimed our heart,
  And every wish were granted,
Patience would die, and hope depart—
  Life would be disenchanted.

And yet in heaven is no more night,
  In heaven is no more sorrow!

Such unimagined new delight
  Fresh grace from pain will borrow.
As the poor seed that underground
  Seeks its true life above it,
Not knowing what will there be found
  When sunbeams kiss and love it;
So we in darkness upward grow,
  And look and long for heaven,
But cannot picture it below,
  Till more of light be given.—*Sunday Magazine.*

THERE'S NOTHING TRUE BUT HEAVEN.

Thomas Moore

THIS world is all a fleeting show
  For man's illusion given;
The smiles of joy, the tears of woe,
Deceitful shine, deceitful flow,—
  There's nothing true but Heaven!

And false the light on Glory's plume,
  As fading hues of even;
And Love, and Hope, and Beauty's bloom,
Are blossoms gathered from the tomb,—
  There's nothing bright but Heaven!

Poor wanderers of a stormy day,
  From wave to wave we're driven,
And Fancy's flash and Reason's ray
Serve but to light the troubled way,—
  There's nothing calm but Heaven!

DEPARTURE OF FRIENDS.

James Montgomery.

FRIEND after friend departs:
  Who hath not lost a friend ?
  There is no union here of hearts,
That finds not here an end.
Were this frail world our only rest,
Living or dying, none were blest.

Beyond the flight of time,
Beyond this vale of death,
There surely is some blessed clime
Where life is not a breath,
Nor life's affection transient fire,
Whose sparks fly upward to expire.

There is a world above,
Where parting is unknown;
A whole eternity of love,
Form'd for the good alone;
And faith beholds the dying here,
Translated to that happier shore.

Thus star by star declines,
Till all are passed away,
As morning high and higher shines,
To pure and perfect day;
Nor sink those stars in empty night,
They hide themselves in heaven's own light.

NO SECTS IN HEAVEN.

Mrs. Elizabeth H. Jocelyn.

TALKING of sects quite late one eve,
What one and another of saints believe,
That night I stood in a troubled dream
By the side of a darkly-flowing stream,
And a "churchman" down to the river came,
When I heard a strange voice call his name:
"Good father, stop; when you cross this tide
You must leave your robes on the other side."

But the aged father did not mind,
And his long gown floated out behind,
As down to the stream his way he took,
His hands held firm of a gilt-edged book.
"I'm bound for Heaven, and when I'm there
I shall want my Book of Common Prayer;
And though I put on a starry crown,
I shall feel quite lost without my gown."

Then he fixed his eyes on the shining track,
But his gown was heavy, and held him back;
And the poor old father tried in vain
A single step in the flood to gain.
I saw him again on the other side,
But his silk gown floated on the tide,
And no one asked, in that blissful spot,
If he belonged to "the church" or not.

NO SECTS IN HEAVEN.

Then down to the river a Quaker strayed,
His dress of sober hue was made,
"My hat and coat must be all of gray,
I cannot go any other way."
Then he buttoned his coat straight up to his chin,
And staidly, solemnly waded in,
And his broad-brimmed hat he pulled down tight
Over his forehead, so cold and white.

But a strong wind carried away his hat,
And he sighed a few moments after that,
And then, as he gazed to the farther shore,
The coat slipped off and was seen no more.
Poor, dying Quaker, thy suit of gray
Is quietly sailing—away—away.
But thou'lt go to heaven as straight as an arrow,
Whether thy brim be broad or narrow.

Next came Dr. Watts with a bundle of psalms,
Tied nicely up in his aged arms,
And hymns as many—a very wise thing,
That the people in heaven, "all round," might sing.
But I thought he heaved an anxious sigh,
As he saw that the river ran broad and high!
And looked rather surprised, as one by one,
The psalms and hymns in the wave went down.

And after him, with his MSS.,
Came Wesley, the pattern of godliness.
But he cried, "Dear me, what shall I do!
The water has soaked them through and through."
And there, on the river, far and wide,

NO SECTS IN HEAVEN.

Away they went on the swollen tide,
And the saint, astonished, passed through alone,
Without his manuscripts, up to the throne.

Then gravely walking, two saints by name,
Down to the stream together came,
But as they stopped at the river's brink,
I saw one saint from the other shrink.
"Sprinkled or plunged, may I ask you, friend,
How you attained to life's great end?"
"*Thus*, with a few drops on our brow."
"But I've been dipped, as you'll see me now.

"And I really think it will hardly do,
As I'm 'close communion,' to cross with you,
You're bound, I know, to the realms of bliss,
But you must go that way, and I'll go this."
And straightway plunging with all his might,
Away to the left—his friend at the right,
Apart they went from this world of sin.
But how did the brethren "enter in?"

And now where the river was rolling on,
A Presbyterian church went down;
Of women there seemed an innumerable throng,
But the men I could count as they passed along,
And concerning the road they could never agree,
The *old* or the *new* way, which it could be;
Nor ever a moment paused to think
That both would lead to the river's brink.

And a sound of murmuring long and loud
Came ever up from the moving crowd,

TO SECTS IN HEAVEN.

"You're in the old way, and I'm in the new,
That is the false, and this is the true,"
Or, "I'm in the old way, and you're in the new,
That is the false, and *this* is the true."
But the *brethren* only seemed to speak,
Modest the sisters walked, and meek.

And if ever one of them chanced to say
What troubles she met with on the way,
How she longed to pass to the other side,
Nor feared to cross over the swelling tide,
A voice arose from the brethren then,
"Let no one speak but the 'holy men,'
For have ye not heard the words of Paul?
'Oh, let the women keep silence all.'"

I watched them long in my curious dream,
Till they stood by the border of the stream,
Then, just as I thought, the two ways met,
But all the brethren were talking yet,
And would talk on, till the heaving tide
Carried them over, side by side;
Side by side, for the way was one,
The toilsome journey of life was done;

And priest and Quaker, and all* who died;
Came out alike on the other side;
No forms, or crosses, or books had they,
No gowns of silk, or suits of gray;
No creeds to guide them, or MSS.,
For all had put on "Christ's Righteousness."

* All seen in the dream.

HEAVEN.

F. W. Faber, D.D.

OH, what is this splendor that beams on me now,
    This beautiful sunrise that dawns on my soul,
While faint and far off land and sea lie below,
    And under my feet the huge golden clouds roll!

To what mighty king doth this city belong,
    With its rich jeweled shrines, and its gardens of flowers,
With its breaths of sweet incense, its measures of song,
    And the light that is gilding its numberless towers?

See! forth from the gates, like a bridal array,
    Come the princes of heaven, how bravely they shine!
'Tis to welcome the stranger, to show me the way,
    And to tell me that all I see round me is mine.

There are millions of saints in their ranks and degrees,
    And each with a beauty and crown of his own;
And there, far outnumbering the sands of the seas,
    The nine rings of angels encircle the throne.

And oh, if the exiles of earth could but win,
    One sight of the beauty of Jesus above,
From that hour they would cease to be able to sin,
    And earth would be heaven; for heaven is love.

But words may not tell of the vision of peace,
    With its worshipful seeming, its marvelous fires;

ANTICIPATION OF HEAVEN.

Where the soul is at large, where its sorrows all cease,
    And the gift has outbidden its boldest desires.

No sickness is here, no bleak, bitter cold,
    No hunger, debt, prison, or weariful toil;
No robbers to rifle our treasures of gold,
    No rust to corrupt, and no canker to spoil.

My God! and it was but a short hour ago,
    That I lay on a bed of unbearable pains;
All was cheerless around me, all weeping and woe;
    Now the wailing is changed to angelical strains.

Because I served Thee, were life's pleasures all lost?
    Was it gloom, pain, or blood, that won heaven for me?
Oh no! one enjoyment alone could life boast,
    And that, dearest Lord! was my service of Thee.

I had hardly to give; 'twas enough to receive,
    Only not to impede the sweet grace from above;
And, this first hour in heaven, I can hardly believe,
    In so great a reward for so little a love.

ANTICIPATION OF HEAVEN.

Thomas Moore.

GO, wing thy flight from star to star,
    From world to luminous world, as far
      As the universe spreads its flaming wall;
Take all the pleasures of all the spheres,
And multiply each through endless years,
One minute of heaven is worth them all.

A HOME IN HEAVEN.

William Hunter.

HOME in heaven! What a joyful thought,
As the poor man toils in his weary lot!
His heart opprest, and with anguish driven
From his home below, to his home in heaven.

A home in heaven! As the sufferer lies
On his bed of pain, and uplifts his eyes
To that bright home; what a joy is given,
With the blessed thought of his home in heaven.

A home in heaven! When our pleasures fade,
And our wealth and fame in the dust are laid,
And strength decays, and our health is riven,
We are happy still with our home in heaven.

A home in heaven! When the faint heart bleeds,
By the Spirit's stroke, for its evil deeds;
Oh! then what bliss in that heart forgiven,
Does the hope inspire of a home in heaven.

A home in heaven! When our friends are fled
To the cheerless gloom of the mouldering dead:
We wait in hope on the promise given;
We will meet up there in our home in heaven.

A home in heaven! When the wheel is broke,
And the golden bowl by the terror-stroke;

When life's bright sun sinks in death's dark even,
We will then fly up to our home in heaven.

Our home in heaven! Oh, the glorious home,
And the Spirit, joined with the bride, says "Come!"
Come, seek His face, and your sins forgiven,
And rejoice in hope of your home in heaven.

THOSE MANSIONS ABOVE.

 FOR a home in those mansions above;
O for a rest in that haven of love;
O to be free from this body of sin,
　This warfare without, these conflicts within!

Give me, dear Saviour, a heart wholly Thine,
A heart that can feel "my Beloved is mine,"
A heart that can say, "I know I am His,"
That, ransomed from woe, I am purchased for bliss.

Give me, O Father, Thy Spirit Divine,
Proving the purchased possession is Thine,
The earnest of joys they only can know
Who walk in the light of the Spirit below.

On me then bestow that armor complete
That covers the head and reaches the feet,
The armor they wear who fight the good fight,
And, having "done all," stand fast in Thy might.

Clad in this armor, sent down from above,
Wrought in the councils of covenant love,

THOSE MANSIONS ABOVE.

Our aim ever upward, our hearts all aglow,
Joyfully onward and homeward we go.

We strain every nerve, we strive for the prize
Of our calling in Christ: a home in the skies:
The battles all fought, the victory won,
We have the reward—" Good servant, well done;

"Come, enter thy home, these mansions above,
Rest in the haven of infinite love;
From sorrow and sin forever released,
Come sit with the guests at the heavenly feast."

All stains washed away, in robes of pure white
We bask in His rays, we shine in His light;
The crown of rejoicing we evermore wear,
The glory of Christ eternally share.

Make me, O Father, more grateful for life,
More willing to bear the turmoil and strife,
More anxious to serve, more like Him to be
Who gave His own life a ransom for me.

That, bearing Christ's image, e'en here below,
My work done in Him, His glory may show,
Till the summons I hear, in accents of love,
"Daughter, come higher, and serve Me above."

What glories await the spirit set free
From fetters of earth, untrammelled to be;
The work begun here is continued above,
And all that blest life is service and love.
—Parish Visitor.

AT HOME IN HEAVEN.

Charles F. Deems, D.D.

WILL any soul that reaches Heaven feel strange there ? Will it seem a foreign country ? Will all its sights, and sounds, and suggestions be totally unfamiliar ? Will they make no responsive note on any chord of the harp of memory ? Will they shed no ray of light on the lens of hope ? There are many of us who are looking forward to a residence in Heaven. Will it be more than a residence ? Will it be a home ? We know the difference between the two when applied to places upon earth. There are many kinds of residences; there is but one home. A lunatic asylum, a penitentiary, the place where we *must* live, but do not want to live, is a residence. The only real home a man has upon earth is the spot in which he would rather be than in any other. The place in which he gets most rest, most comfort, most solace, most satisfaction to every craving of his nature—that is home. How do we look forward toward Heaven ? Is it simply the termination of the journey, where, in the natural course of things, the pilgrimage ceases ? Such a state of affairs may occur to a man who has gone from his home, and whose business or duty has taken him across the ocean to a foreign port. There he may have to stay all the days of his life, and behind him leave wife and children, father and mother. He looks forward with interest to his arrival. He would rather be there than on the stormy ocean. But it is not home. Now, how do we feel toward Heaven ? Is 't simply the end of the road we must travel as Christians, and which we must terminate somewhere, sometime; or have we longings for it ? Does it come into our dreams? Do thoughts of it often lift our souls as the tides lift up the seas? Do we feel that every other residence is a tent, but heaven is our mansion; that we go to every other place because we *must*, but are stretching ourselves to be in heaven because we *would?* Are we heavenly-minded and heavenly-hearted? If so, we shall be at home in Heaven. It may be so sweet, so delicious, so satisfactory, so fulfilling, as to come in sudden and sublime contrast with all our previous experience. In this sense it may, for a brief season, be startling and somewhat strange; but if we have been spiritually-minded upon earth, each new moment of heaven will bring us the fulfillment of some hope, or the completion, in shouts of laughter, of some song which we had begun upon earth, and which had been drowned in sobs. It will be the being "forever with the Lord" that will make our heaven everlasting.

"Forever with the Lord?" Why not *now* with the Lord? Is not our present life a part of "forever?" If now with the Lord—if our communion be with Him—if we are learning His ways and walking in His companionship here, and are to be learning His ways and walking in His companionship in heaven, why should we not be at home in heaven?

The angels come down to earth. They have their mission of ministry. Their duties probably take them, sometimes, into places where they feel very strange; but there must be other spots amid the circumstances of which even angels must feel very much at home. Where a family is consecrated to God—where perfect love prevails—where Jesus reigns—where the Father's will is done in earth as it is in heaven, oh! surely there the good angels must feel at home.

How blessed is the work of the angels and the men who are striving more and more to make earth like heaven, so that the denizens of the one shall be the citizens of the other.

MEETNESS FOR HEAVEN.

IN visiting an art gallery or conservatory of music, our enjoyment will be in the ratio of the previous training and development of our tastes and sympathies in this direction. As those entertainments would be to the blind or deaf, so would the joys of heaven be to the sinner. Place him under the very shadow of the tree of life, and he would say, "I don't want to be here."

Heaven must be begun upon earth. We must carry its bud in our hearts here, or we can never see its full blossom hereafter. Entrance into heaven is not the result of a projectile force lifting as into an unknown sphere. It is the result of a process begun in time. The Church is God's training school, where the appetites and affections for the joys of heaven are developed. Our great work is not merely to get men into heaven, but to prepare them for it. When they are ready they will be there soon enough.

Our characters are now catching colors which will survive the judgment day. What gigantic importance this gives to time! As we sit before the artist's camera while our photograph is being impressed upon the sensitive plate, how important it is that we maintain the right position. A slight move will spoil the picture. So during our brief years on earth our characters are impressed for eternity. Death will be the artist closing the watch, and announcing the process completed, and the impression then made cannot be altered. The soldiers used to say when a comrade fell, "Poor fellow, he has received his discharge." But death is not a discharge. It is only a transfer. It takes us to the judgment seat and leaves us as it found us. The direction which the main current of our affections and aspirations has taken upon earth will there become fixed. Let us not lose the opportunities now passing or we lose the inheritance. Let us not miss the tide or it will be forever too late.—*United Presbyterian.*

FORETOKENS OF HEAVEN.
R. W. Hamilton.

LET the traveler, however remote his stray, find something congenial to his own latitude and country, and the sense of alienation is redeemed. Should he unexpectedly discover the daisy of his native fields, or catch the wood-note that had caroled from his native groves—should he hear his mother tongue—should he enjoy the right and protection of some institution at which his youthful heart had learned to bound—though the earth's diameter struck through between his sojourn and his own land, even that sojourn would be less to him than home. And the Christian has now much akin to heaven. His heart is there. Eternal life abides in him. Now he possesses the principles which heaven but matures, and cherishes the affections which it but expands.

BLESSED are they that are homesick, for they shall come at last to the Father's house.

Henrich Stillings.

JOYS OF HEAVEN.

Nancy A. W. Priest

BEYOND these chilling winds and gloomy skies,
    Beyond Death's cloudy portal—
There is a land where beauty never dies,
    And love becomes immortal.

A land whose light is never dimmed by shade,
    Whose fields are ever vernal,
Where nothing beautiful can ever fade,
    But blooms for aye eternal.

We may not know how sweet its balmy air,
    How bright and fair its flowers;
We may not hear the songs that echo there,
    Through those enchanted bowers.

The city's shining towers we may not see,
    With our dim earthly vision:
For Death, the silent warder, keeps the key
    That opes those gates elysian.

But sometimes, where adown the western sky
    The fiery sunset lingers,
Its golden gates swing inward noiselessly,
    Unlocked by silent fingers.

And while they stand a moment half ajar,
    Gleams from the inner glory,

UNVEILED HEAVEN.

Stream lightly through the azure vault afar,
   And half reveal the story.

O land unknown! O land of love divine!
   Father all-wise, eternal,
Guide, guide, these wandering, way-worn feet of mine,
   Unto those pastures vernal.

UNVEILED HEAVEN.
Ernst Lange, D.D.

WHAT no human eye hath seen, what no mortal ear hath heard,
   What on thought hath never been, in its noblest flights, conferred—
      This hath God prepared in store
      For His people evermore!

When the shaded pilgrim-land fades before the closing eye,
Then revealed on ether, heaven's own scenery shall lie;
   Then the veil of flesh shall fall,
   Now concealing, darkening all.

When this aching head shall rest, all its busy pulses o'er,
From her mortal robes undrest, shall my spirit upward soar,
   Then shall unimagined joy
   All my thoughts and powers employ.

WHAT is the heaven our God bestows?
   No prophet yet, no angel knows.
John Keble.

IMMORTALITY.

George D. Prentice.

IT cannot be that earth is man's only abiding place. It cannot be that our life is a bubble, cast up by the ocean of eternity, to float another moment upon its surface, and then sink into nothingness and darkness forever. Else why is it that the high and glorious aspirations which leap like angels from the temples of our hearts, are forever wandering abroad, satisfied?

Why is it that the rainbow and the cloud come over us with a beauty that is not of earth, and then pass off and leave us to muse on their faded loveliness?

Why is it that the stars which hold their festival around the midnight throne are set above the grasp of our limited faculties, and are forever mocking us with their unapproachable glory?

Finally, why is it that bright forms of human beauty are presented to the view, and then taken from us, leaving the thousand streams of the affections to flow back in an Alpine torrent upon our hearts?

We are born for a higher destiny than that of earth. There is a realm where the rainbow never fades; where the stars will be spread out before us like the islands that slumber on the ocean; and where the beautiful beings that here pass before us like visions will stay in our presence forever!

RELIGION is the best armor a man can have, but the worst cloak.

TIME AND ETERNITY.

Horatius Bonar.

IT is not Time that flies;
   'Tis we, 'tis we are flying:
It is not Life that dies;
   'Tis we, 'tis we are dying.
Time and Eternity are one;
Time is Eternity begun;
Life changes, yet without decay;
'Tis we alone who pass away.

It is not Truth that flies;
   'Tis we, 'tis we are flying:
It is not Faith that dies;
   'Tis we, 'tis we are dying.
O ever-during faith and truth,
Whose youth is age, whose age is youth!
Twin stars of immortality,
Ye cannot perish from our sky.

It is not Hope that flies;
   'Tis we, 'tis we are flying;
It is not Love that dies;
   'Tis we, 'tis we are dying.
Twin streams, that have in heaven your birth,
Ye glide in gentle joy through earth,
We fade, like flowers beside you sown;
Ye are still flowing, flowing on.

Yet we do but die to live;
   It is from death we're flying;
Forever lives our Life;
   For us there is no dying.
We die but as the Spring-bud dies,
In Summer's golden glow to rise.
These be our days of April bloom;
Our Summer is beyond the tomb.

NO NIGHT IN HEAVEN.

NO night shall be in heaven; no gathering gloom
Shall o'er that glorious landscape ever come;
No tears shall fall in sadness o'er those flowers
That breathe their fragrance through celestial bowers.

No night shall be in heaven; forbid to sleep,
These eyes no more their mournful vigils keep;
Their fountains dried, their tears all wiped away,
They gaze undazzled on eternal day.

No night shall be in heaven; no sorrow reign,
No secret anguish, no corporeal pain,
No shivering limbs, no burning fever there,
No soul's eclipse, no winter of despair.

No night shall be in heaven, but endless noon;
No fast declining sun, no waning moon;
But there the Lamb shall yield perpetual light
'Mid pastures green and waters ever bright.

No night shall be in heaven; no darkened room,
No bed of death, nor silence of the tomb,
But breezes ever fresh with love and truth
Shall brace the frame with an immortal youth.

No night shall be in heaven, but night is here,
The night of sorrow, and the night of fear;
I mourn the ills that now my steps attend,
And shrink from others that may yet impend.

No night shall be in heaven. Oh, had I faith,
To rest in what the faithful witness saith,
That faith should make these hideous phantoms flee,
And leave no night henceforth on earth to me.—*Anonymous.*

NO SORROW THERE.
Daniel March, D.D.

THIS earthly life has been fitly characterized as a pilgrimage through a vale of tears. In the language of poetry, man himself has been called a pendulum betwixt a smile and a tear. Everything in this world is characterized by imperfection. The best people have many faults. The clearest mind only sees through a glass darkly. The purest heart is not without spot. All the intercourse of society, all the transactions of business, all our estimates of human conduct and motive must be based upon the sad assumption that we cannot wholly trust either ourselves or our fellow-men. Every heart has its grief, every house has its skeleton, every character is marred with weakness and imperfection. And all these aimless conflicts of our minds, and unanswered longings of our hearts should lead us to rejoice the more in the divine assurance that a time is coming when night shall melt into noon, and the mystery shall be clothed with glory.

FAREWELL LIFE, WELCOME LIFE.

Thomas Hood.

FAREWELL, life! My senses swim,
    And the world is growing dim;
    Thronging shadows crowd the light,
Like the advent of the night;
Colder, colder, colder still,
Upward steals a vapor chill;
Strong the earthly odor grows—
I smell the mould above the rose!

Welcome, life! The spirit strives!
Strength returns, and hope revives!
Cloudy fears and shapes forlorn
Fly like shadows at the morn:
O'er the earth there comes a bloom,
Sunny light for sullen gloom,
Warm perfume for vapor cold—
I smell the rose above the mould!

THE END.

HAVE you, my dear reader, thought seriously of the *end?* the end of *this day*, the end of *this month*, the end of *this year*, the end of *this life?* Indeed, the end of *all earthly things?* The *end* is *surely coming!* It may be *near*.

THE END.

The end will come soon. This life is *short* and *uncertain* at the best. A few more rising and setting suns, and we shall be gone—numbered with the dead.

The end may come when you are not looking for it. Long life, many days yet, you may be saying, "To-morrow shall be as this day and much more abundant." But God may say to you, as he did to the rich man of old, "Thou fool, this night thy soul shall be required of thee; then whose shall those things be which thou hast provided?"

The end may come suddenly, like the flash of the lightning, or *stealthily as a thief in the night.* "For in such an hour as ye think not the Son of man cometh."

The end may come when you are not prepared for it—not prepared *at all,* or *poorly* prepared for it. *Are you* prepared for it *now?* What assurance have *you* that you *would be* in the *future?*

"Procrastination is the thief of time."

O, what shall the end of all earthly things be to you—to *you* as an individual? Would sudden death be sudden glory?

"And if the righteous scarcely be saved, where shall the ungodly and the sinner appear?" "But sin, when it is finished, bringeth forth death." "For the wages of sin is death; but the gift of God is eternal life through Jesus Christ our Lord."

> "That awful day will surely come,
>   The appointed hour makes haste,
> When I must stand before my Judge,
>   And pass the solemn test.
>
> "If now thou standest at the door,
>   O, let me feel thee near;
> And make my peace with God, before
>   I at thy bar appear."

—Anonymous.

✥BENEDICTION.✥

"MAY the blessings of thy God wait upon thee and the sun of Glory shine around thy head, may the gates of plenty, honor, and happiness be always open to thee and thine.

"May no strife disturb thy days, nor sorrow distress thy nights, and may the pillow of Peace kiss thy cheek, and pleasures of imagination attend thy dreams; and when length of years makes thee tired of earthly joys, and the curtains of death gently close round the scene of thy existence, may the angels of God attend thy bed, and take care that the expiring lamp of life shall not receive one rude blast to hasten its extinction; and, finally, may the SAVIOUR's blood wash thee from all impurities and prepare thee to enter into the land of everlasting FELICITY."

www.ingramcontent.com/pod-product-compliance
Lightning Source LLC
Chambersburg PA
CBHW022143300426
44115CB00006B/323